# BATMAN FACES

## MATT WAGNER
STORY AND ART

### WILLIE SCHUBERT
LETTERS

### STEVE OLIFF
COLORS

INTRODUCTION BY JOE R. LANSDALE

BATMAN CREATED BY BOB KANE

DAN DIDIO
SENIOR VP-EXECUTIVE EDITOR

ARCHIE GOODWIN
EDITOR-ORIGINAL SERIES

BILL KAPLAN
ASSISTANT EDITOR-ORIGINAL SERIES

BOB KAHAN
EDITOR-COLLECTED EDITION

ROBBIN BROSTERMAN
SENIOR ART DIRECTOR

PAUL LEVITZ
PRESIDENT & PUBLISHER

GEORG BREWER
VP-DESIGN & DC DIRECT CREATIVE

RICHARD BRUNING
SENIOR VP-CREATIVE DIRECTOR

PATRICK CALDON
EXECUTIVE VP-FINANCE & OPERATIONS

CHRIS CARAMALIS
VP-FINANCE

JOHN CUNNINGHAM
VP-MARKETING

TERRI CUNNINGHAM
VP-MANAGING EDITOR

ALISON GILL
VP-MANUFACTURING

DAVID HYDE
VP-PUBLICITY

HANK KANALZ
VP-GENERAL MANAGER, WILDSTORM

JIM LEE
EDITORIAL DIRECTOR-WILDSTORM

PAULA LOWITT
SENIOR VP-BUSINESS & LEGAL AFFAIRS

MARY ELLEN MCLAUGHLIN
VP-ADVERTISING & CUSTOM PUBLISHING

JOHN NEE
SENIOR VP-BUSINESS DEVELOPMENT

GREGORY NOVECK
SENIOR VP-CREATIVE AFFAIRS

SUE POHJA
VP-BOOK TRADE SALES

STEVE ROTTERDAM
SENIOR VP-SALES & MARKETING

CHERYL RUBIN
SENIOR VP-BRAND MANAGEMENT

JEFF TROJAN
VP-BUSINESS DEVELOPMENT, DC DIRECT

BOB WAYNE
VP-SALES

COVER PAINTING BY MATT WAGNER.

BATMAN: FACES

DC COMICS, 1700 BROADWAY, NEW YORK, NY 10019
A WARNER BROS. ENTERTAINMENT COMPANY
PRINTED IN CANADA. SECOND PRINTING.

ISBN: 978-1-56389-126-7

# INTRODUCTION BY
## JOE R. LANSDALE

**W**hen I was asked to write the introduction to Matt Wagner's FACES, a Batman versus Two-Face story, I jumped at the chance.

Why?

I'm a Matt Wagner fan, pure and simple. I like this fella's work. He knows what he's doing. He's a good storyteller, but beyond that, he works on a subterranean level. Even if when reading Wagner I'm not always aware of exactly what's going on beneath my feet, I can feel the rumble of action below. It's that old thing about there being more going on in the scene than just the scene.

As a writer, I know this little trick is a lot harder to pull off than one might expect. Wagner, he's got it down.

Another reason I jumped at the chance to write this introduction is simple. I'm a Batman fan. Batman was one of the first comics I ever read. Superman was briefly my favorite as a child, but then, gradually, Batman took over.

I admired his honor. The fact that he was a human with no special powers, other than those he had honed for himself. An athletic body, a proficiency in martial arts, knowledge of a variety of esoteric disciplines, and he got to wear a neat black hat with ears on it.

I remember my mother made me my own Batman hat. My ears wouldn't stand up. The cape looked pretty cool though. And I had my own Robin. My poor nephew had to wear that costume, God love him.

But that's another story.

Batman. Gee, boys and girls, I love him. And, Two-Face, what a villain. He's one of the more fascinating metaphors ever created for our Dark Knight to battle. A man whose decisions, no matter how extreme, are decided by the mere flip of a coin. Yes sir, duality, my friends, duality. No one better represents the two extremes of humanity—good and evil—better than Two-Face.

From what I can tell, like me, Matt loves the concept of the dual mind. No one is all good or all evil, and in one sense we all have masks behind which we hide other intentions. Or *faces*, if you will.

This is not to say that behind every smile there lurks a set of bared fangs. Far from it. But behind every face *are* other faces, some more scarred than others. And behind some scarred or deformed countenances lie faces of beauty and serenity.

But keep this in mind.

Behind the faces of some, there *do* lie faces so dark that if we actually had the ability to view them, their mere gazes would turn us to stone or drive us to madness.

Faces. Think about it.

Ted Bundy.

Jeffrey Dahmer.

Very ordinary-looking folks. No fangs. No green goo dripping from their eyes. No wild and savage expressions.

Bundy was the boy next door. Only the boy next door had a knife. And Dahmer was the nerd next door, only in his refrigerator...well, no further explanation is necessary.

Evil can be housed in beauty. Evil can be housed in the plain and the ordinary.

And what about Jack the Ripper? What was his every-day face? A mild-mannered school teacher? An aristocrat?

Think about it. But don't think about it too long;

Matt Wagner, other than showing these dual sides of humankind carried to the extreme with Two-Face as the primary threat, is also a humanist. He knows how to switch the focus from our hero to the villain, and even to the "minor" players in his drama. Note his poignant handling of the "freaks" in this story. The way he deals with the sad little realtor. The realtor is not just a patsy; he's a pathetic human being with a desire to be special. Just like all of us.

Everyone has a secret in this story, another side to their soul. Wagner addresses both sides—or in some cases, several sides. He's also giving vanity a kick in the butt here. I'm not suggesting we quit combing our hair before we go out, stop brushing our teeth or stop trying to keep up a pleasant appearance, but think. In these times, is anything sold anymore without a pretty face or muscular body to advertise it? Cars with big-busted women leaning across them. Aftershaves with handsome male faces being shaved, the aftershave being slapped on by the hands of a beautiful woman. Like maybe she just hangs out in the john waiting for this guy to shave, lives for the moment when she can put this mess on her hands and rub it into his face.

Guy sitting around in his underwear, drinking a beer, sees that on TV, and secretly, in the stupid part of his head, he thinks, I had me some of that, I'd get the gal too. I'd be a hot potato. A part of him knows this is foolish, but if it didn't work to some extent, didn't prey on our vanity or our desire to be attractive like the next man or woman, didn't somehow address our hidden fantasies, our other faces, hell, it wouldn't sell soap.

Matt knows it sells soap. He knows what fools we are, and with this nice little slice of blackness called FACES, he tells us about it.

Masterful business. And another thing I like:

Batman is a detective here. I admit a few of the clues seemed a little too vague for anyone to pick up on, but then again, Batman is Batman. He's the masked Ellery Queen of the night set. He works on a higher plane than you or I, and from experience; his instincts are good.

Yeah, I liked the mystery element, the detecting. There's not enough of that in Batman anymore. Too much of the avenger angle. It's a good angle, but it's sort of worn out its welcome. That's another reason I found FACES so appealing: it didn't follow the crowd.

In summary:

Thanks, DC Comics, I'm glad you published this fine story.

Thanks, Bob Kane, for Batman. He is one neat and singular hero.

But above all, thanks, Matt Wagner, for knowing what to do with this one neat and singular hero, as well as the unique and fascinating villain Two-Face. Thanks for a marvelous and haunting story.

And—

—do it again, Matt! Do it again!

Joe R. Lansdale
(his own self)

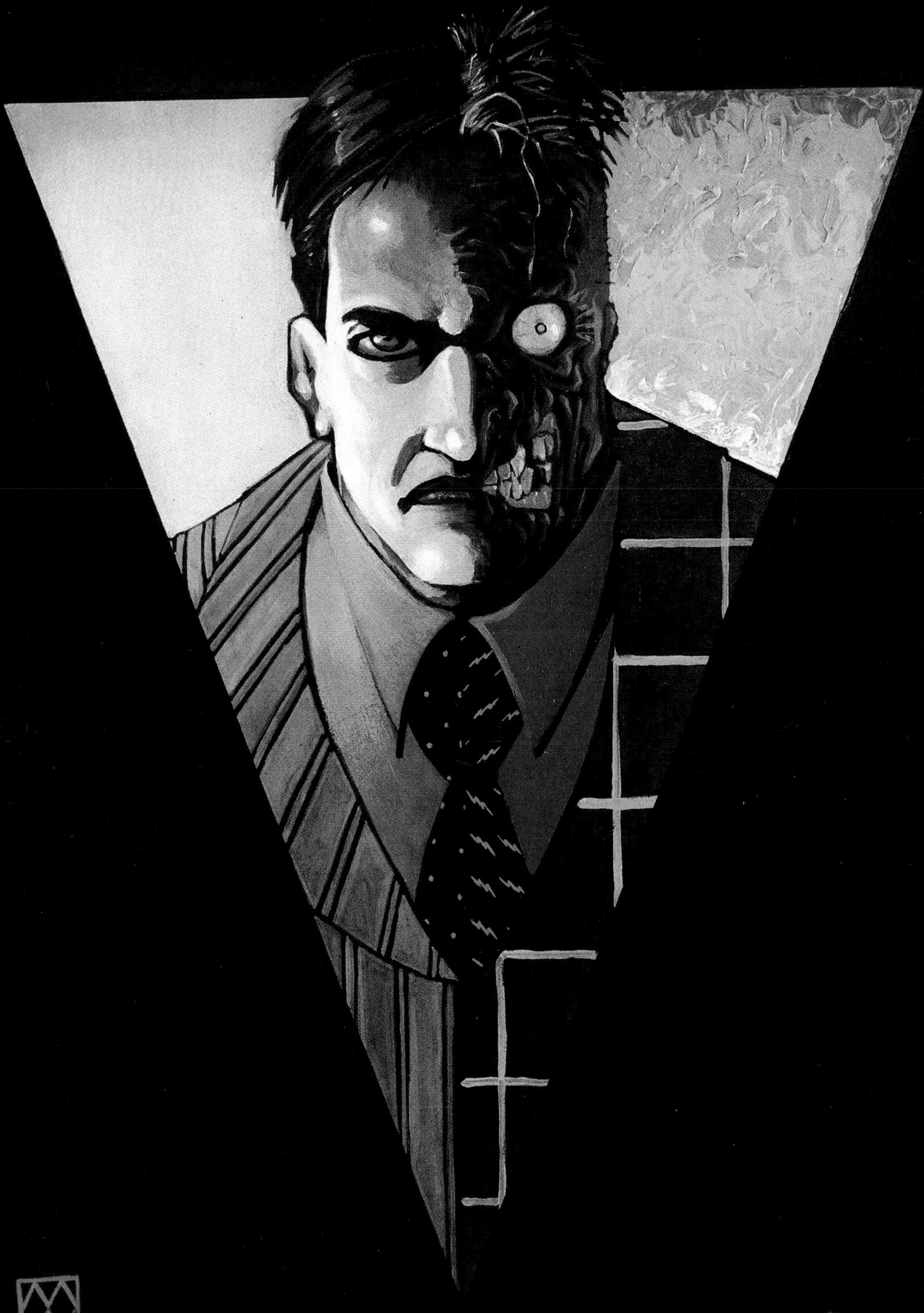

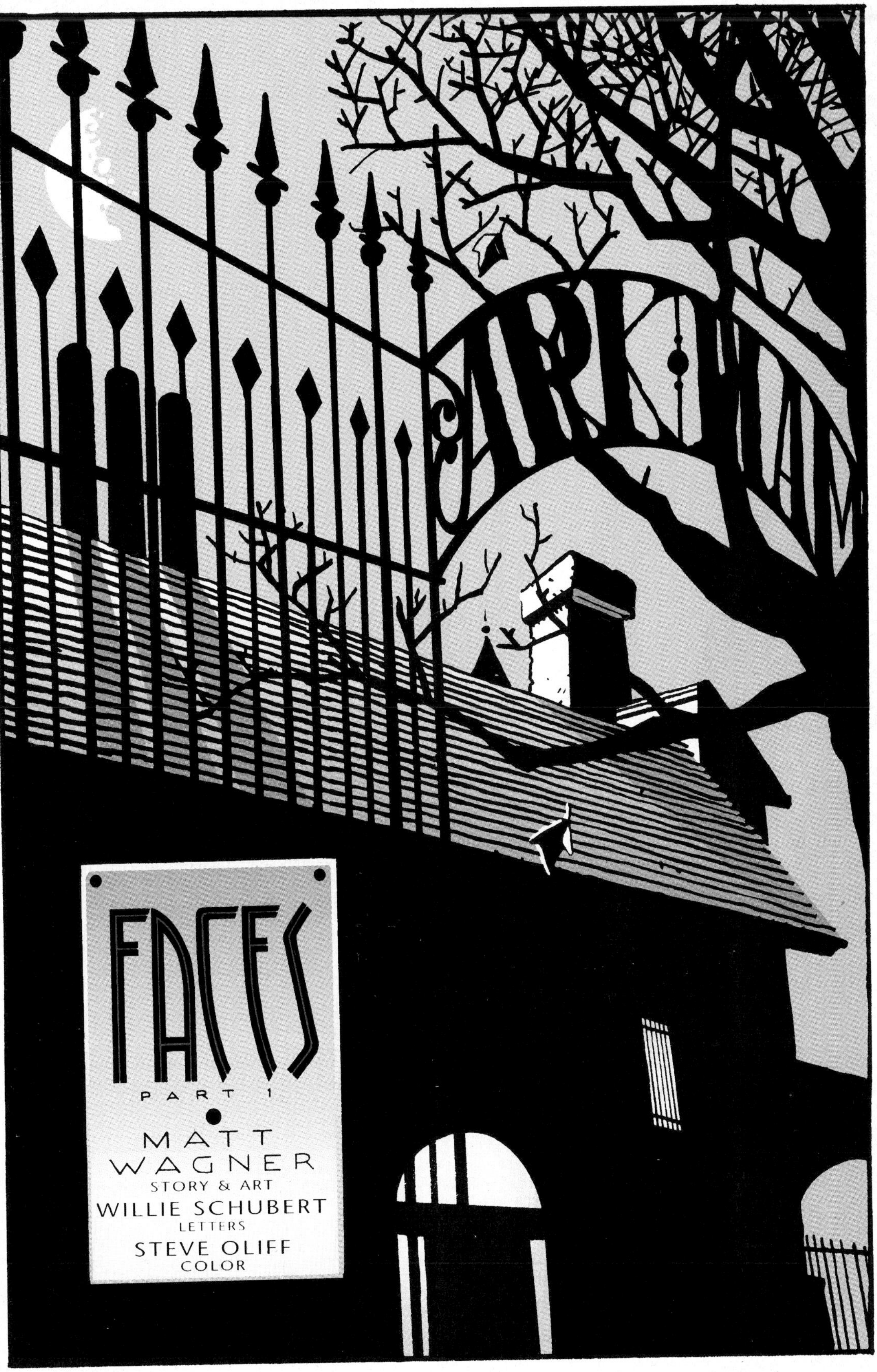
FACES
PART 1
MATT WAGNER
STORY & ART
WILLIE SCHUBERT
LETTERS
STEVE OLIFF
COLOR

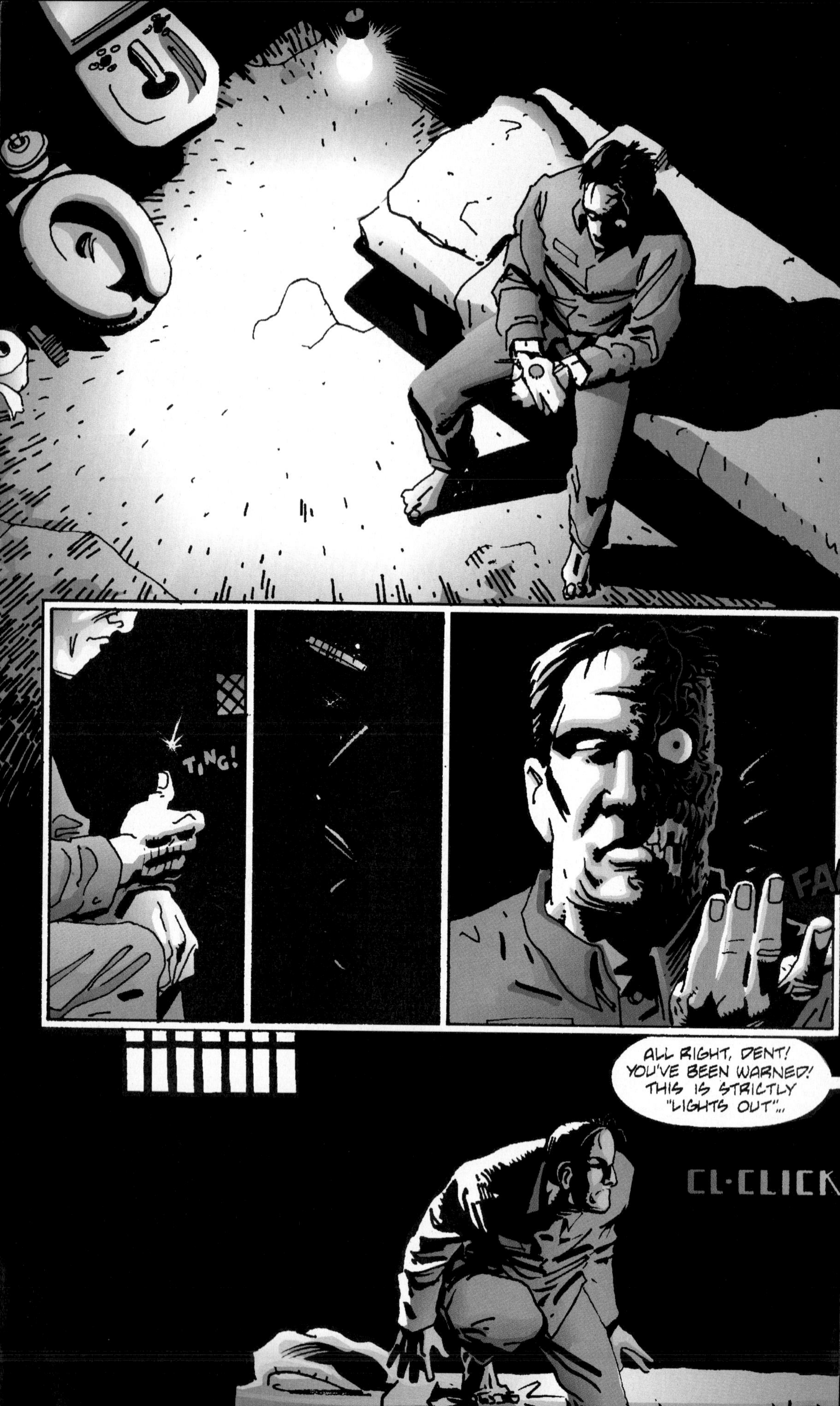
TING!
FA
ALL RIGHT, DENT! YOU'VE BEEN WARNED! THIS IS STRICTLY "LIGHTS OUT"...
CL-CLICK

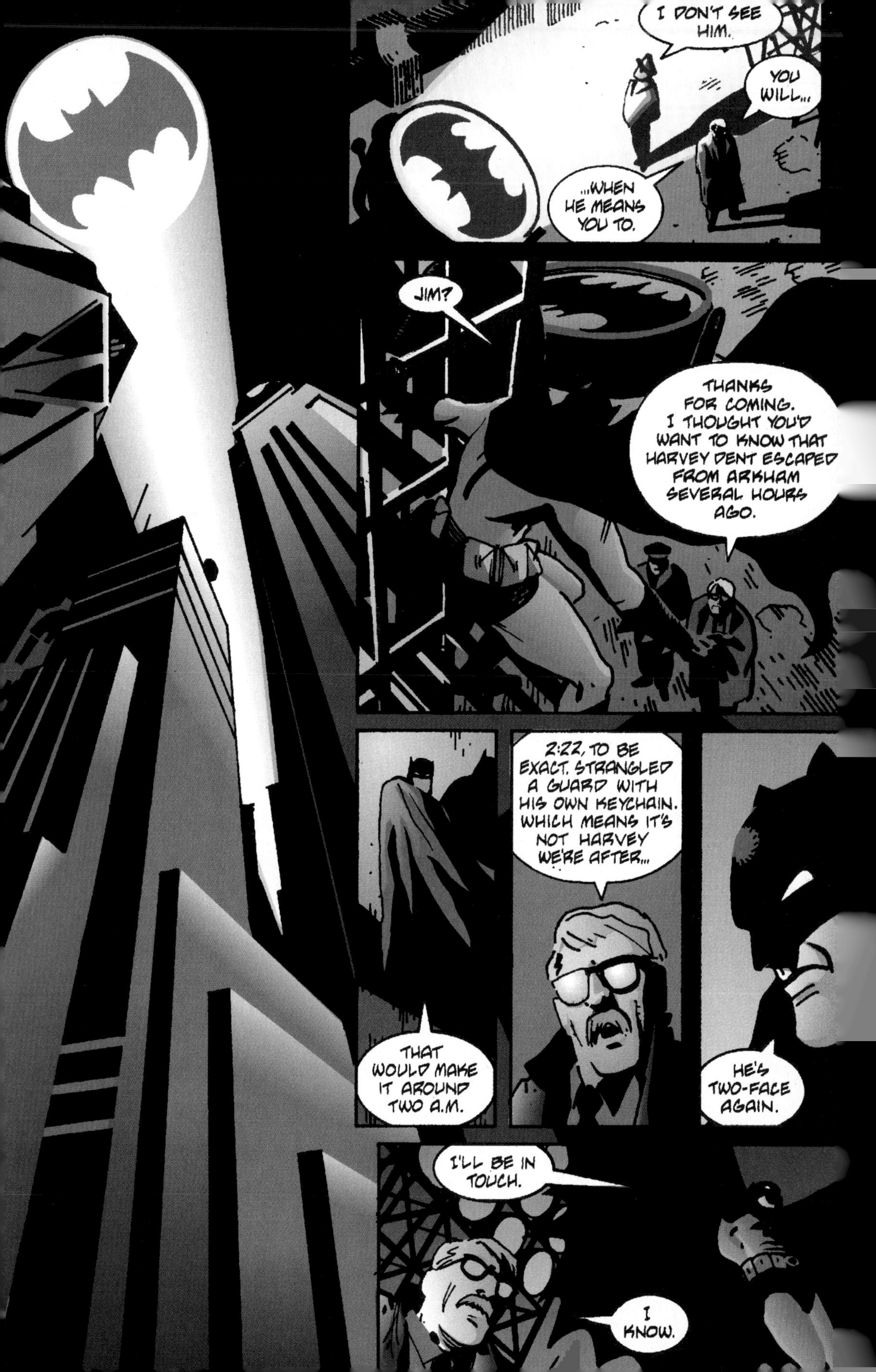
I DON'T SEE HIM.
YOU WILL...
...WHEN HE MEANS YOU TO.
JIM?
THANKS FOR COMING. I THOUGHT YOU'D WANT TO KNOW THAT HARVEY DENT ESCAPED FROM ARKHAM SEVERAL HOURS AGO.
THAT WOULD MAKE IT AROUND TWO A.M.
2:22, TO BE EXACT. STRANGLED A GUARD WITH HIS OWN KEYCHAIN. WHICH MEANS IT'S NOT HARVEY WE'RE AFTER...
HE'S TWO-FACE AGAIN.
I'LL BE IN TOUCH.
I KNOW.

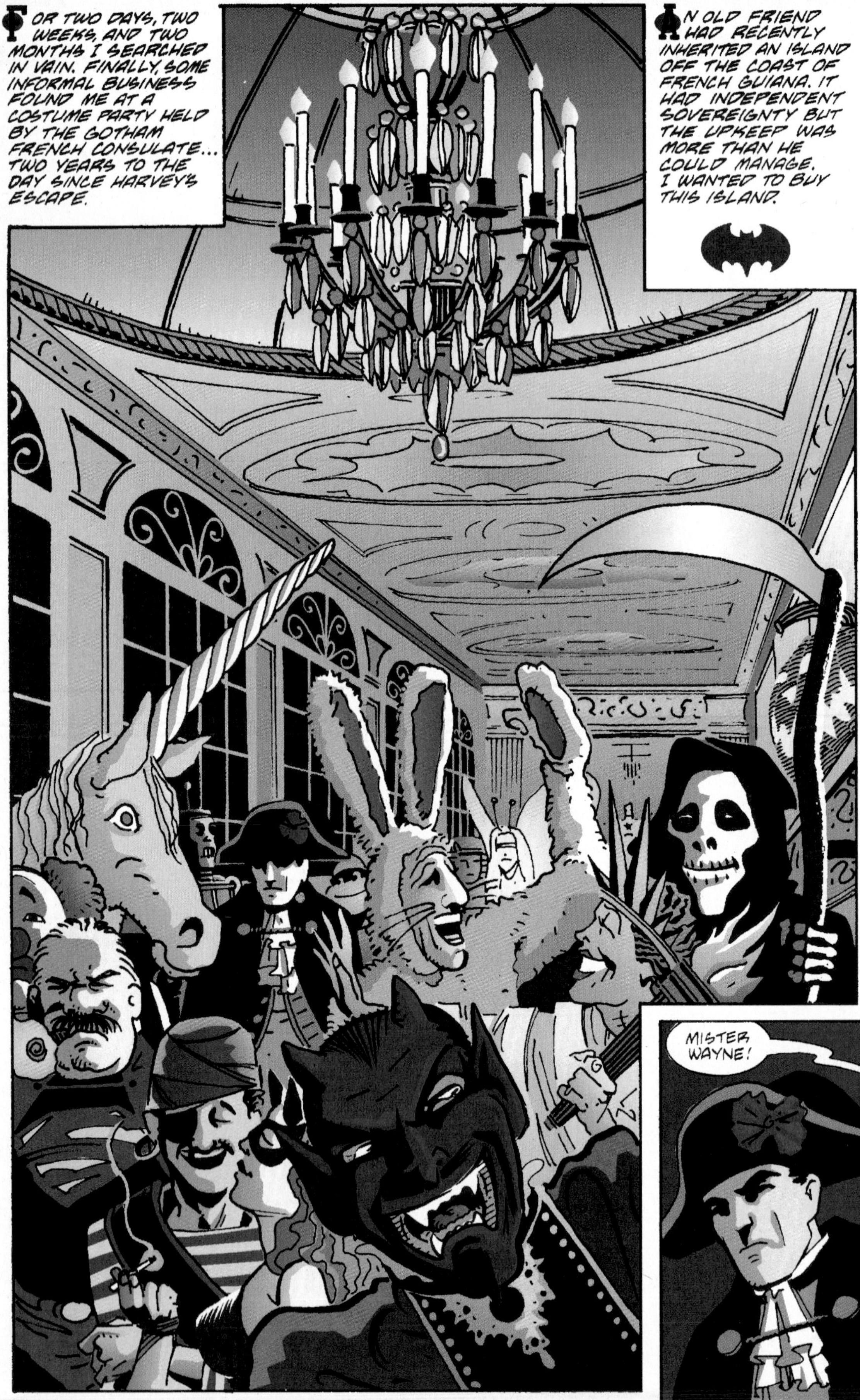
FOR TWO DAYS, TWO WEEKS, AND TWO MONTHS I SEARCHED IN VAIN. FINALLY, SOME INFORMAL BUSINESS FOUND ME AT A COSTUME PARTY HELD BY THE GOTHAM FRENCH CONSULATE... TWO YEARS TO THE DAY SINCE HARVEY'S ESCAPE.
AN OLD FRIEND HAD RECENTLY INHERITED AN ISLAND OFF THE COAST OF FRENCH GUIANA. IT HAD INDEPENDENT SOVEREIGNTY BUT THE UPKEEP WAS MORE THAN HE COULD MANAGE. I WANTED TO BUY THIS ISLAND.
MISTER WAYNE!

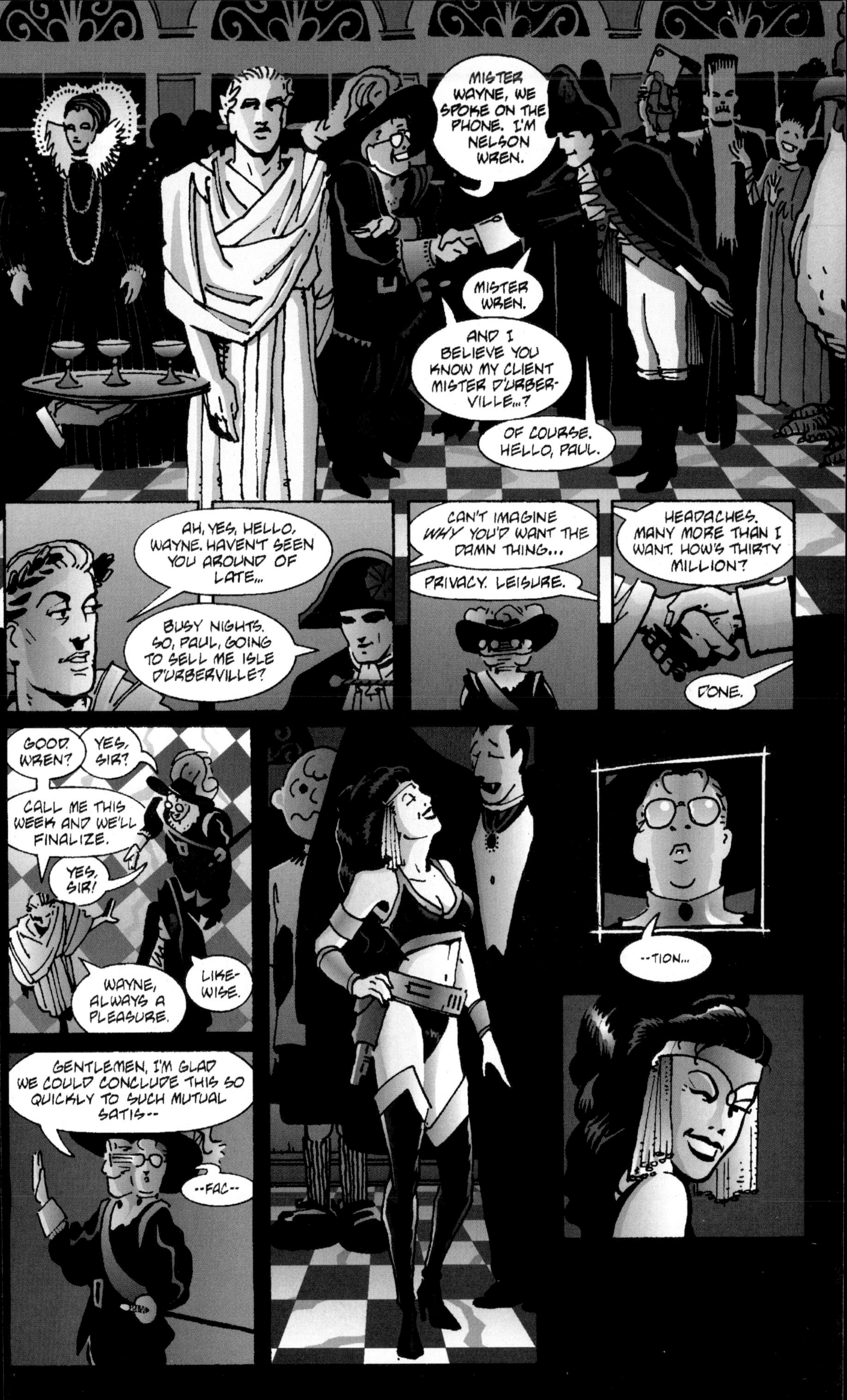
MISTER WAYNE, WE SPOKE ON THE PHONE. I'M NELSON WREN.
MISTER WREN.
AND I BELIEVE YOU KNOW MY CLIENT MISTER D'URBERVILLE...?
OF COURSE. HELLO, PAUL.
AH, YES, HELLO, WAYNE. HAVEN'T SEEN YOU AROUND OF LATE...
BUSY NIGHTS. SO, PAUL, GOING TO SELL ME ISLE D'URBERVILLE?
CAN'T IMAGINE WHY YOU'D WANT THE DAMN THING...
PRIVACY. LEISURE.
HEADACHES. MANY MORE THAN I WANT. HOW'S THIRTY MILLION?
DONE.
GOOD. WREN?
YES, SIR?
CALL ME THIS WEEK AND WE'LL FINALIZE.
YES, SIR!
WAYNE, ALWAYS A PLEASURE.
LIKE-WISE.
GENTLEMEN, I'M GLAD WE COULD CONCLUDE THIS SO QUICKLY TO SUCH MUTUAL SATIS--
--FAC--
--TION...

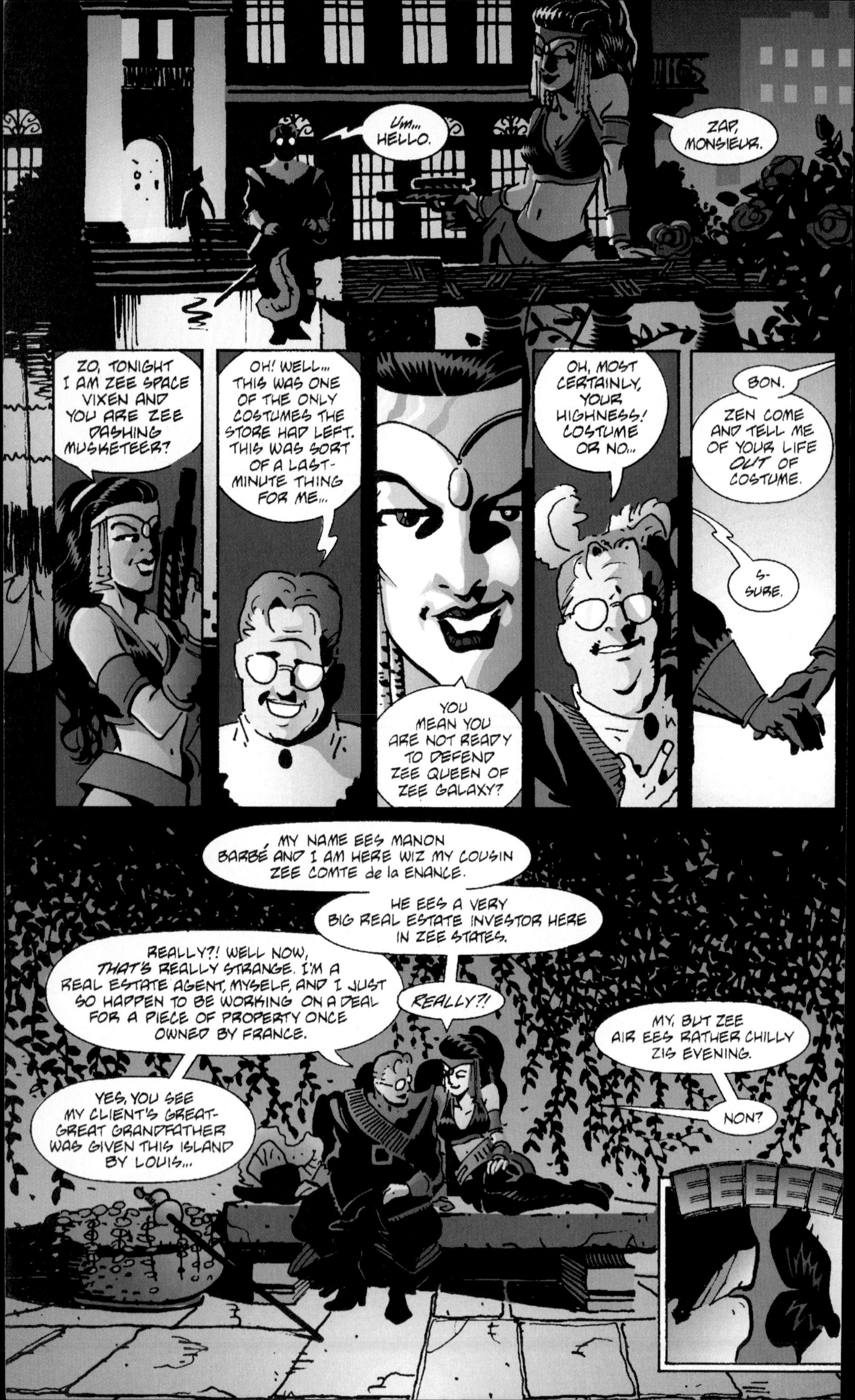
UM... HELLO.
ZAP, MONSIEUR.
ZO, TONIGHT I AM ZEE SPACE VIXEN AND YOU ARE ZEE DASHING MUSKETEER?
OH! WELL... THIS WAS ONE OF THE ONLY COSTUMES THE STORE HAD LEFT. THIS WAS SORT OF A LAST-MINUTE THING FOR ME...
YOU MEAN YOU ARE NOT READY TO DEFEND ZEE QUEEN OF ZEE GALAXY?
OH, MOST CERTAINLY, YOUR HIGHNESS! COSTUME OR NO...
BON.
ZEN COME AND TELL ME OF YOUR LIFE OUT OF COSTUME.
S-SURE.
MY NAME EES MANON BARBÉ AND I AM HERE WIZ MY COUSIN ZEE COMTE de la ENANCE.
HE EES A VERY BIG REAL ESTATE INVESTOR HERE IN ZEE STATES.
REALLY?! WELL NOW, THAT'S REALLY STRANGE. I'M A REAL ESTATE AGENT, MYSELF, AND I JUST SO HAPPEN TO BE WORKING ON A DEAL FOR A PIECE OF PROPERTY ONCE OWNED BY FRANCE.
REALLY?!
MY, BUT ZEE AIR EES RATHER CHILLY ZIS EVENING.
YES, YOU SEE MY CLIENT'S GREAT-GREAT GRANDFATHER WAS GIVEN THIS ISLAND BY LOUIS...
NON?

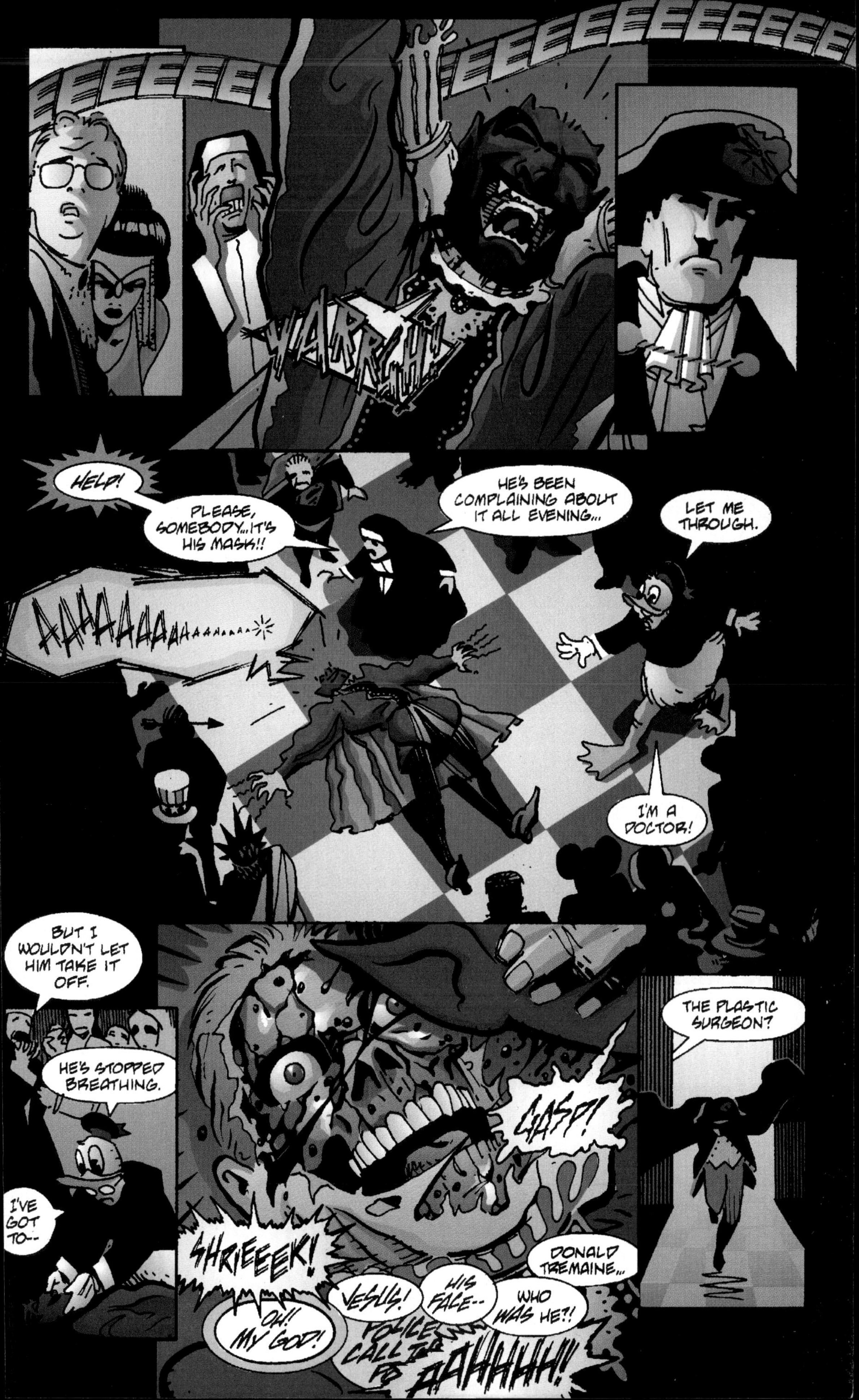
EEEEEEEEEEEEEEEEEEEEEE
YARRGH!
HELP!
PLEASE, SOMEBODY...IT'S HIS MASK!!
HE'S BEEN COMPLAINING ABOUT IT ALL EVENING...
LET ME THROUGH.
AAAAAAAaaaaaaaa
I'M A DOCTOR!
BUT I WOULDN'T LET HIM TAKE IT OFF.
HE'S STOPPED BREATHING.
I'VE GOT TO--
GASP!
THE PLASTIC SURGEON?
SHRIEEEK!
OH!! MY GOD!
JESUS!
HIS FACE--
WHO WAS HE?!
DONALD TREMAINE...
POLICE
CALL
AAHHHH!!

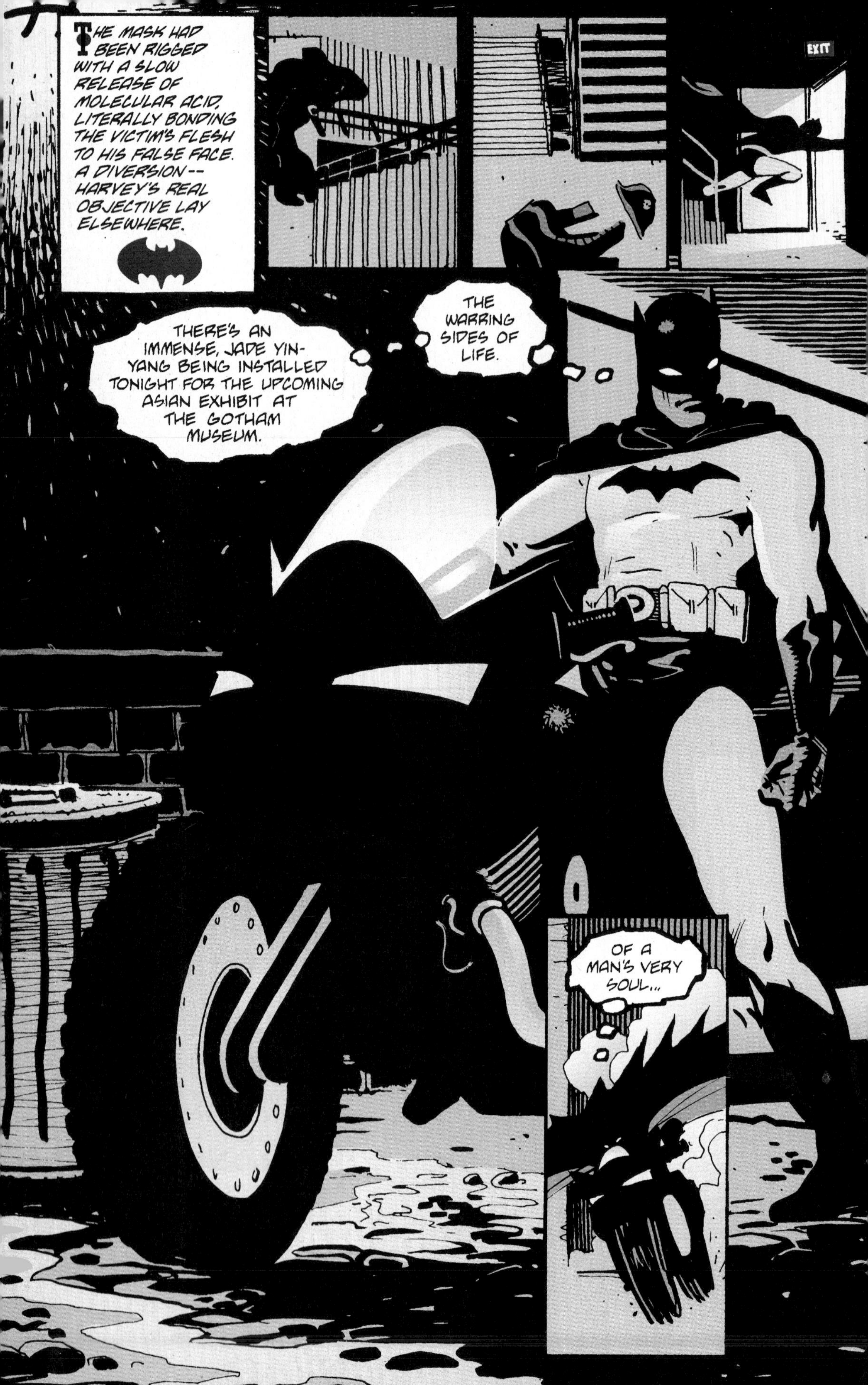
THE MASK HAD BEEN RIGGED WITH A SLOW RELEASE OF MOLECULAR ACID, LITERALLY BONDING THE VICTIM'S FLESH TO HIS FALSE FACE. A DIVERSION-- HARVEY'S REAL OBJECTIVE LAY ELSEWHERE.
EXIT
THERE'S AN IMMENSE, JADE YIN-YANG BEING INSTALLED TONIGHT FOR THE UPCOMING ASIAN EXHIBIT AT THE GOTHAM MUSEUM.
THE WARRING SIDES OF LIFE.
OF A MAN'S VERY SOUL...

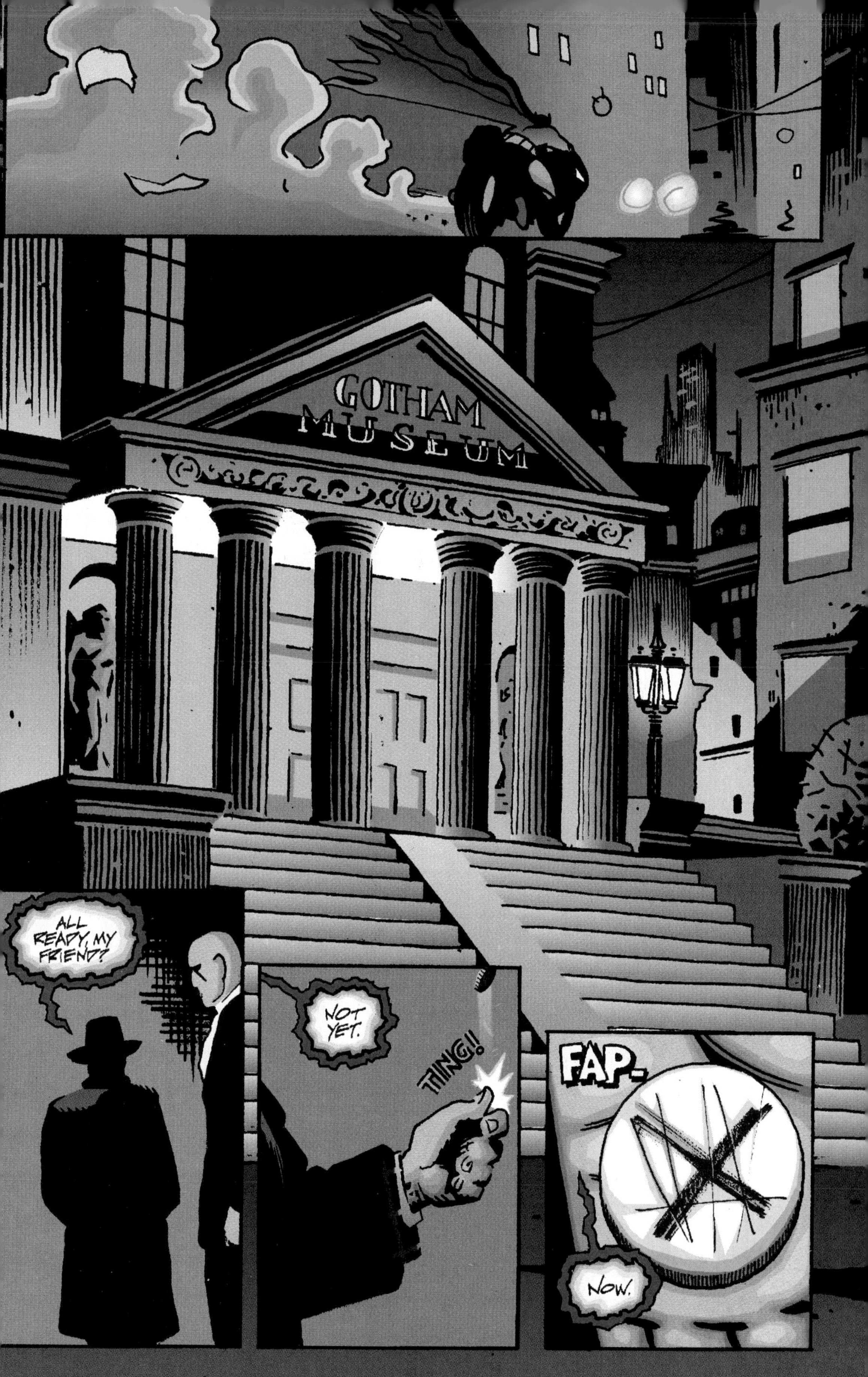
GOTHAM MUSEUM
ALL READY, MY FRIEND?
NOT YET.
TING!
FAP-
NOW.

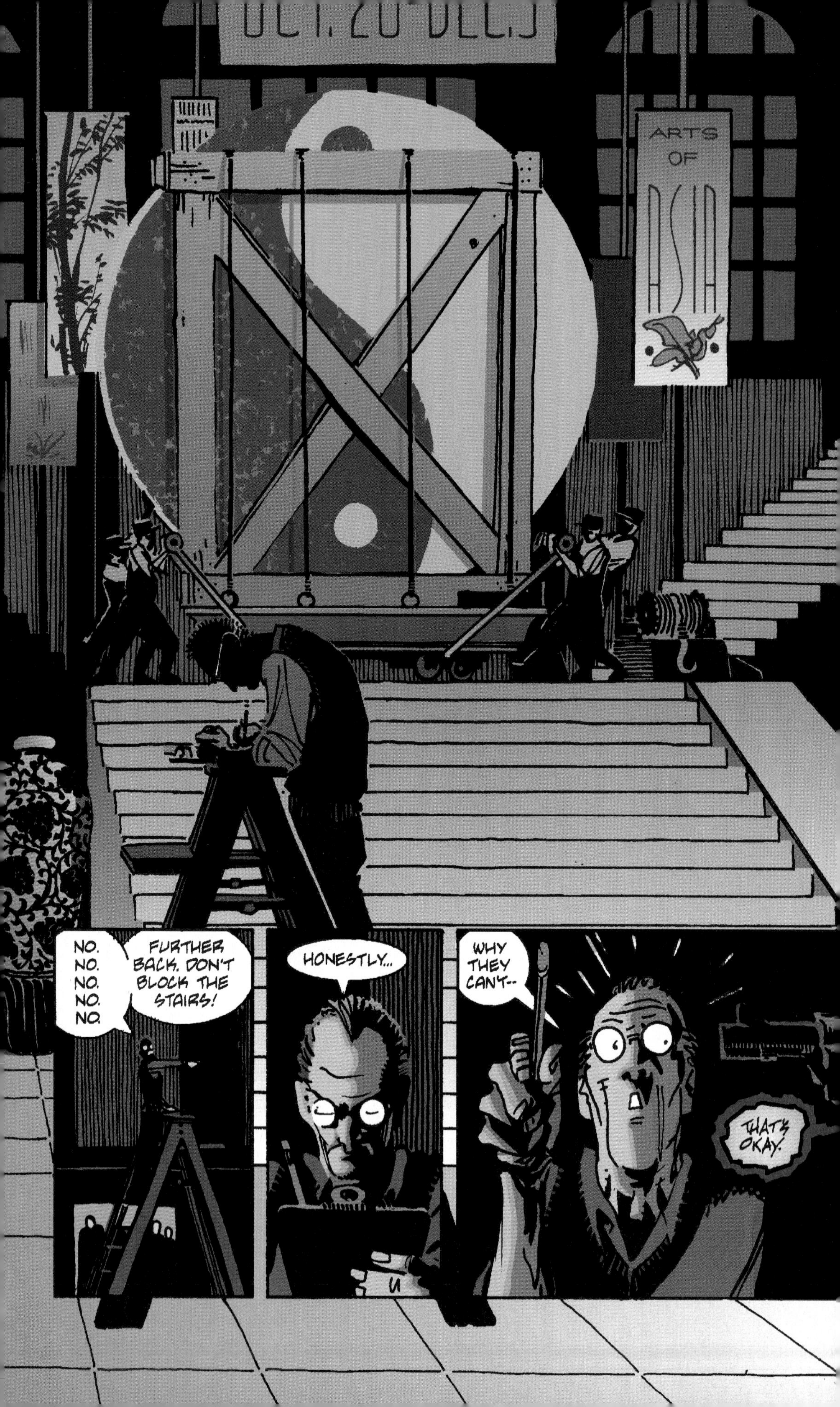
ARTS OF ASIA
NO. NO. NO. NO. NO.
FURTHER BACK. DON'T BLOCK THE STAIRS!
HONESTLY...
WHY THEY CAN'T--
THAT'S OKAY.

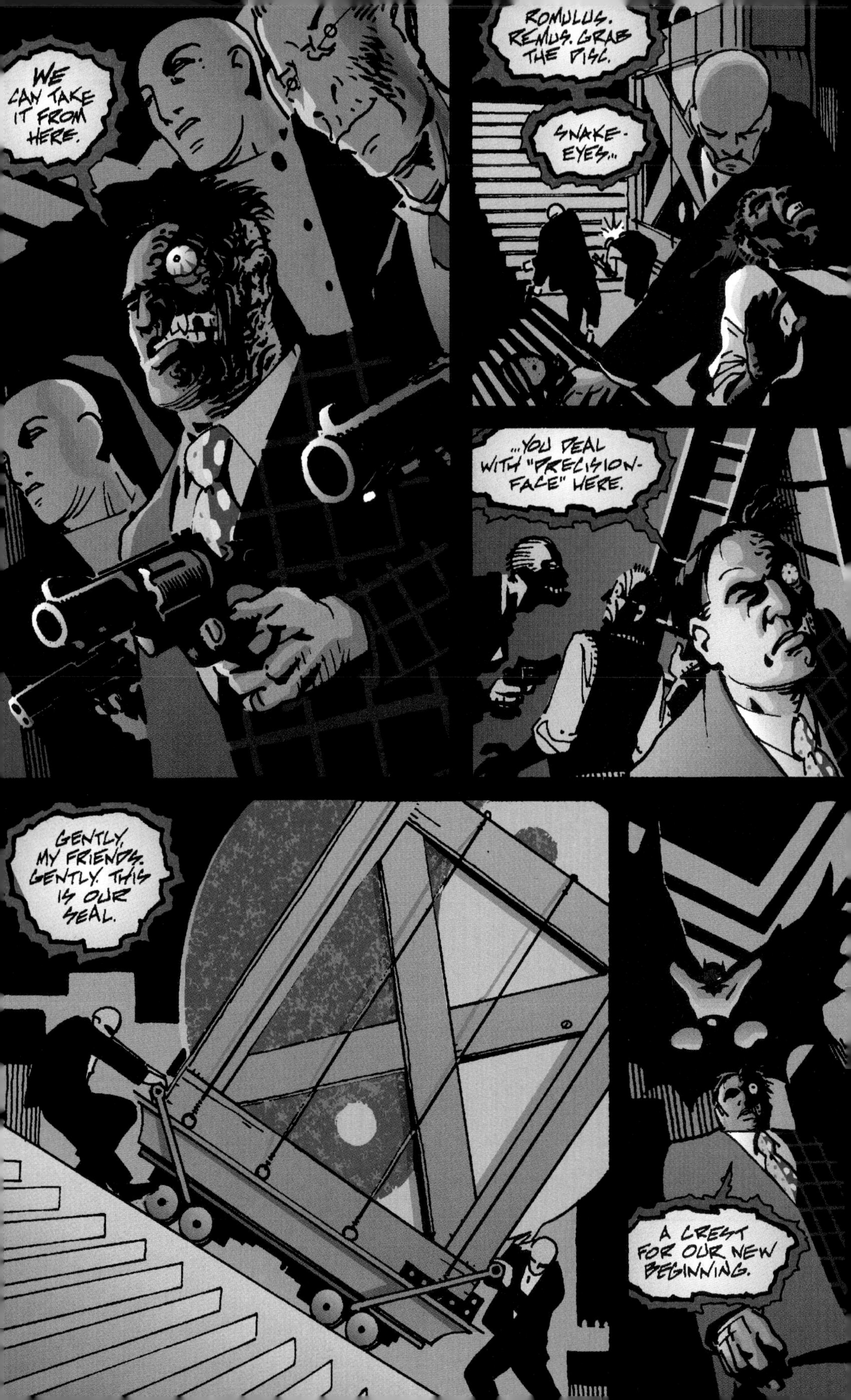
WE CAN TAKE IT FROM HERE.
ROMULUS. REMUS. GRAB THE DISC.
SNAKE-EYES...
...YOU DEAL WITH "PRECISION-FACE" HERE.
GENTLY, MY FRIENDS. GENTLY. THIS IS OUR SEAL.
A CREST FOR OUR NEW BEGINNING.

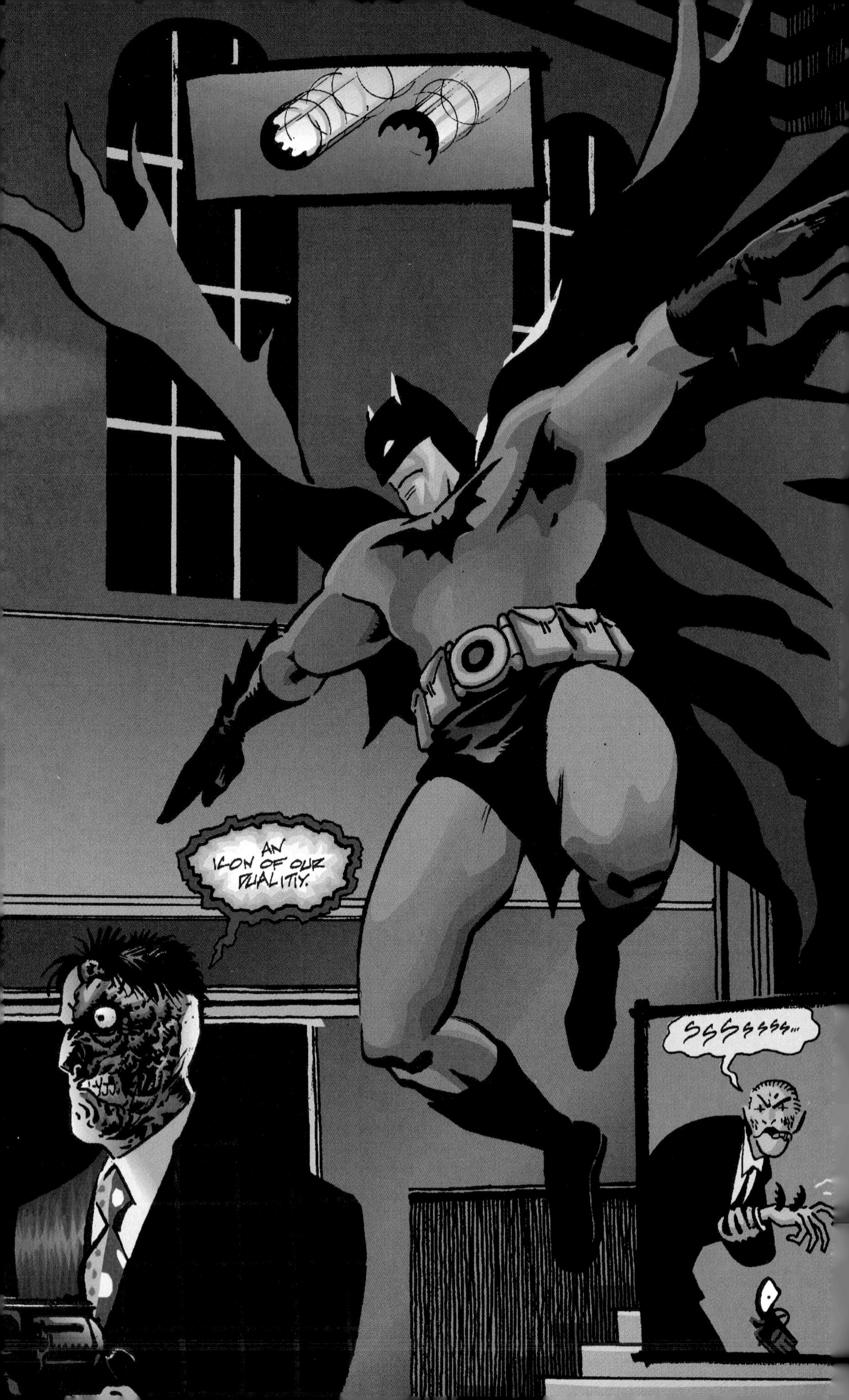
AN ICON OF OUR DUALITIY.
SSSSSSS...

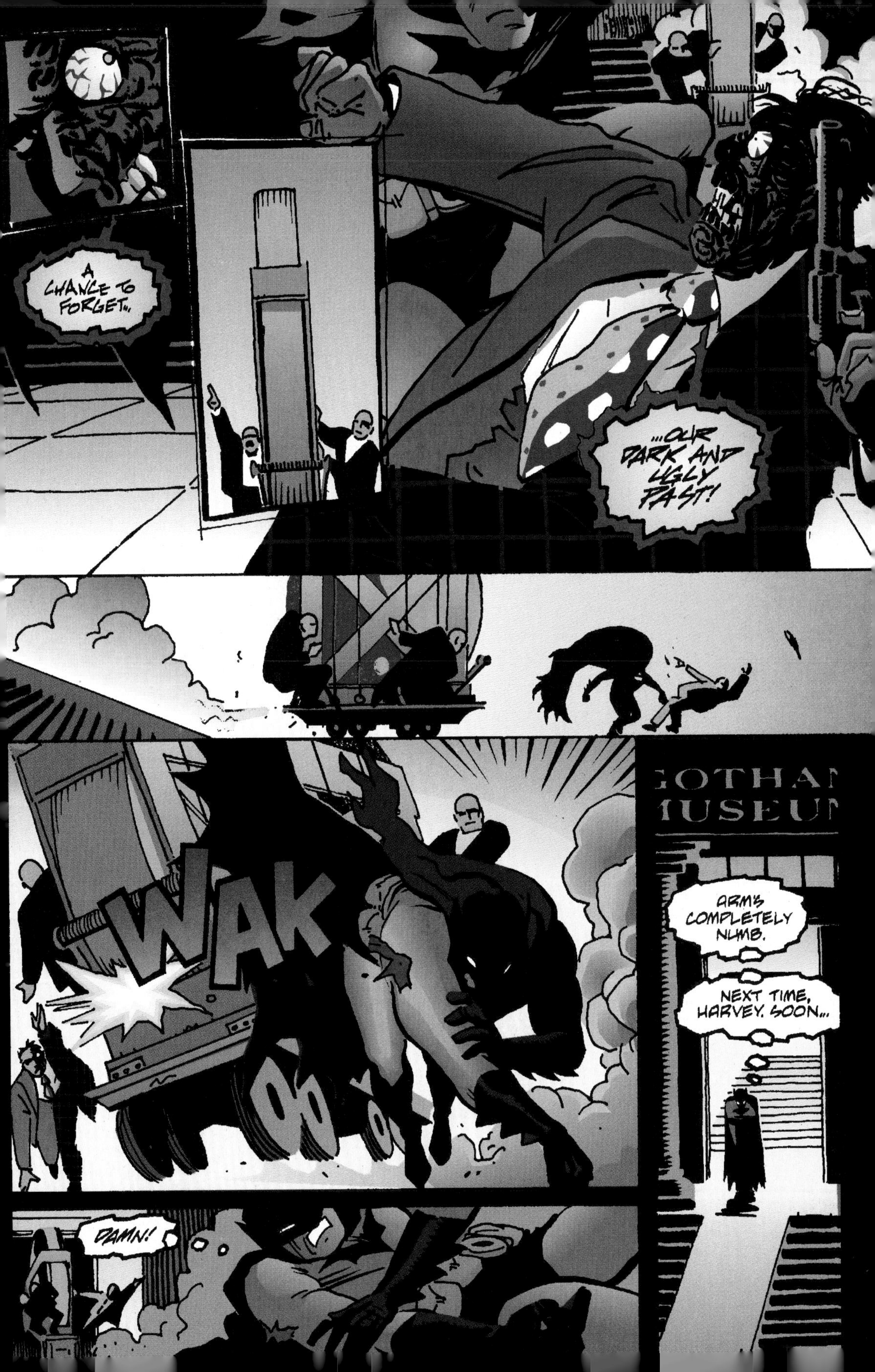
A CHANCE TO FORGET...
...OUR DARK AND UGLY PAST!
WAK
GOTHAM MUSEUM
ARM'S COMPLETELY NUMB.
NEXT TIME, HARVEY. SOON...
DAMN!

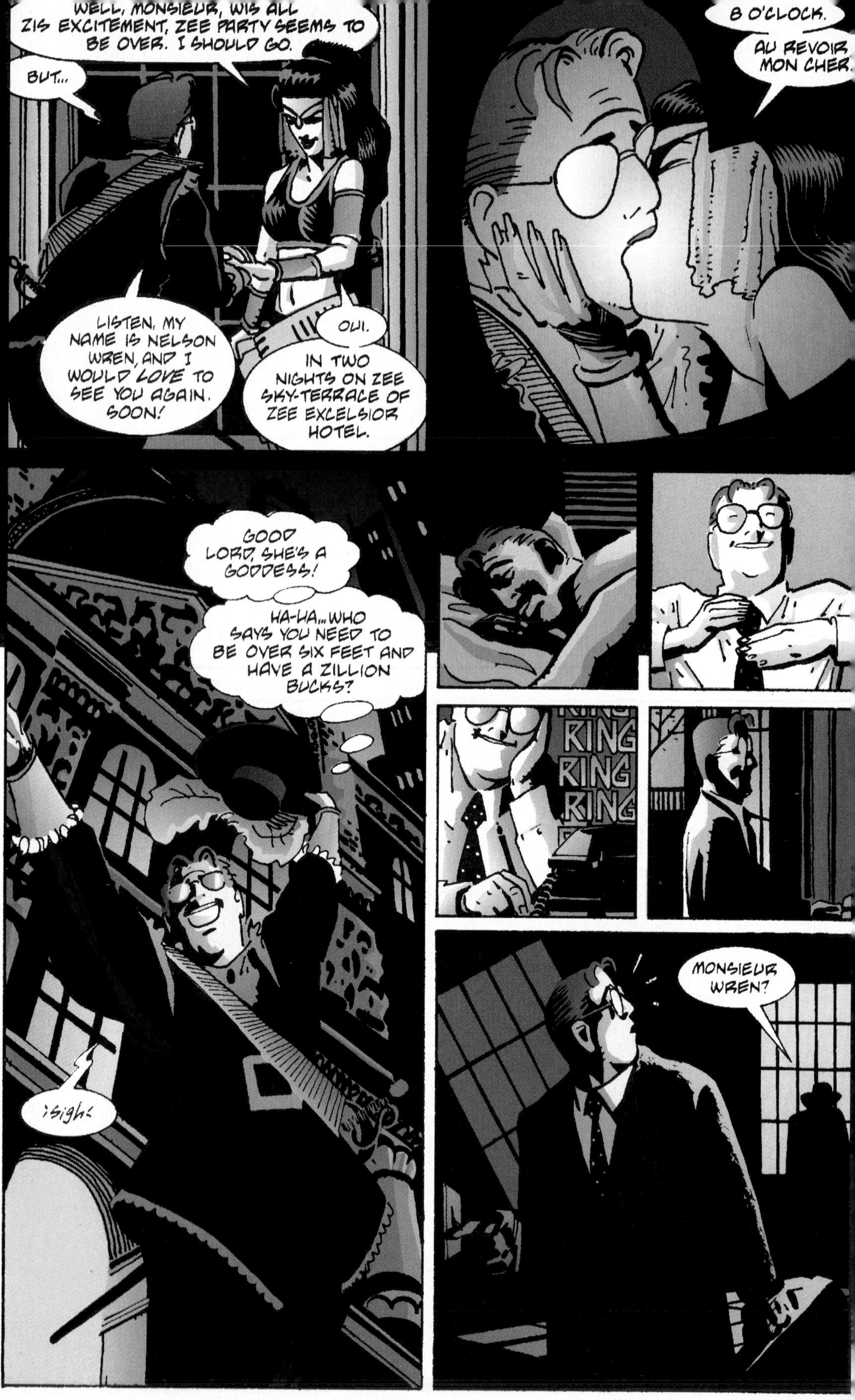
WELL, MONSIEUR, WIS ALL ZIS EXCITEMENT, ZEE PARTY SEEMS TO BE OVER. I SHOULD GO.
BUT...
LISTEN, MY NAME IS NELSON WREN, AND I WOULD LOVE TO SEE YOU AGAIN. SOON!
OUI.
IN TWO NIGHTS ON ZEE SKY-TERRACE OF ZEE EXCELSIOR HOTEL.
8 O'CLOCK.
AU REVOIR MON CHER.
GOOD LORD, SHE'S A GODDESS!
HA-HA... WHO SAYS YOU NEED TO BE OVER SIX FEET AND HAVE A ZILLION BUCKS?
¡sigh¡
RING
RING
RING
RING
MONSIEUR WREN?

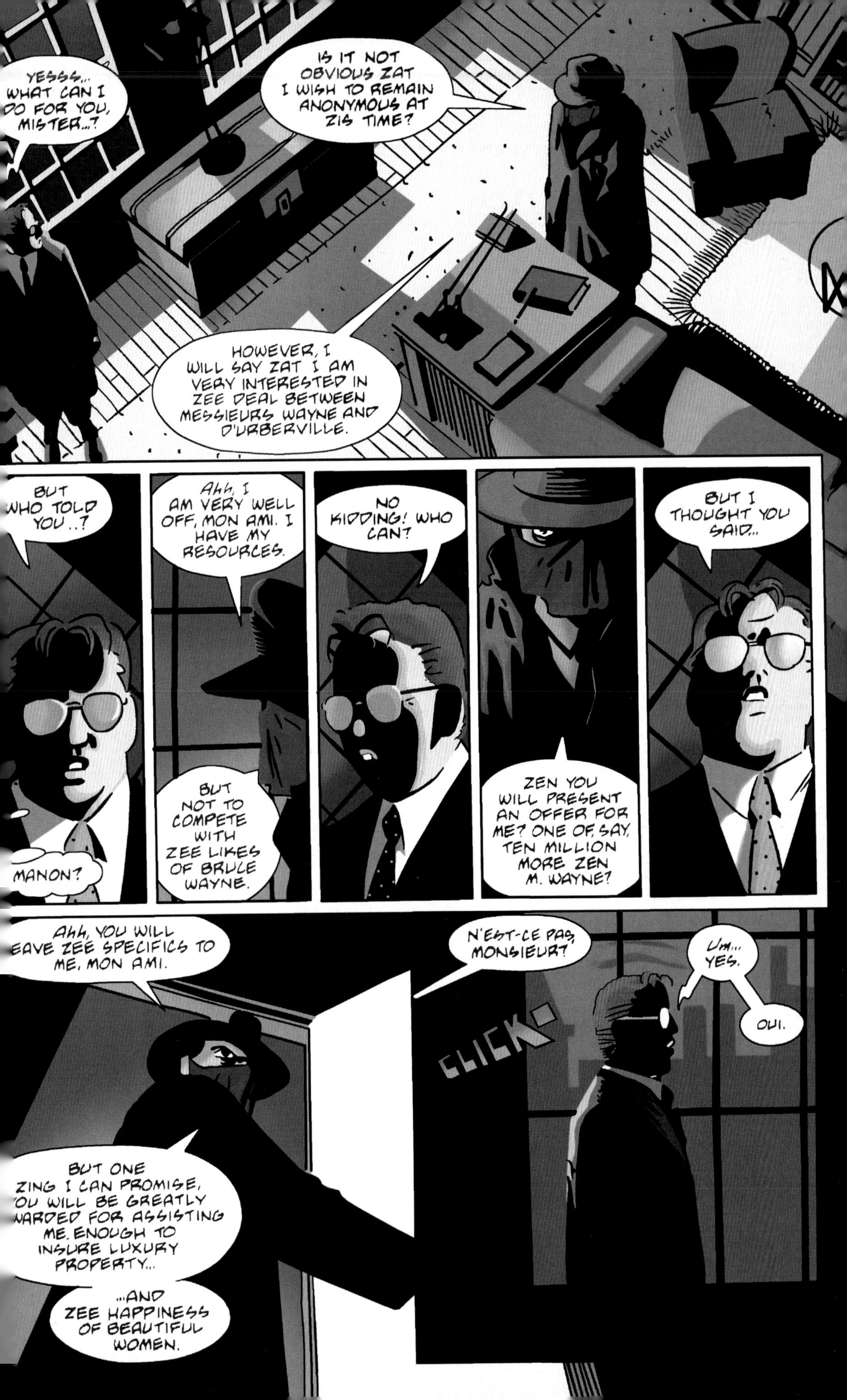
YESSS... WHAT CAN I DO FOR YOU, MISTER...?
IS IT NOT OBVIOUS ZAT I WISH TO REMAIN ANONYMOUS AT ZIS TIME?
HOWEVER, I WILL SAY ZAT I AM VERY INTERESTED IN ZEE DEAL BETWEEN MESSIEURS WAYNE AND D'URBERVILLE.
BUT WHO TOLD YOU..?
MANON?
AHH, I AM VERY WELL OFF, MON AMI. I HAVE MY RESOURCES.
BUT NOT TO COMPETE WITH ZEE LIKES OF BRUCE WAYNE.
NO KIDDING! WHO CAN?
ZEN YOU WILL PRESENT AN OFFER FOR ME? ONE OF, SAY, TEN MILLION MORE ZEN M. WAYNE?
BUT I THOUGHT YOU SAID...
AHH, YOU WILL EAVE ZEE SPECIFICS TO ME, MON AMI.
BUT ONE ZING I CAN PROMISE, OU WILL BE GREATLY WARDED FOR ASSISTING ME. ENOUGH TO INSURE LUXURY PROPERTY...
...AND ZEE HAPPINESS OF BEAUTIFUL WOMEN.
N'EST-CE PAS, MONSIEUR?
CLICK
UM... YES.
OUI.

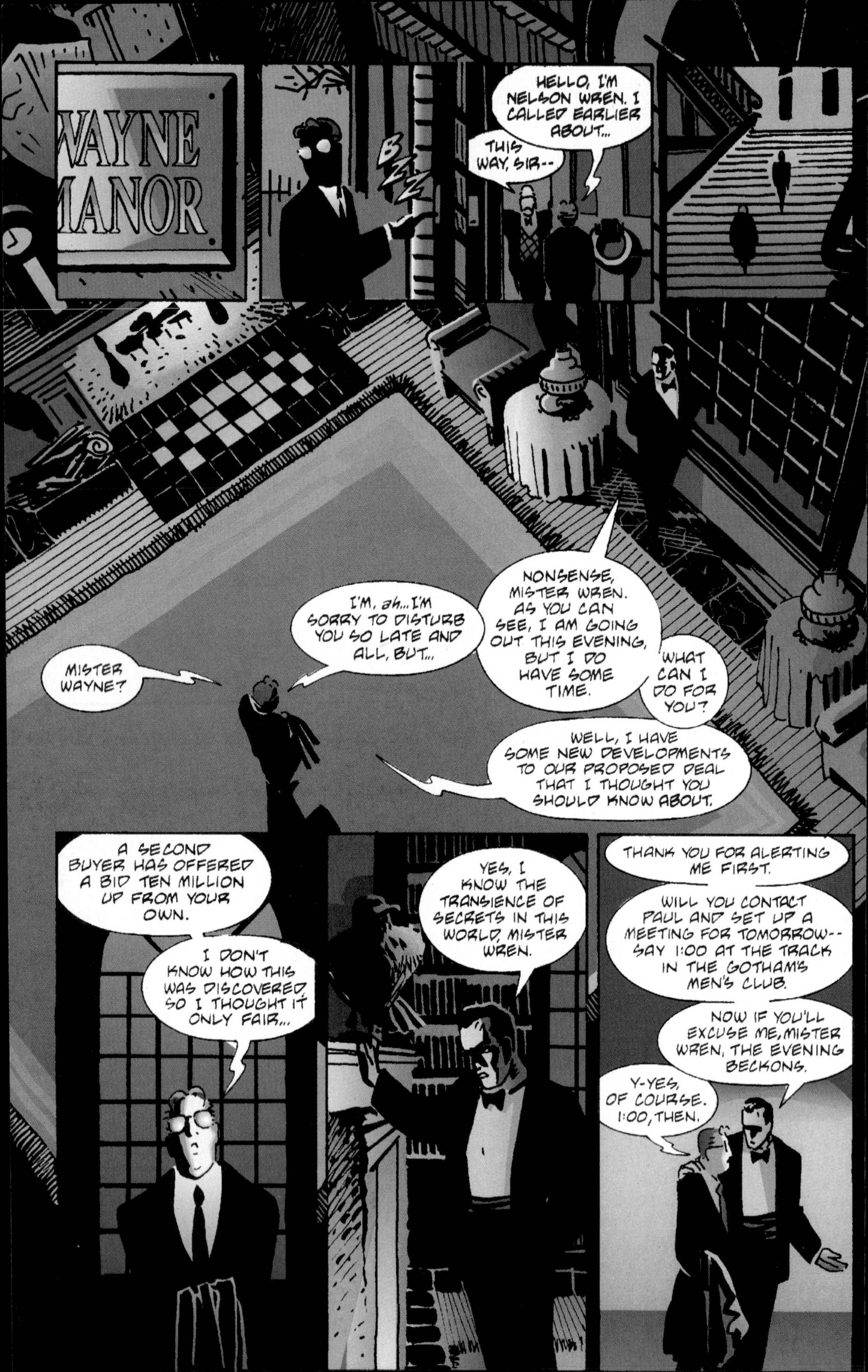
WAYNE MANOR
BZZZ
HELLO, I'M NELSON WREN. I CALLED EARLIER ABOUT...
THIS WAY, SIR--
MISTER WAYNE?
I'M, ah... I'M SORRY TO DISTURB YOU SO LATE AND ALL, BUT...
NONSENSE, MISTER WREN. AS YOU CAN SEE, I AM GOING OUT THIS EVENING, BUT I DO HAVE SOME TIME.
WHAT CAN I DO FOR YOU?
WELL, I HAVE SOME NEW DEVELOPMENTS TO OUR PROPOSED DEAL THAT I THOUGHT YOU SHOULD KNOW ABOUT.
A SECOND BUYER HAS OFFERED A BID TEN MILLION UP FROM YOUR OWN.
I DON'T KNOW HOW THIS WAS DISCOVERED SO I THOUGHT IT ONLY FAIR...
YES, I KNOW THE TRANSIENCE OF SECRETS IN THIS WORLD, MISTER WREN.
THANK YOU FOR ALERTING ME FIRST.
WILL YOU CONTACT PAUL AND SET UP A MEETING FOR TOMORROW-- SAY 1:00 AT THE TRACK IN THE GOTHAM'S MEN'S CLUB.
NOW IF YOU'LL EXCUSE ME, MISTER WREN, THE EVENING BECKONS.
Y-YES, OF COURSE. 1:00, THEN.

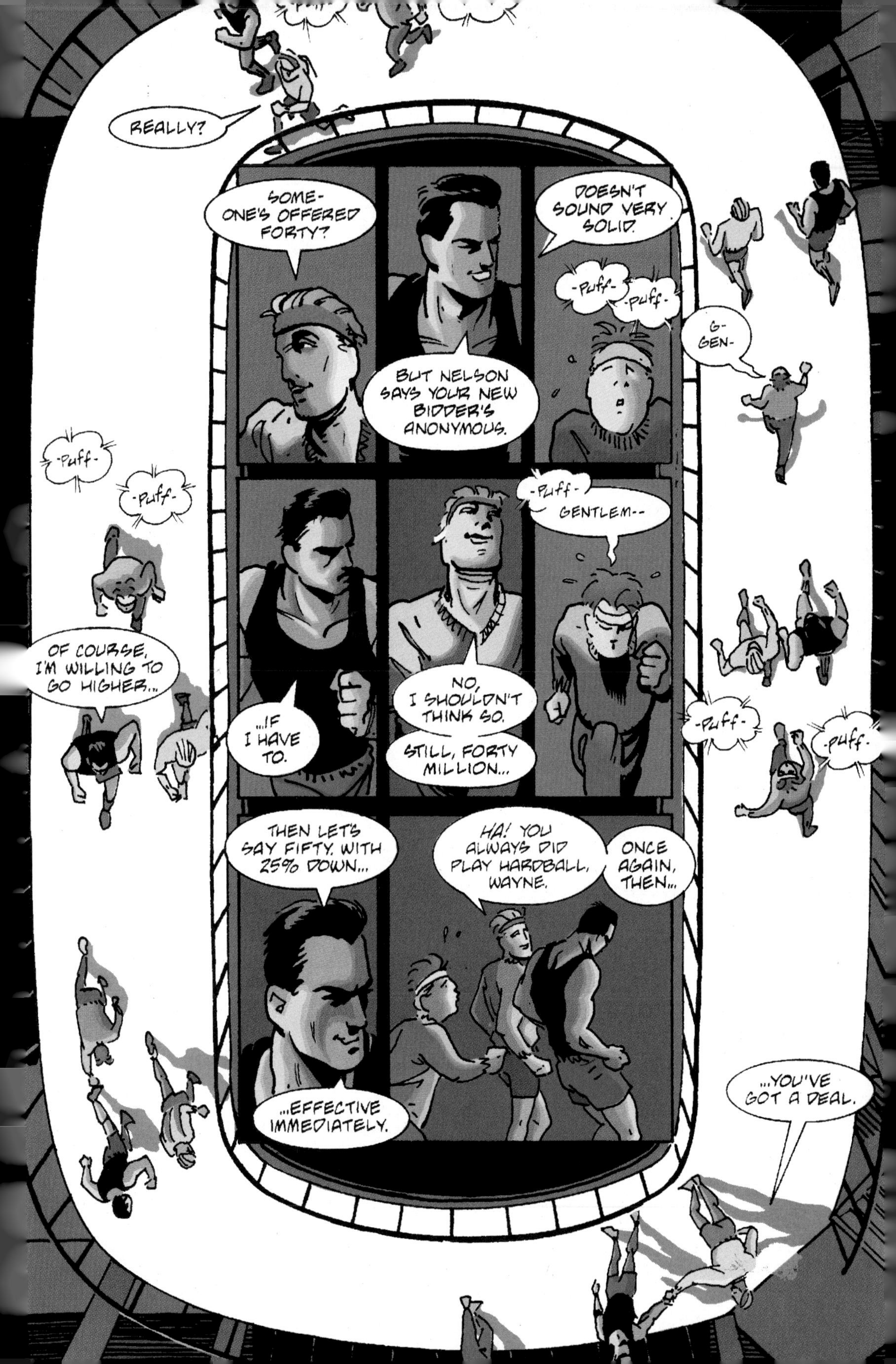
REALLY?
SOME-ONE'S OFFERED FORTY?
BUT NELSON SAYS YOUR NEW BIDDER'S ANONYMOUS.
DOESN'T SOUND VERY SOLID.
-Puff-
-puff-
G-GEN-
-Puff-
-puff-
OF COURSE, I'M WILLING TO GO HIGHER...
...IF I HAVE TO.
NO, I SHOULDN'T THINK SO.
STILL, FORTY MILLION...
-Puff-
GENTLEM--
-Puff-
-puff-
THEN LET'S SAY FIFTY, WITH 25% DOWN...
...EFFECTIVE IMMEDIATELY.
HA! YOU ALWAYS DID PLAY HARDBALL, WAYNE.
ONCE AGAIN, THEN...
...YOU'VE GOT A DEAL.

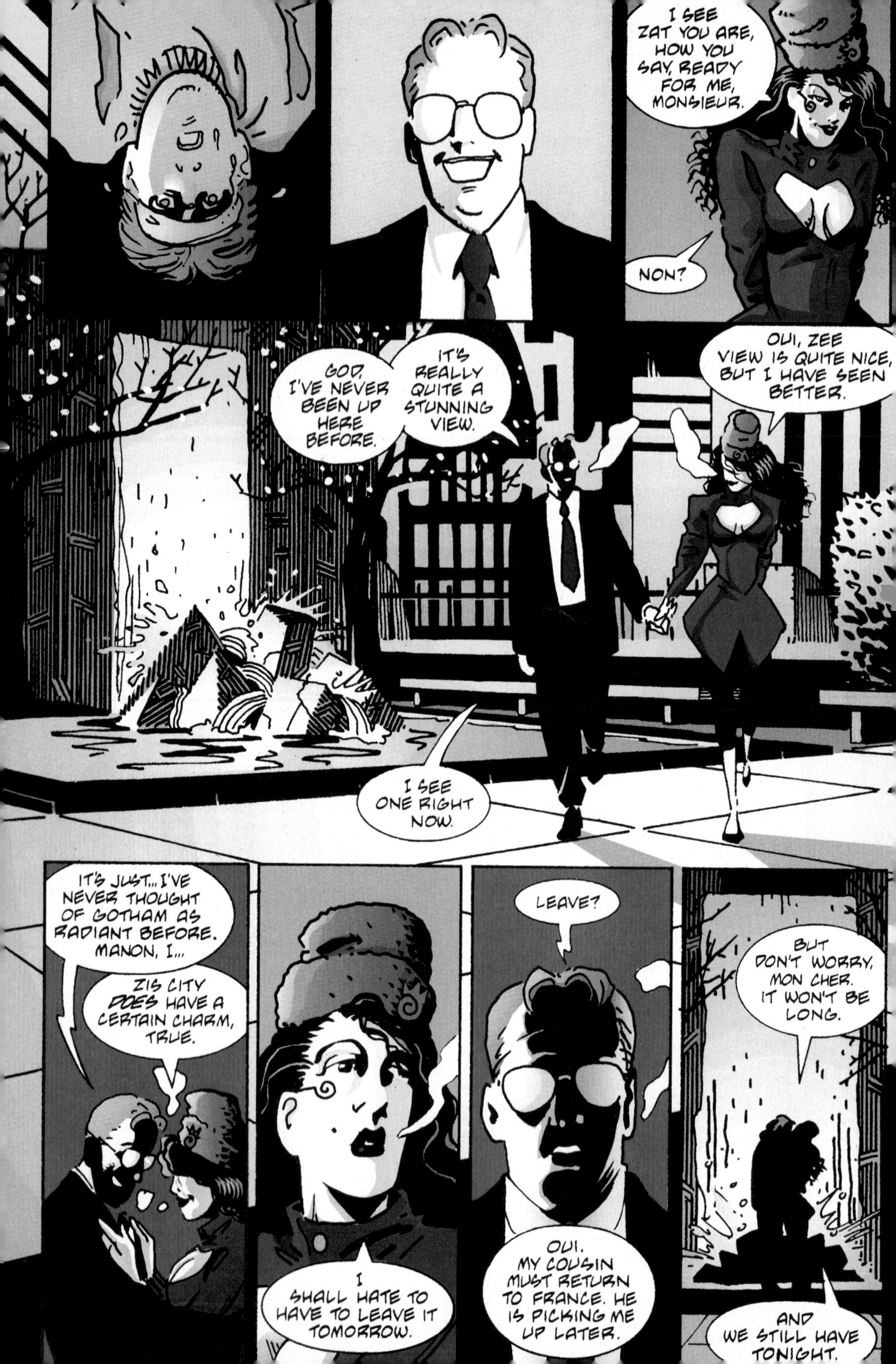
I SEE ZAT YOU ARE, HOW YOU SAY, READY FOR ME, MONSIEUR.
NON?
GOD, I'VE NEVER BEEN UP HERE BEFORE.
IT'S REALLY QUITE A STUNNING VIEW.
OUI, ZEE VIEW IS QUITE NICE, BUT I HAVE SEEN BETTER.
I SEE ONE RIGHT NOW.
IT'S JUST... I'VE NEVER THOUGHT OF GOTHAM AS RADIANT BEFORE. MANON, I...
ZIS CITY DOES HAVE A CERTAIN CHARM, TRUE.
I SHALL HATE TO HAVE TO LEAVE IT TOMORROW.
LEAVE?
OUI. MY COUSIN MUST RETURN TO FRANCE. HE IS PICKING ME UP LATER.
BUT DON'T WORRY, MON CHER. IT WON'T BE LONG.
AND WE STILL HAVE TONIGHT.

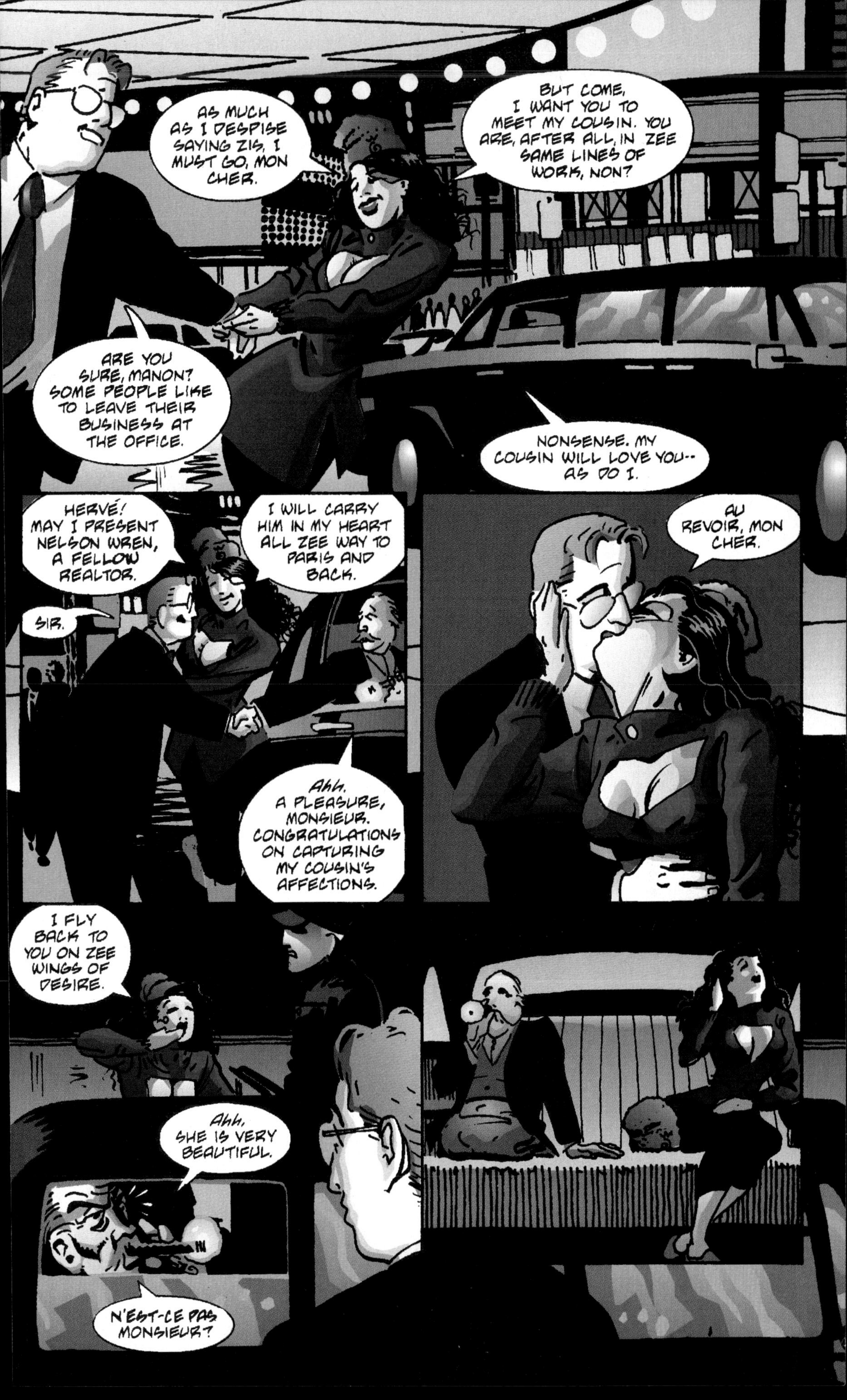
AS MUCH AS I DESPISE SAYING ZIS, I MUST GO, MON CHER.
BUT COME, I WANT YOU TO MEET MY COUSIN. YOU ARE, AFTER ALL, IN ZEE SAME LINES OF WORK, NON?
ARE YOU SURE, MANON? SOME PEOPLE LIKE TO LEAVE THEIR BUSINESS AT THE OFFICE.
NONSENSE. MY COUSIN WILL LOVE YOU-- AS DO I.
HERVÉ! MAY I PRESENT NELSON WREN, A FELLOW REALTOR.
I WILL CARRY HIM IN MY HEART ALL ZEE WAY TO PARIS AND BACK.
SIR.
Ahh. A PLEASURE, MONSIEUR. CONGRATULATIONS ON CAPTURING MY COUSIN'S AFFECTIONS.
AU REVOIR, MON CHER.
I FLY BACK TO YOU ON ZEE WINGS OF DESIRE.
Ahh, SHE IS VERY BEAUTIFUL.
N'EST-CE PAS MONSIEUR?

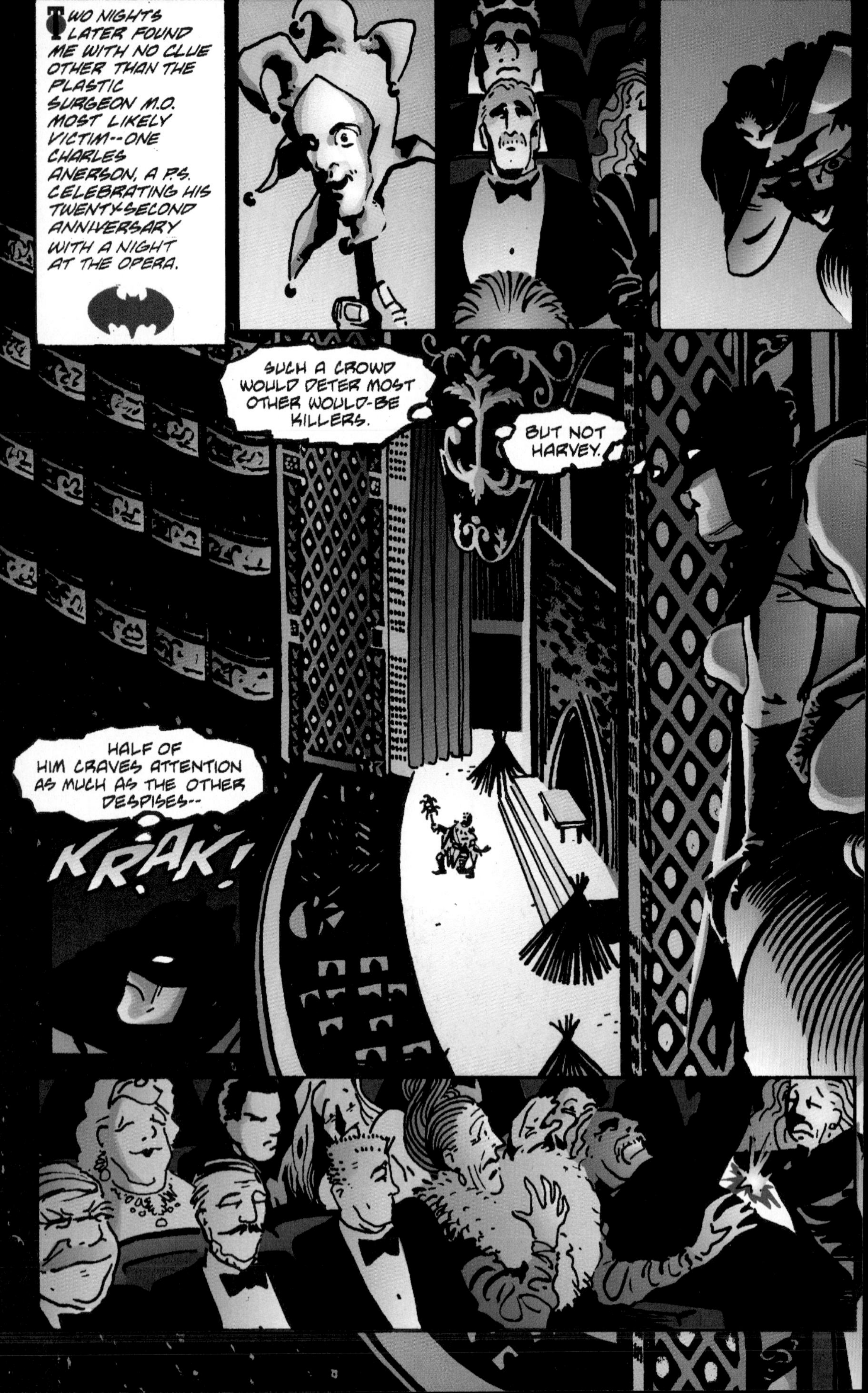
TWO NIGHTS LATER FOUND ME WITH NO CLUE OTHER THAN THE PLASTIC SURGEON M.O. MOST LIKELY VICTIM--ONE CHARLES ANERSON, A P.S. CELEBRATING HIS TWENTY-SECOND ANNIVERSARY WITH A NIGHT AT THE OPERA.
SUCH A CROWD WOULD DETER MOST OTHER WOULD-BE KILLERS.
BUT NOT HARVEY.
HALF OF HIM CRAVES ATTENTION AS MUCH AS THE OTHER DESPISES--
KRAK!

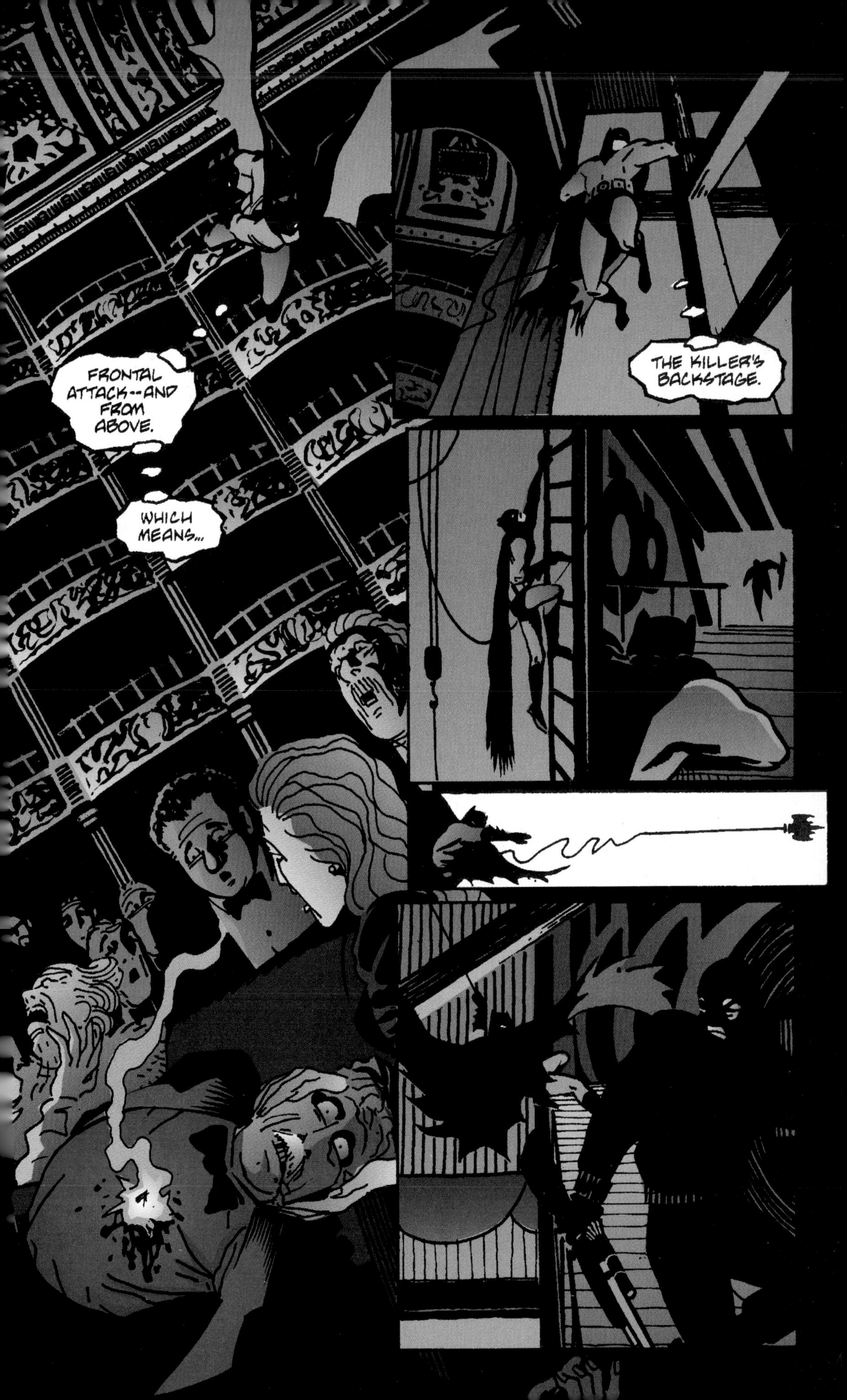
FRONTAL ATTACK--AND FROM ABOVE.
WHICH MEANS...
THE KILLER'S BACKSTAGE.

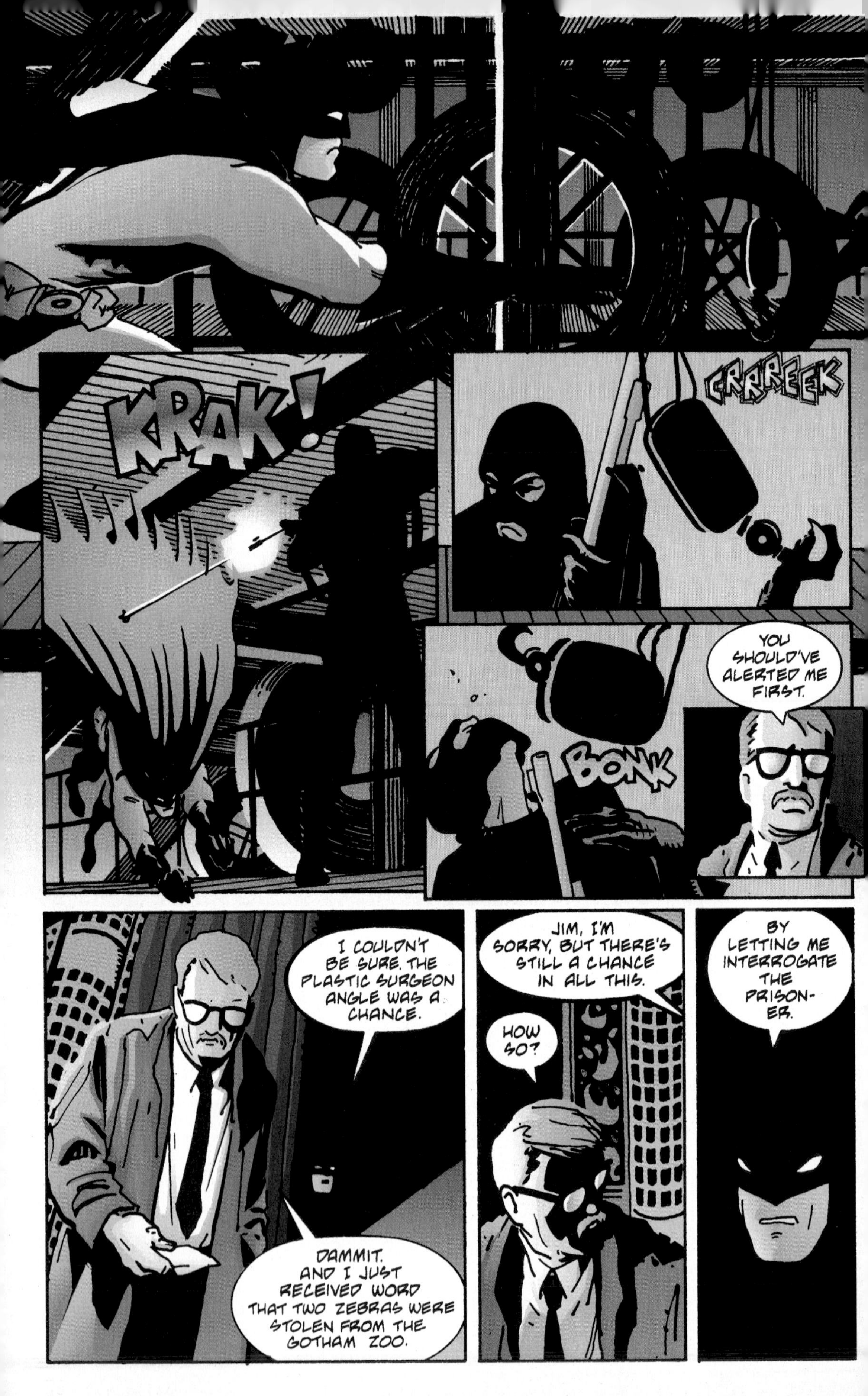
KRAK!
CRRREEK
BONK
YOU SHOULD'VE ALERTED ME FIRST.
I COULDN'T BE SURE. THE PLASTIC SURGEON ANGLE WAS A CHANCE.
DAMMIT. AND I JUST RECEIVED WORD THAT TWO ZEBRAS WERE STOLEN FROM THE GOTHAM ZOO.
JIM, I'M SORRY, BUT THERE'S STILL A CHANCE IN ALL THIS.
HOW SO?
BY LETTING ME INTERROGATE THE PRISON-ER.

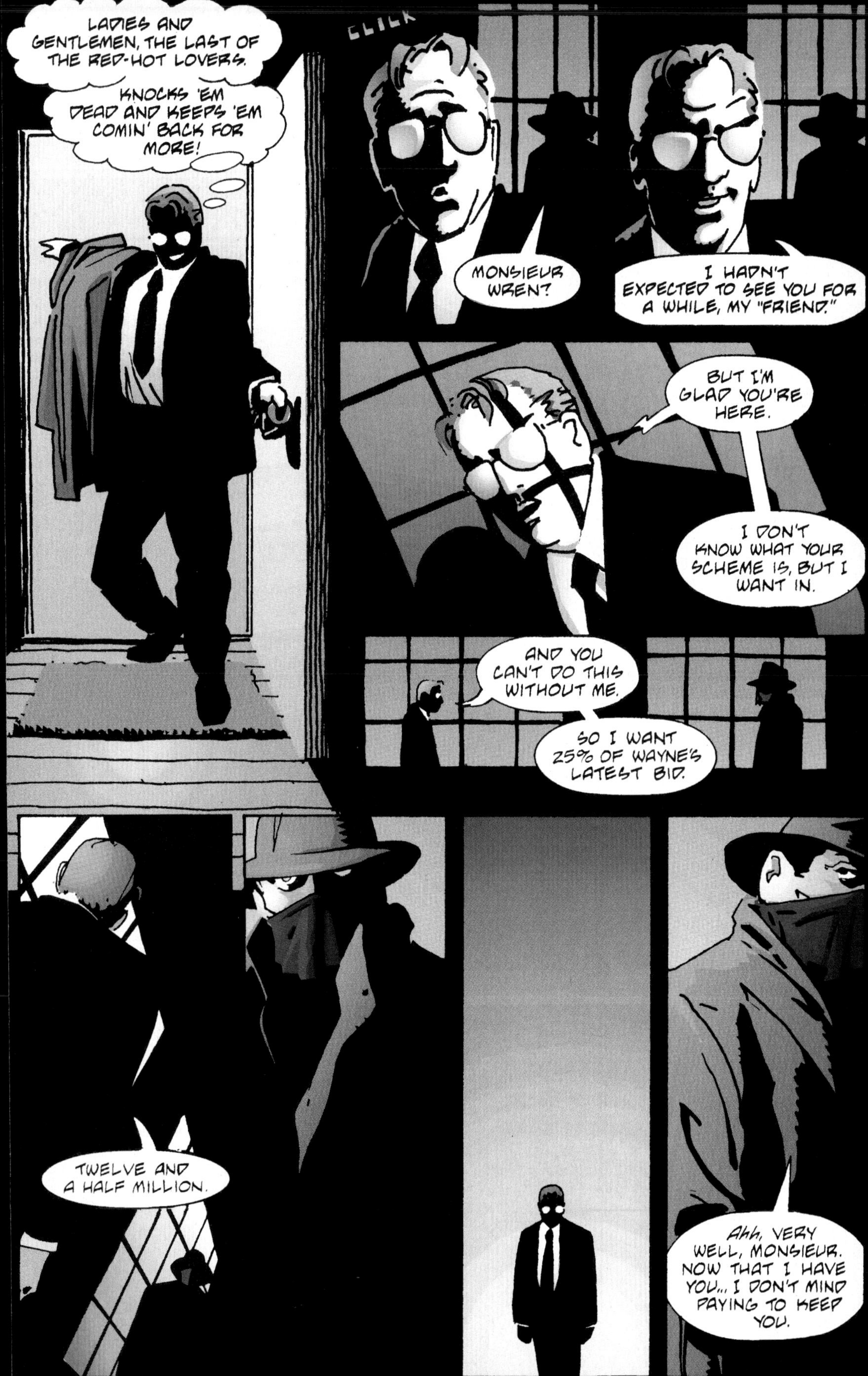
LADIES AND GENTLEMEN, THE LAST OF THE RED-HOT LOVERS.
KNOCKS 'EM DEAD AND KEEPS 'EM COMIN' BACK FOR MORE!
CLICK
MONSIEUR WREN?
I HADN'T EXPECTED TO SEE YOU FOR A WHILE, MY "FRIEND."
BUT I'M GLAD YOU'RE HERE.
I DON'T KNOW WHAT YOUR SCHEME IS, BUT I WANT IN.
AND YOU CAN'T DO THIS WITHOUT ME.
SO I WANT 25% OF WAYNE'S LATEST BID.
TWELVE AND A HALF MILLION.
AHH, VERY WELL, MONSIEUR. NOW THAT I HAVE YOU... I DON'T MIND PAYING TO KEEP YOU.

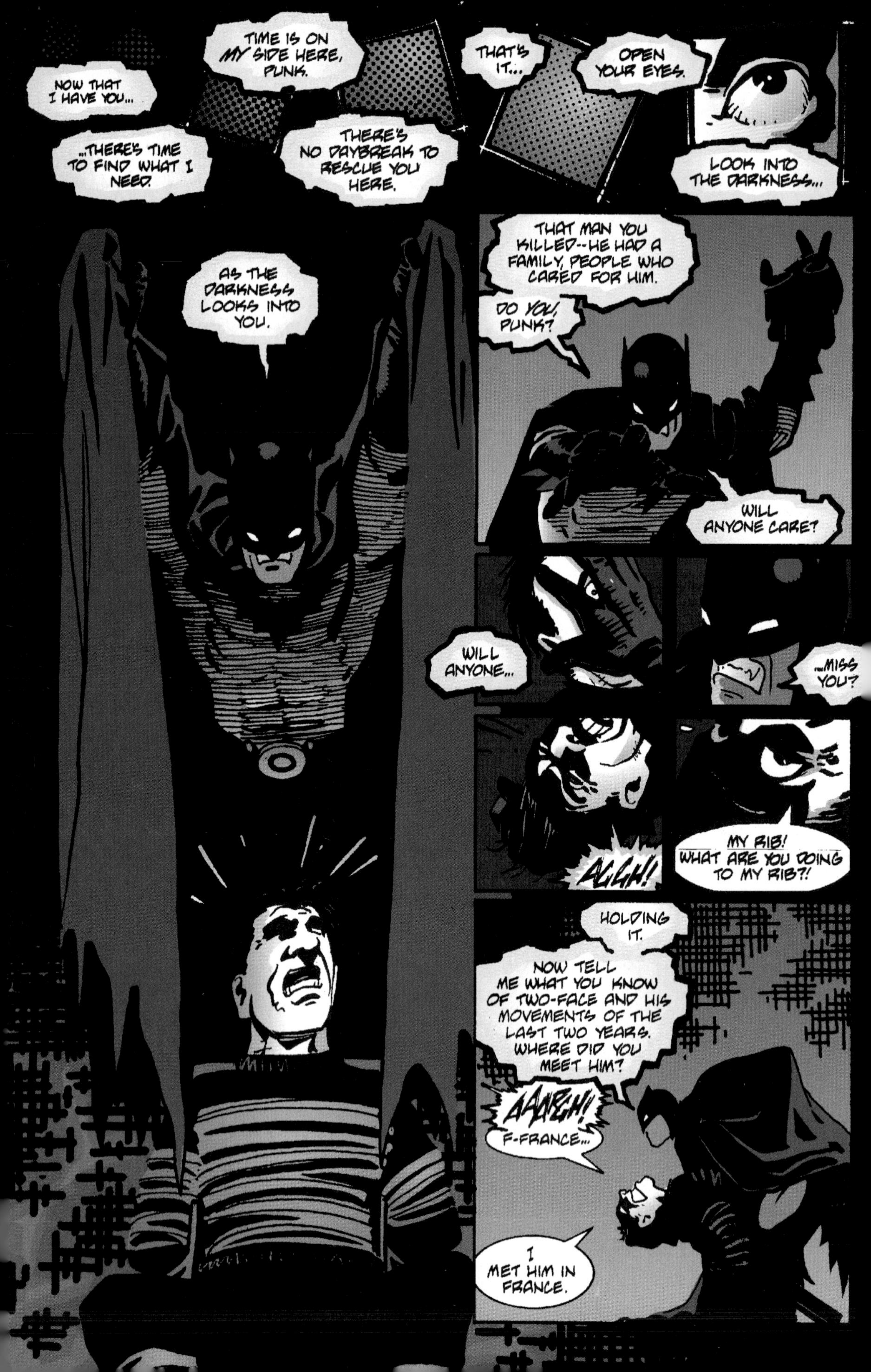
NOW THAT I HAVE YOU...
...THERE'S TIME TO FIND WHAT I NEED.
TIME IS ON MY SIDE HERE, PUNK.
THERE'S NO DAYBREAK TO RESCUE YOU HERE.
THAT'S IT...
OPEN YOUR EYES.
LOOK INTO THE DARKNESS...
AS THE DARKNESS LOOKS INTO YOU.
THAT MAN YOU KILLED--HE HAD A FAMILY, PEOPLE WHO CARED FOR HIM.
DO YOU, PUNK?
WILL ANYONE CARE?
WILL ANYONE...
...MISS YOU?
AGGH!
MY RIB! WHAT ARE YOU DOING TO MY RIB?!
HOLDING IT.
NOW TELL ME WHAT YOU KNOW OF TWO-FACE AND HIS MOVEMENTS OF THE LAST TWO YEARS. WHERE DID YOU MEET HIM?
AAARGH! F-FRANCE...
I MET HIM IN FRANCE.

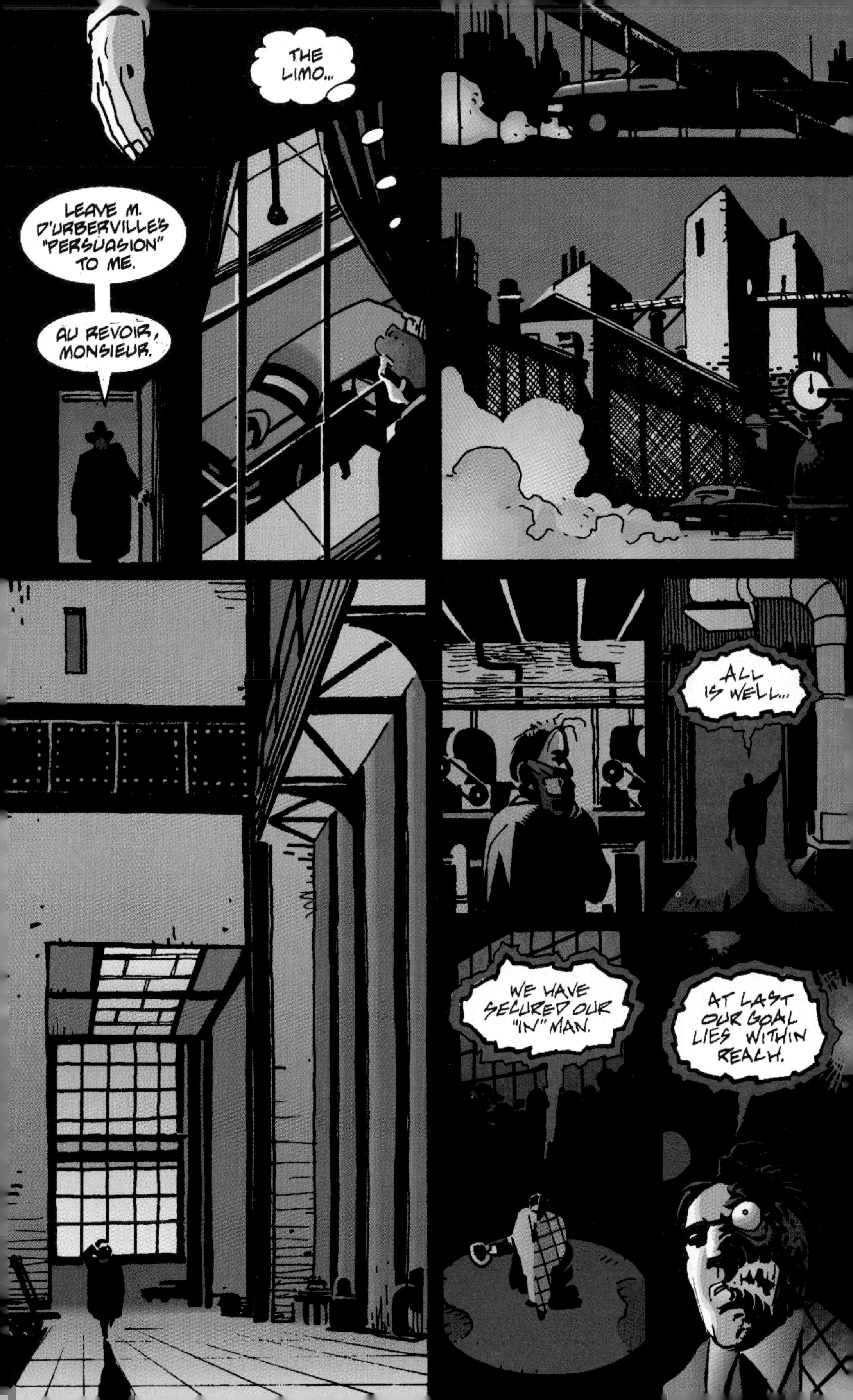
THE LIMO...
LEAVE M. D'URBERVILLE'S "PERSUASION" TO ME.
AU REVOIR, MONSIEUR.
ALL IS WELL...
WE HAVE SECURED OUR "IN" MAN.
AT LAST OUR GOAL LIES WITHIN REACH.

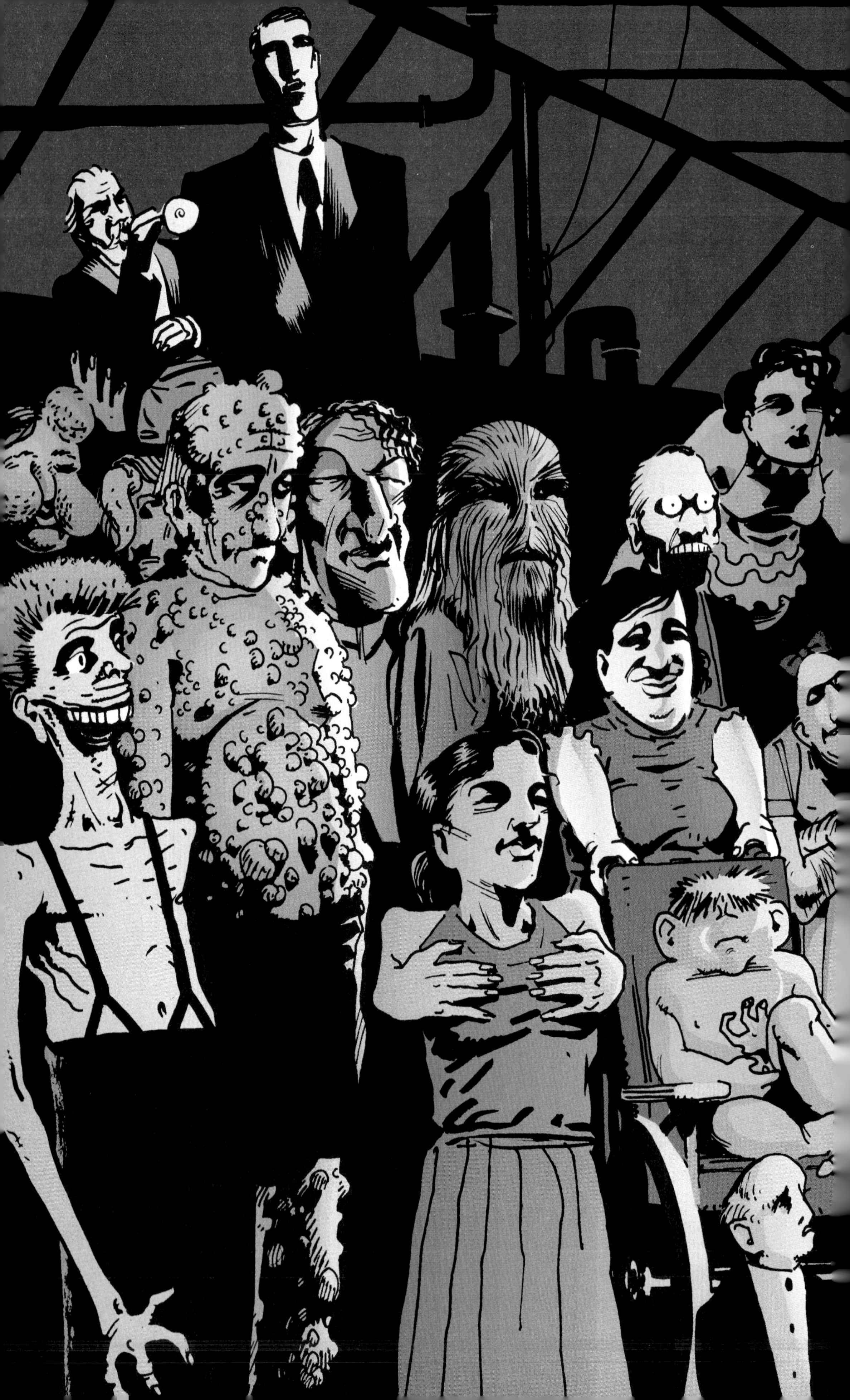

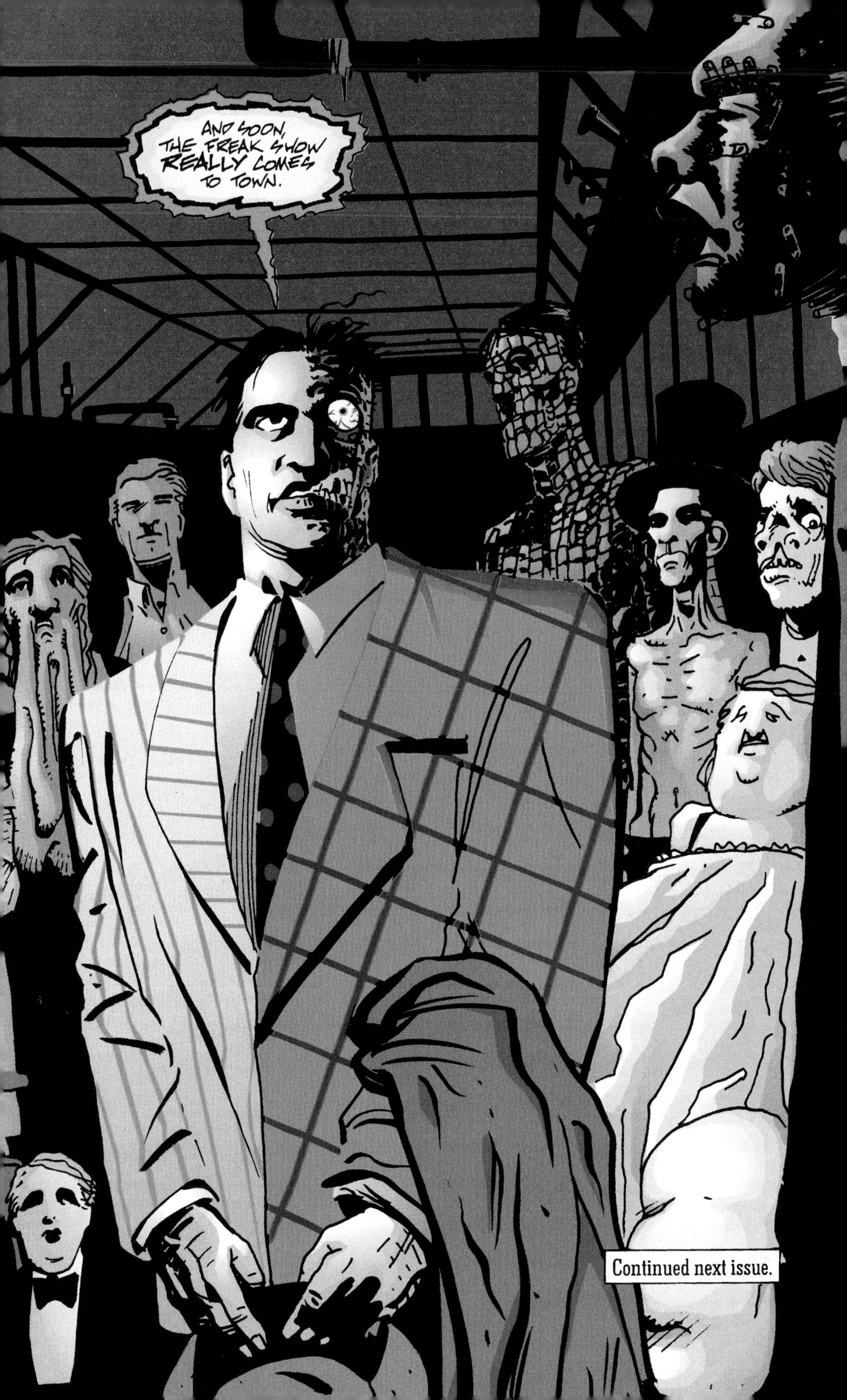
AND SOON, THE FREAK SHOW REALLY COMES TO TOWN.
Continued next issue.

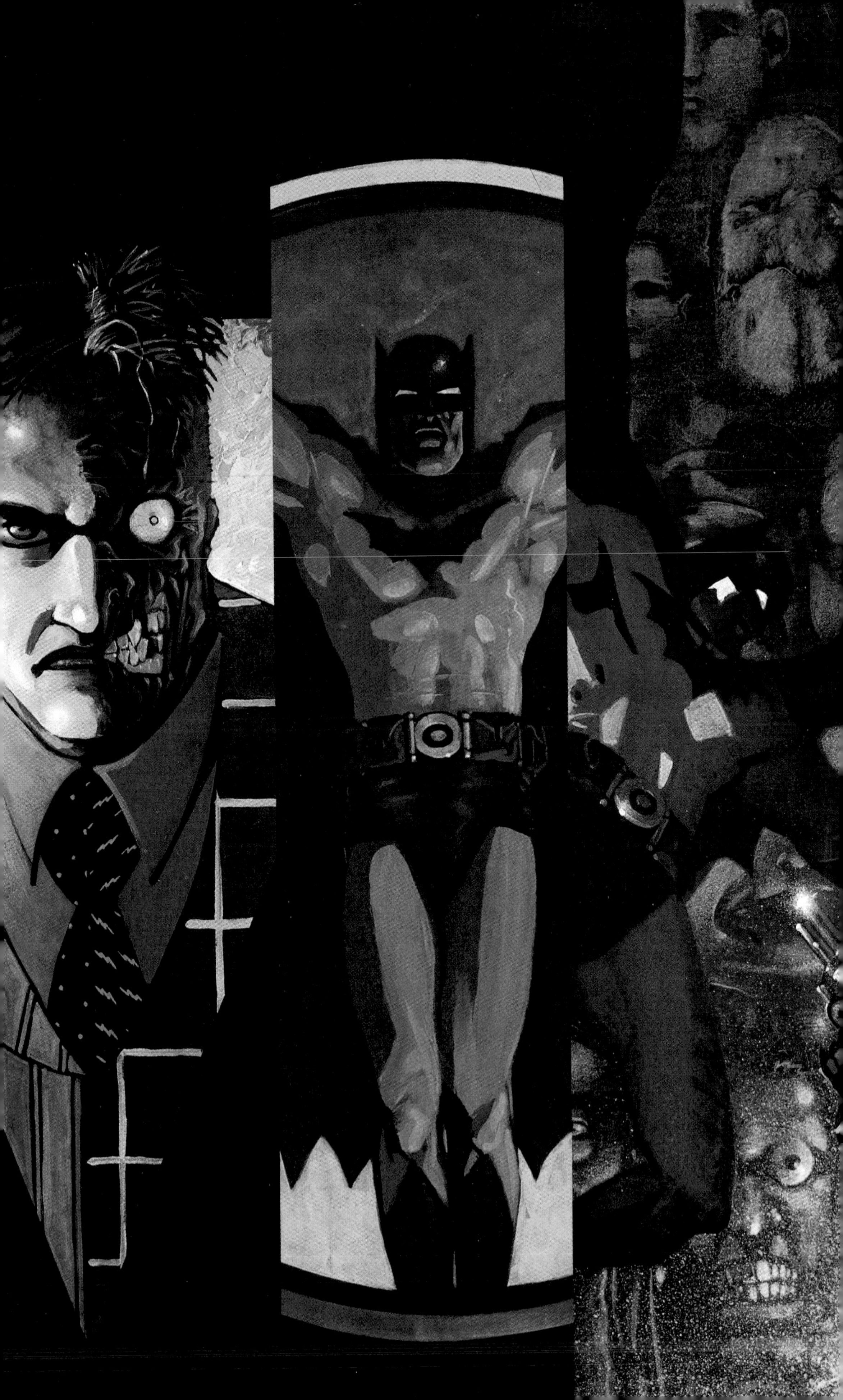

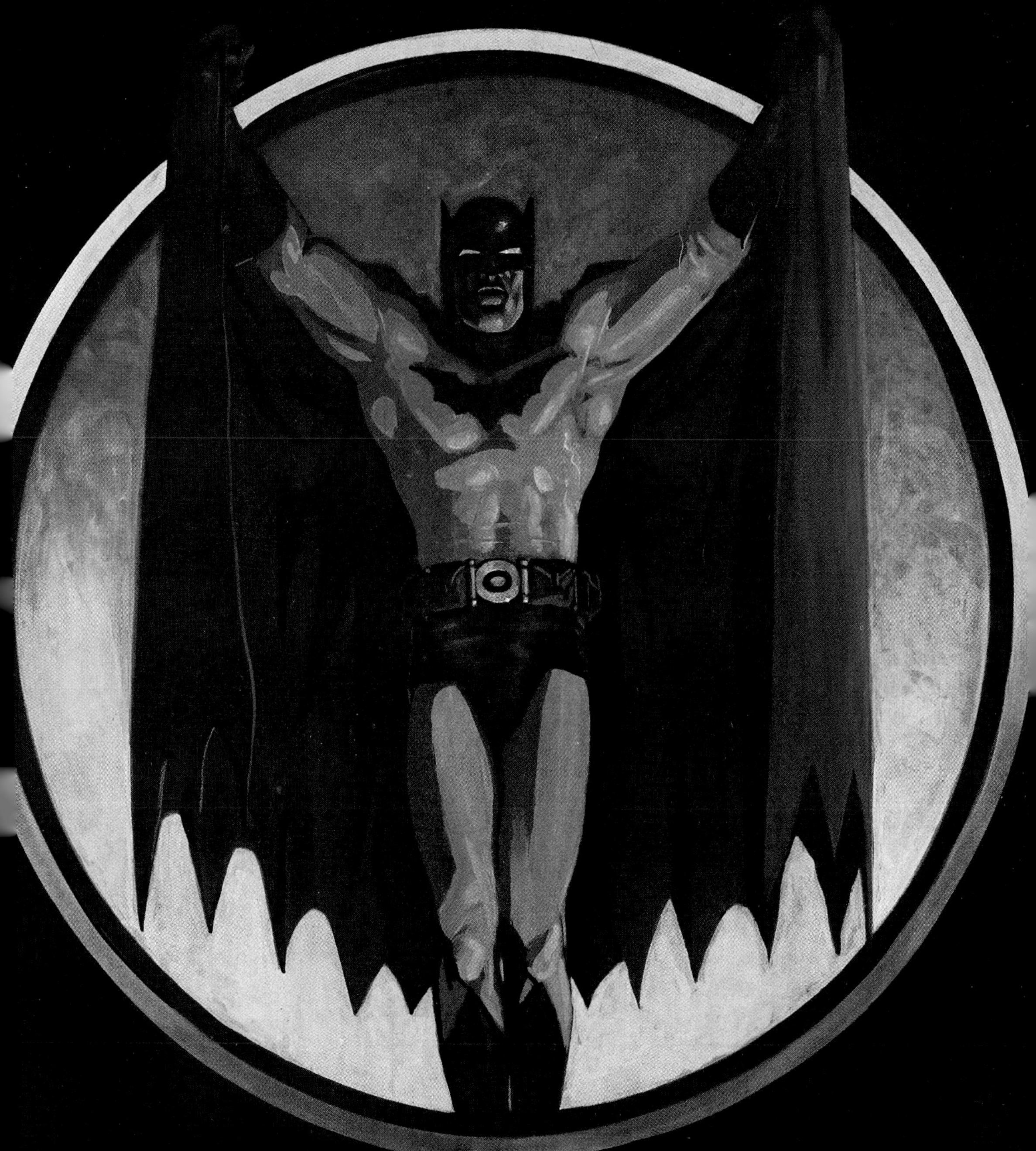

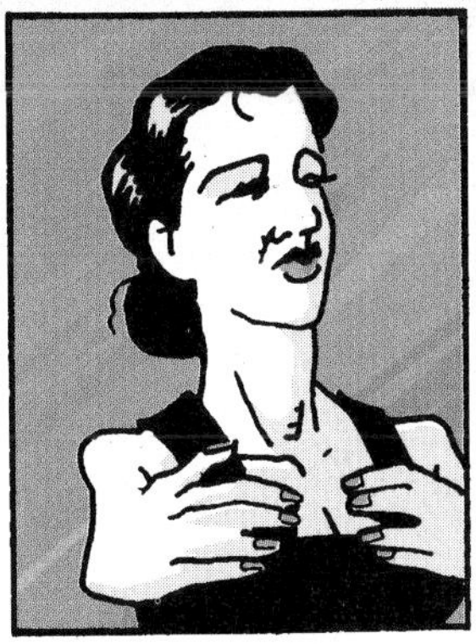

Violette Fournier--Thalidomide casualty. Missing for twenty months.

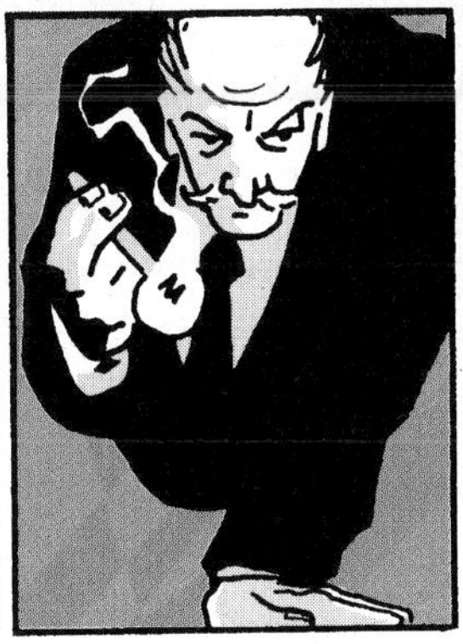

Anton Ecole--Born legless. Missing for seventeen months.

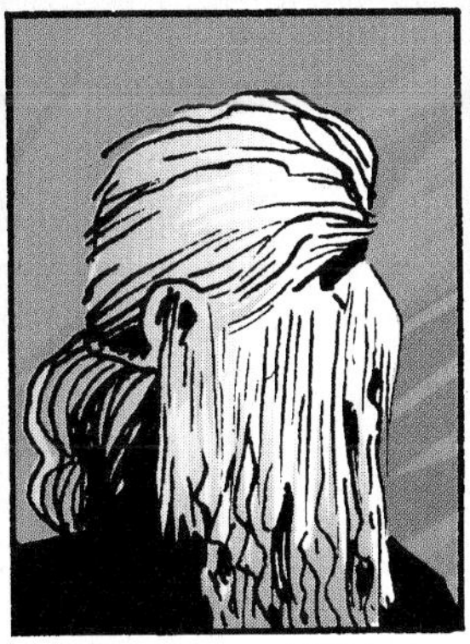

Josef Auger--Afflicted with hypertrichosis. Missing for six months.

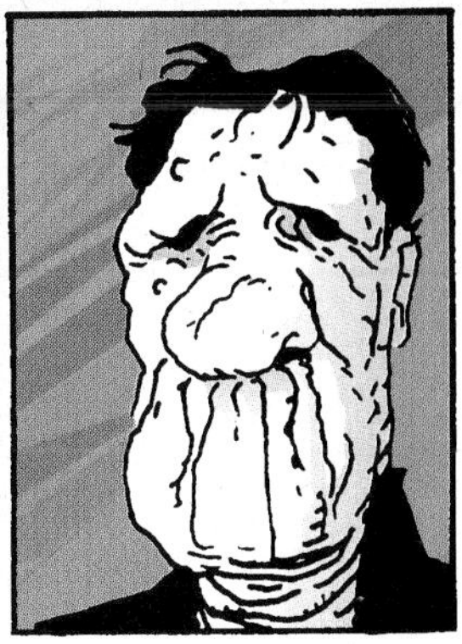

Frances Devere--Undiagnosed facial deformity. Believed kidnapped.

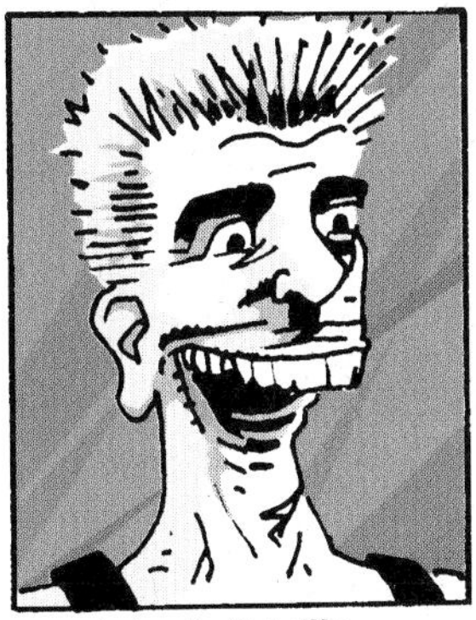

Antonio Patrillo--Born with no lower jawbone. Missing for over a year.

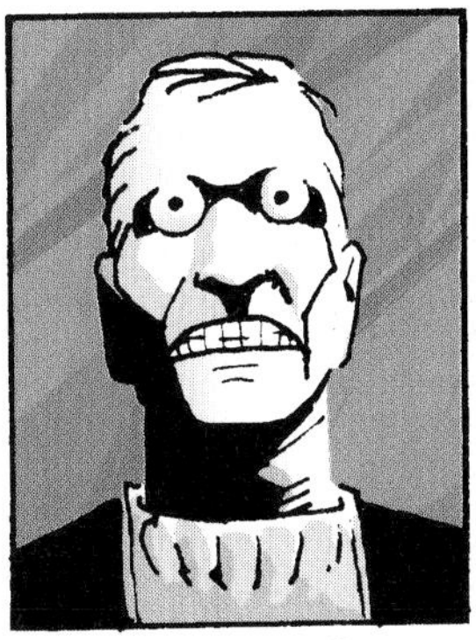

Alain Rachins--Born with no eyelids or lips. Believed kidnapped.

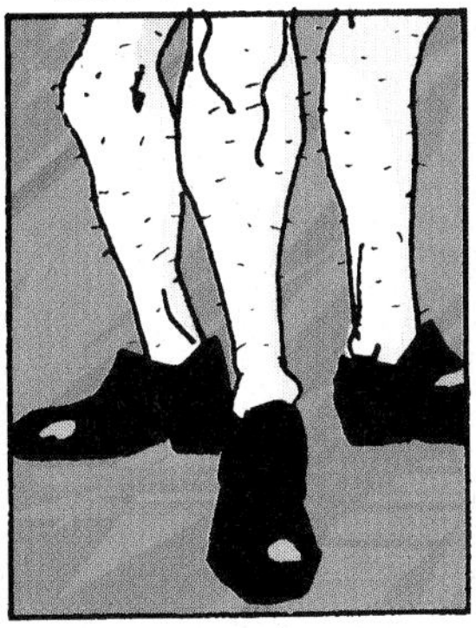

Renée Machon--Born with a third leg. Missing for eight months.

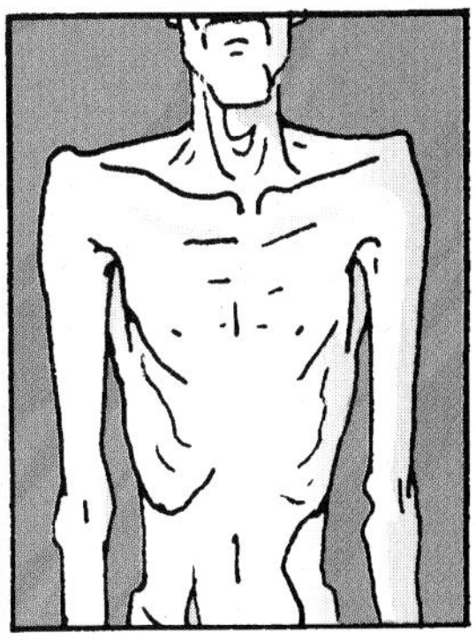

Rudolph Petruchka--Adult weight of 67 pounds. Believed kidnapped.

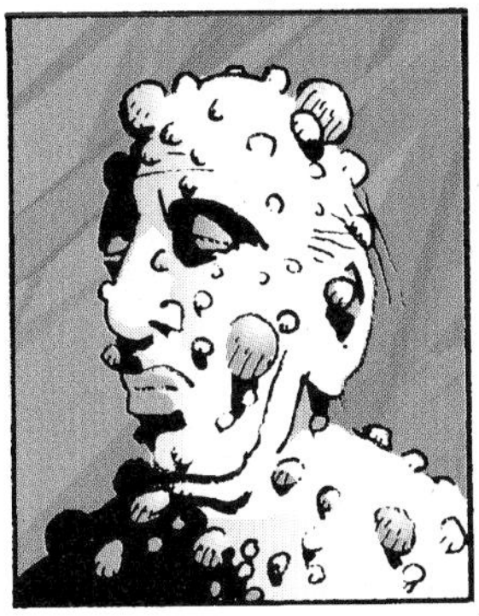

Herve Pierre--Body covered with tumorous lumps. Missing for fourteen months.

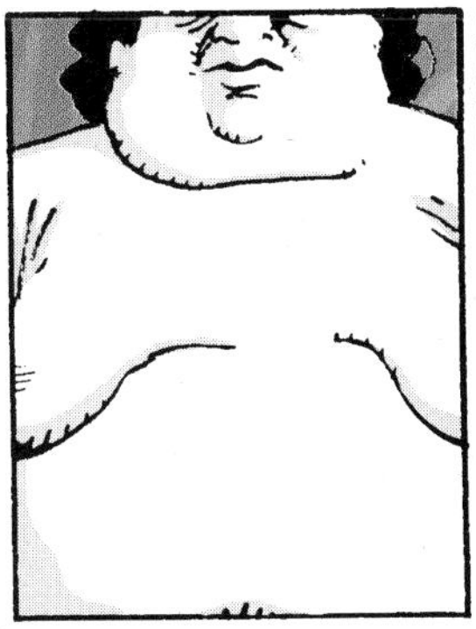

Dora Lang--Adult weight of 673 pounds. Missing for four months.

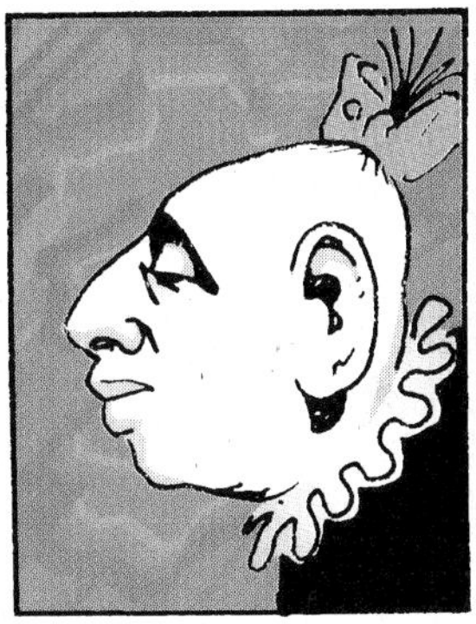

"Booshka" Granger--Born with microcephalia. Believed kidnapped.

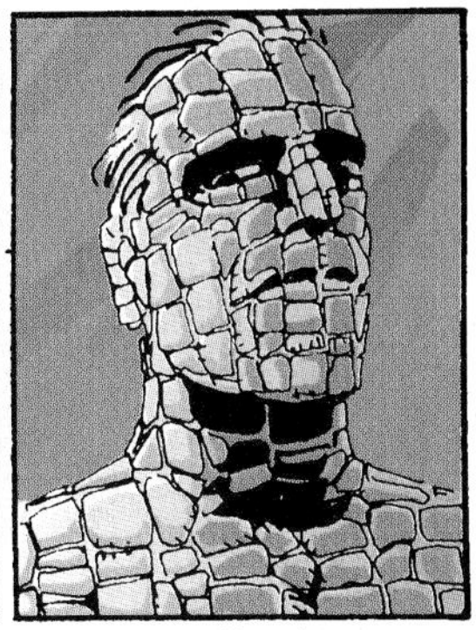

Etienne Frazier--Afflicted with hyperexema. Believed kidnapped.

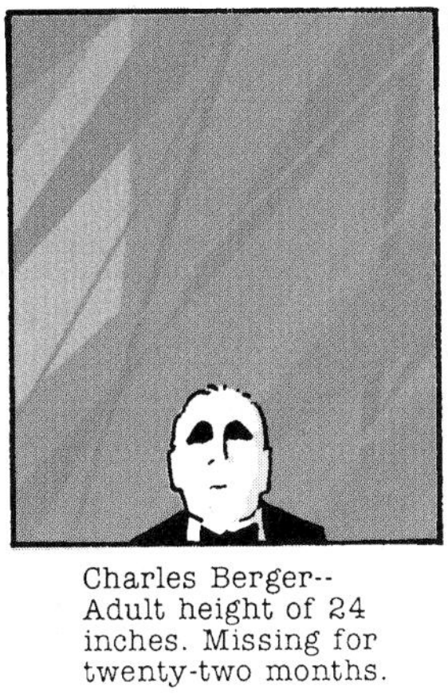

Charles Berger--Adult height of 24 inches. Missing for twenty-two months.

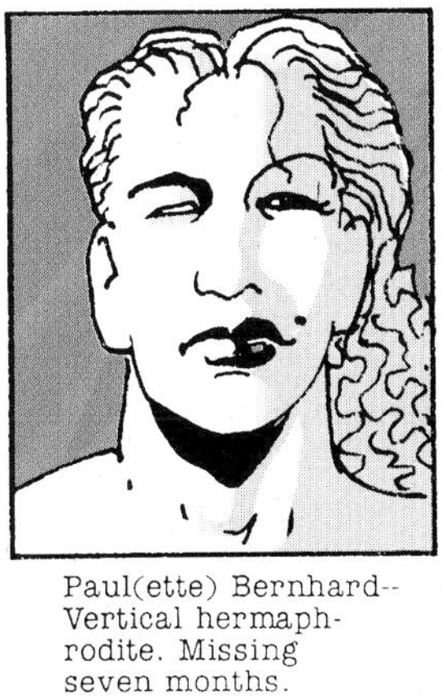

Paul(ette) Bernhard--Vertical hermaphrodite. Missing seven months.

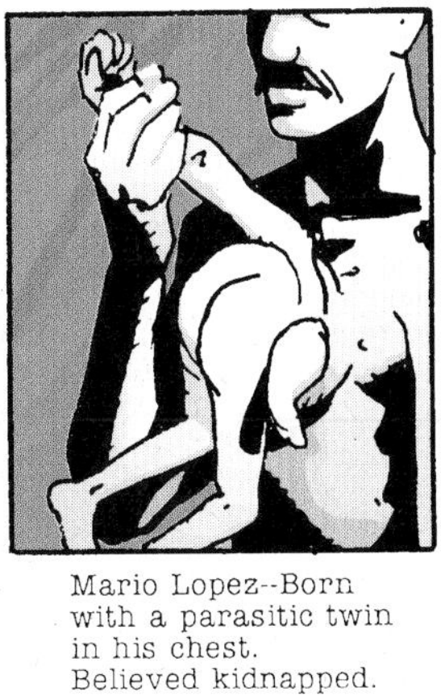

Mario Lopez--Born with a parasitic twin in his chest. Believed kidnapped.

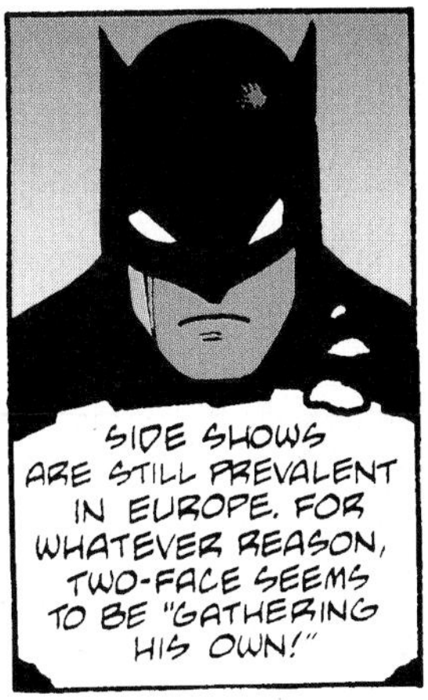
SIDE SHOWS ARE STILL PREVALENT IN EUROPE. FOR WHATEVER REASON, TWO-FACE SEEMS TO BE "GATHERING HIS OWN!"

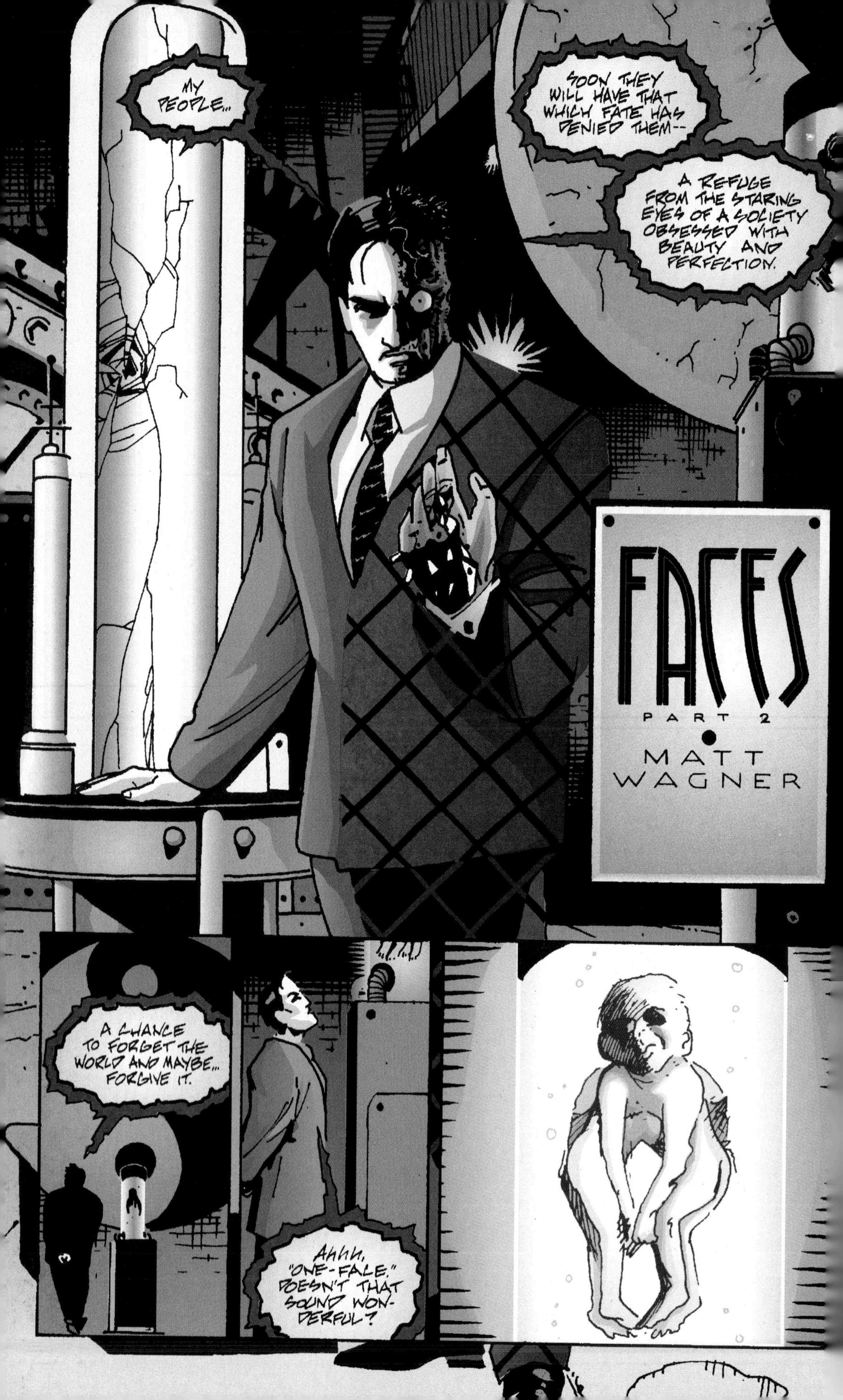
MY PEOPLE...
SOON THEY WILL HAVE THAT WHICH FATE HAS DENIED THEM--
A REFUGE FROM THE STARING EYES OF A SOCIETY OBSESSED WITH BEAUTY AND PERFECTION.
FACES
PART 2
MATT WAGNER
A CHANCE TO FORGET THE WORLD AND MAYBE... FORGIVE IT.
AHHH, "ONE-FACE." DOESN'T THAT SOUND WON-DERFUL?

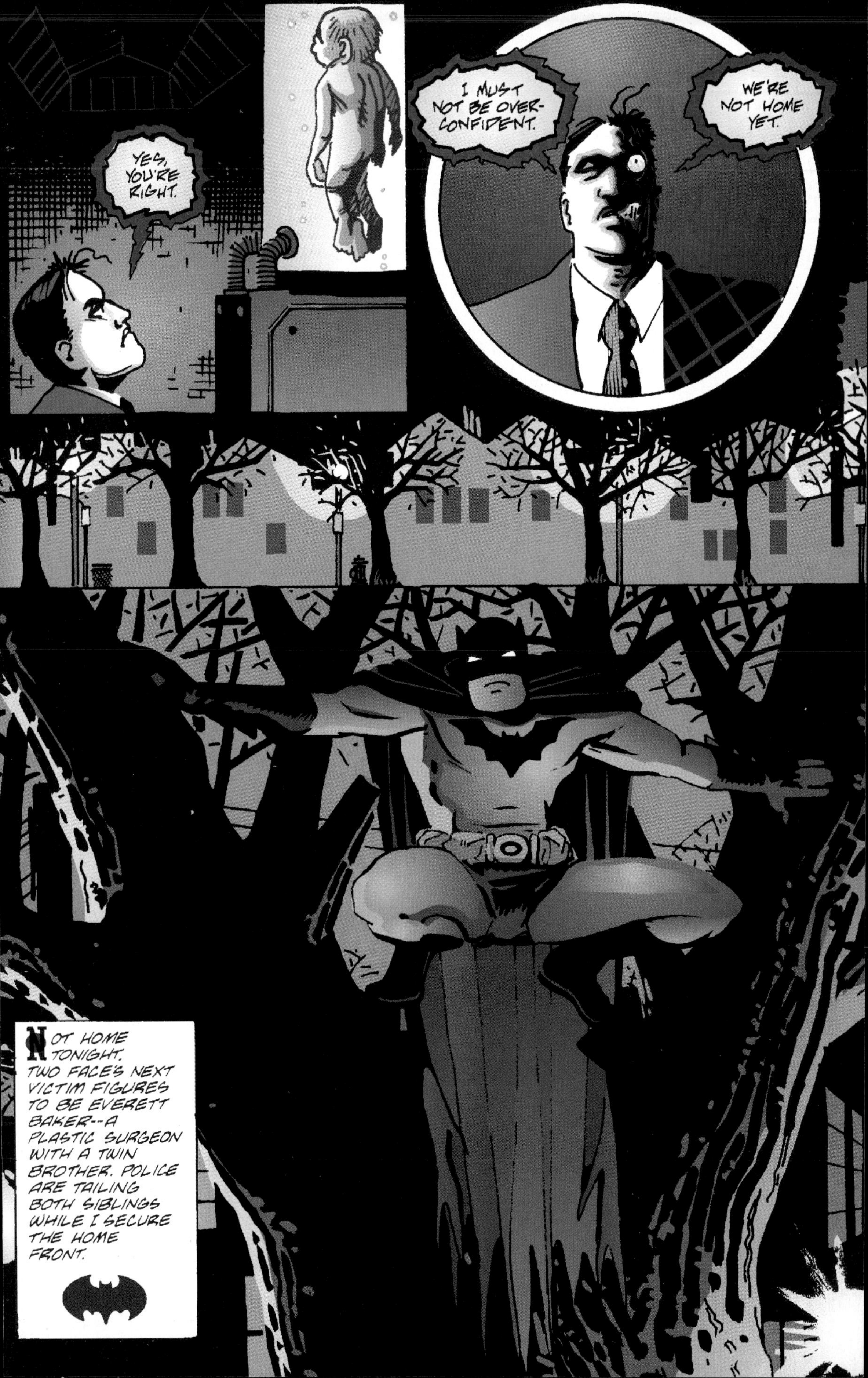
YES, YOU'RE RIGHT.
I MUST NOT BE OVER-CONFIDENT.
WE'RE NOT HOME YET.
NOT HOME TONIGHT. TWO FACE'S NEXT VICTIM FIGURES TO BE EVERETT BAKER--A PLASTIC SURGEON WITH A TWIN BROTHER. POLICE ARE TAILING BOTH SIBLINGS WHILE I SECURE THE HOME FRONT.

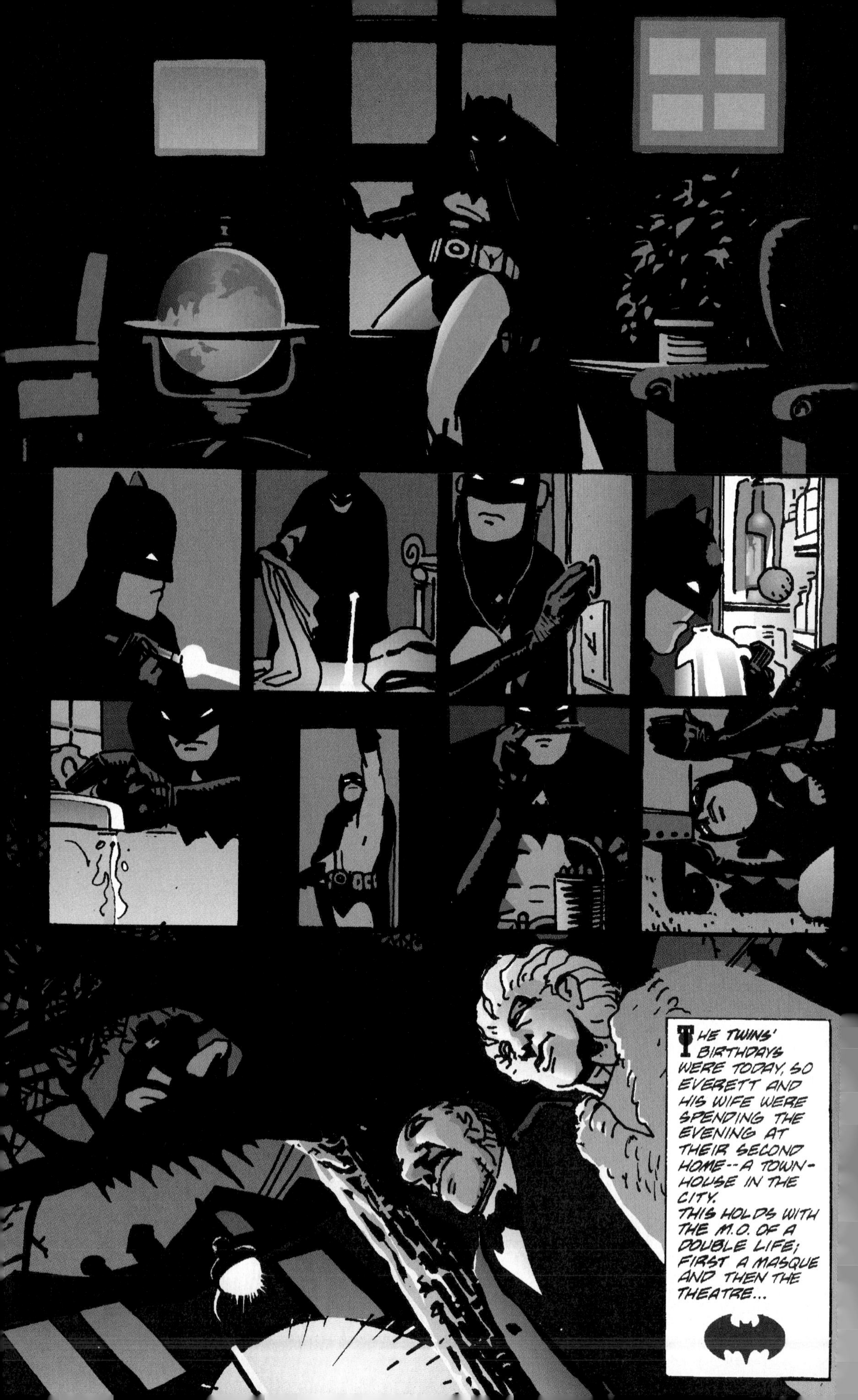
THE TWINS' BIRTHDAYS WERE TODAY, SO EVERETT AND HIS WIFE WERE SPENDING THE EVENING AT THEIR SECOND HOME--A TOWN-HOUSE IN THE CITY.
THIS HOLDS WITH THE M.O. OF A DOUBLE LIFE; FIRST A MASQUE AND THEN THE THEATRE...

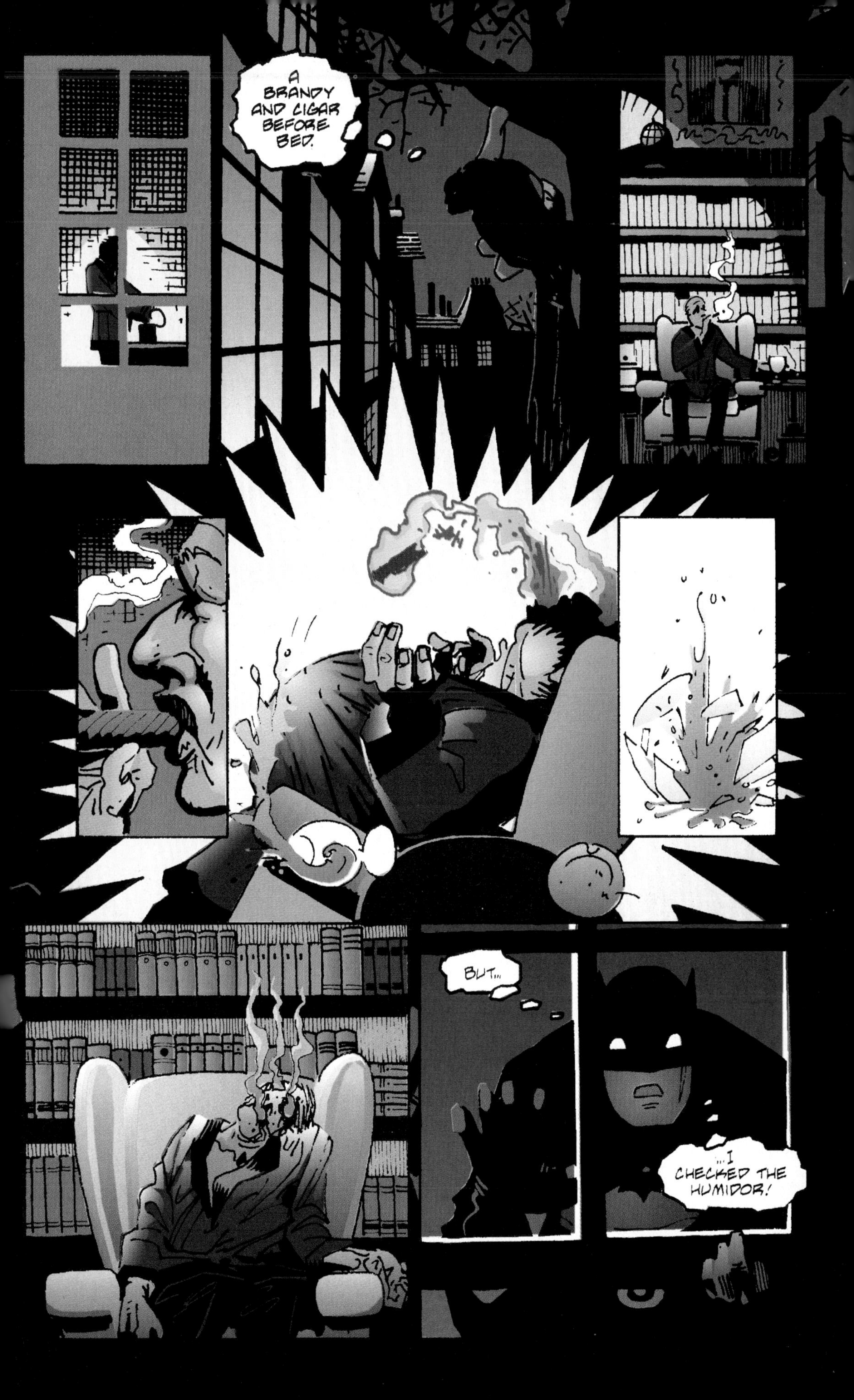
A BRANDY AND CIGAR BEFORE BED.
BUT...
...I CHECKED THE HUMIDOR!

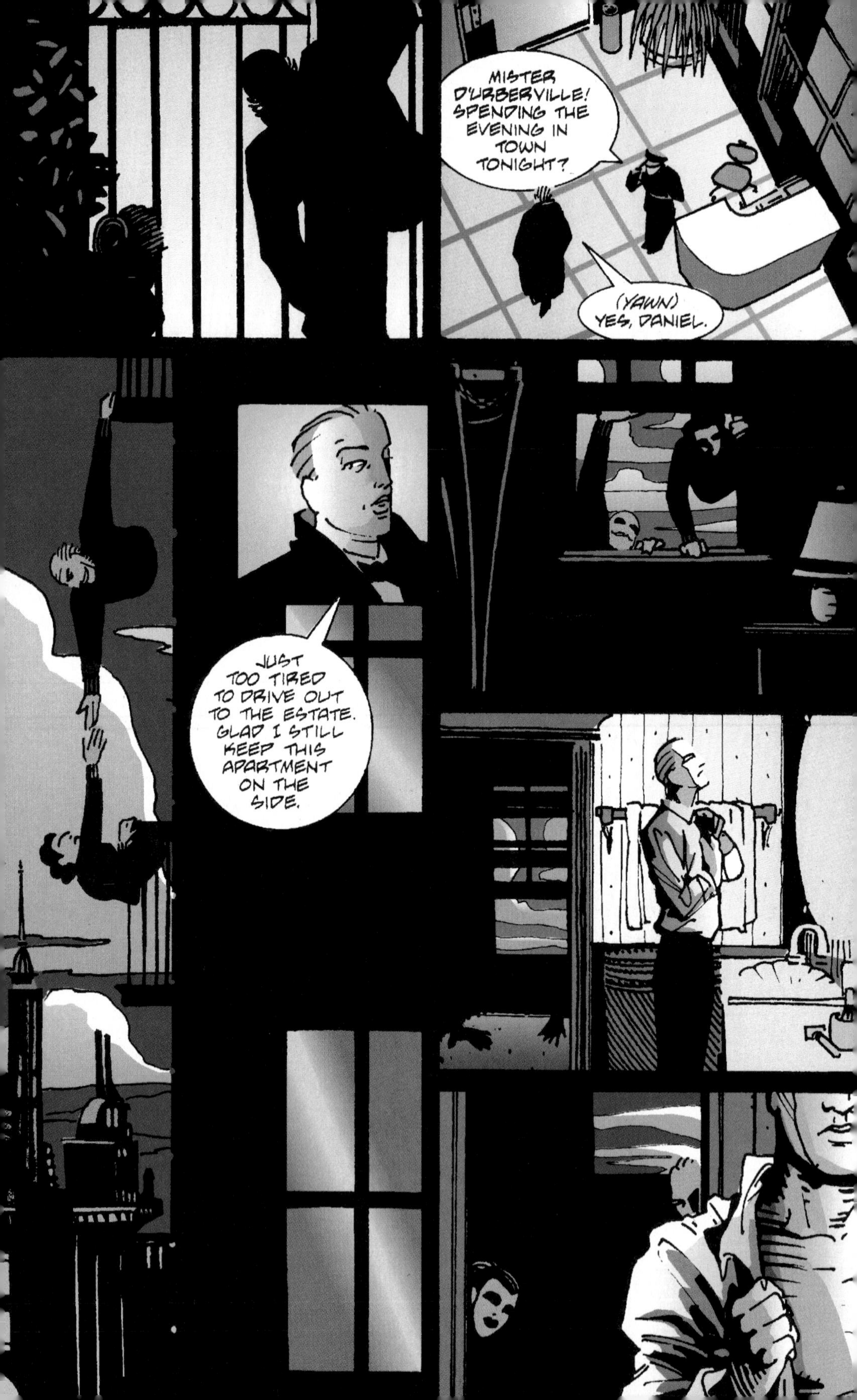
MISTER D'URBERVILLE! SPENDING THE EVENING IN TOWN TONIGHT?
(YAWN) YES, DANIEL.
JUST TOO TIRED TO DRIVE OUT TO THE ESTATE. GLAD I STILL KEEP THIS APARTMENT ON THE SIDE.

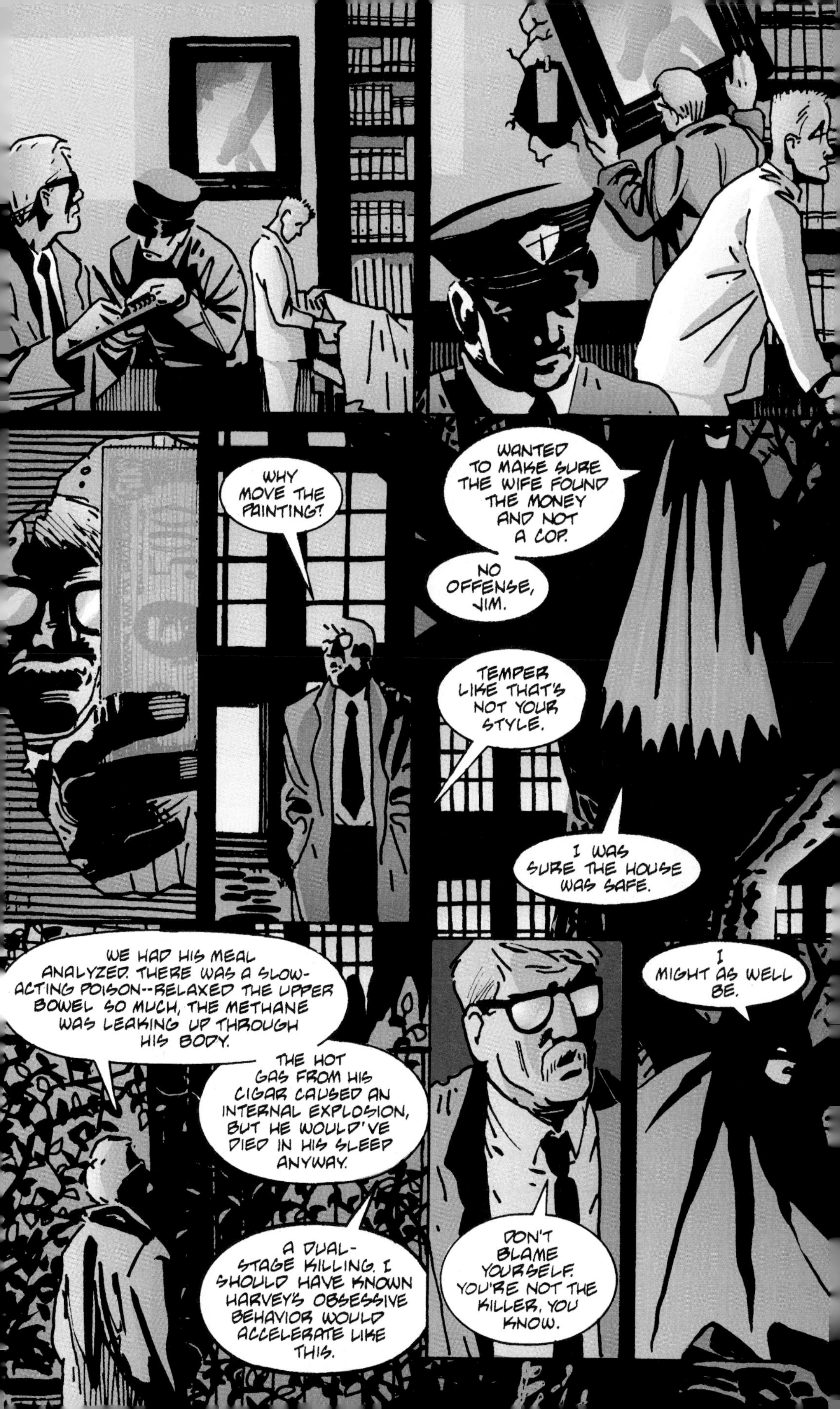
WHY MOVE THE PAINTING?
WANTED TO MAKE SURE THE WIFE FOUND THE MONEY AND NOT A COP.
NO OFFENSE, JIM.
TEMPER LIKE THAT'S NOT YOUR STYLE.
I WAS SURE THE HOUSE WAS SAFE.
WE HAD HIS MEAL ANALYZED. THERE WAS A SLOW-ACTING POISON--RELAXED THE UPPER BOWEL SO MUCH, THE METHANE WAS LEAKING UP THROUGH HIS BODY.
THE HOT GAS FROM HIS CIGAR CAUSED AN INTERNAL EXPLOSION, BUT HE WOULD'VE DIED IN HIS SLEEP ANYWAY.
A DUAL-STAGE KILLING. I SHOULD HAVE KNOWN HARVEY'S OBSESSIVE BEHAVIOR WOULD ACCELERATE LIKE THIS.
I MIGHT AS WELL BE.
DON'T BLAME YOURSELF. YOU'RE NOT THE KILLER, YOU KNOW.

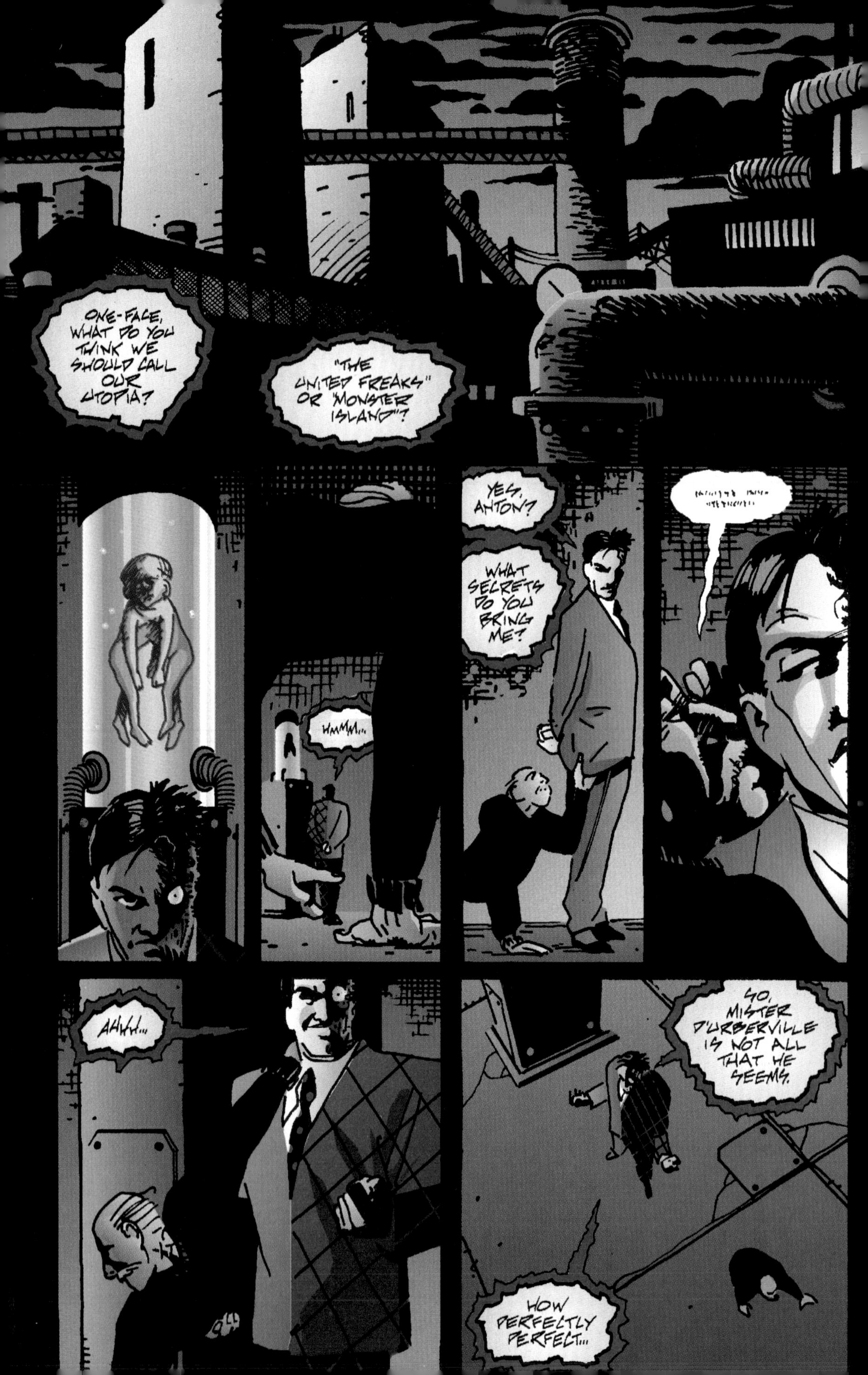

ONE-FACE, WHAT DO YOU THINK WE SHOULD CALL OUR UTOPIA?
"THE UNITED FREAKS" OR "MONSTER ISLAND"?
HMMM...
YES, ANTON?
WHAT SECRETS DO YOU BRING ME?
AHHH...
SO, MISTER D'URBERVILLE IS NOT ALL THAT HE SEEMS.
HOW PERFECTLY PERFECT...

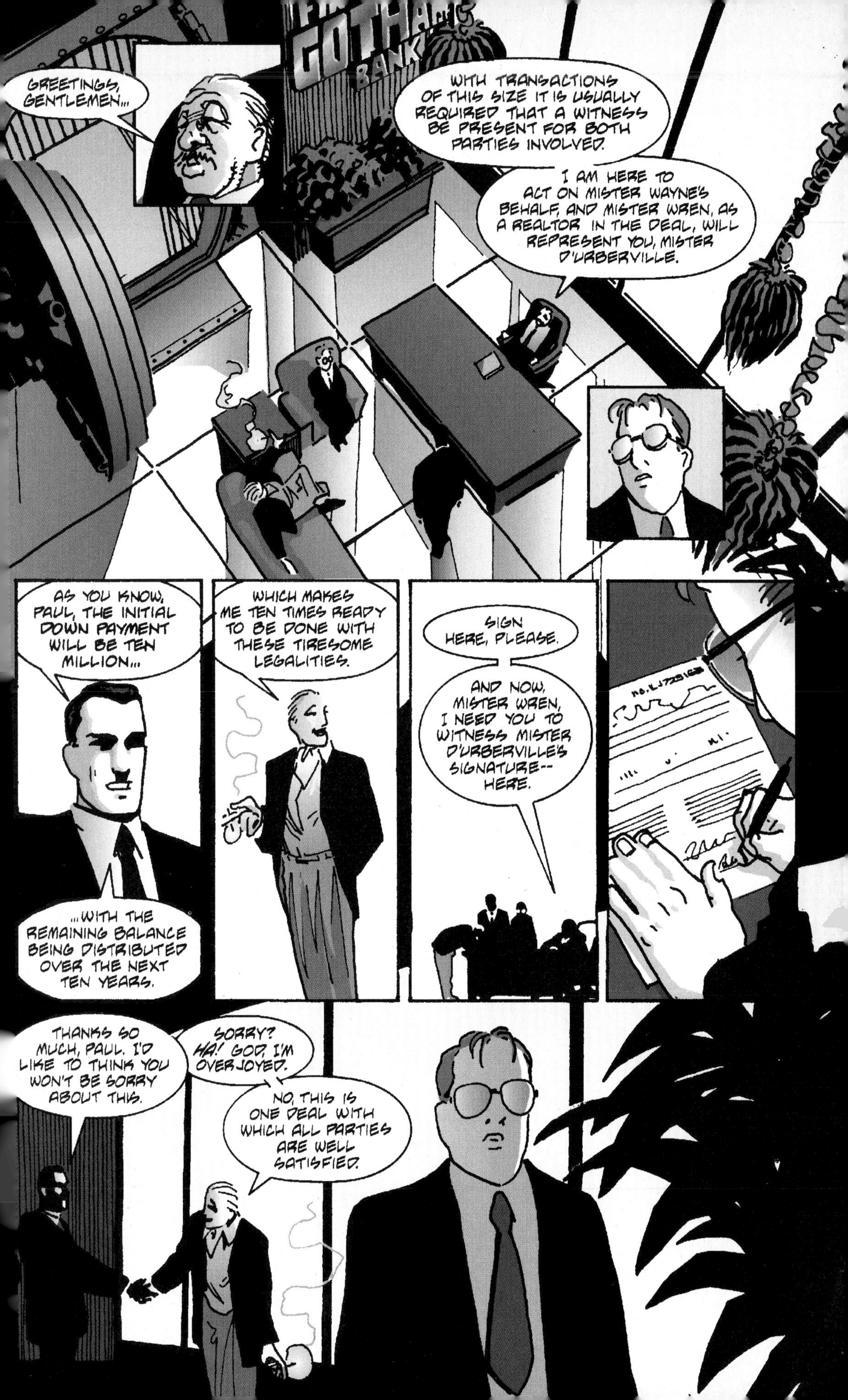
GOTHAM BANK
GREETINGS, GENTLEMEN...
WITH TRANSACTIONS OF THIS SIZE IT IS USUALLY REQUIRED THAT A WITNESS BE PRESENT FOR BOTH PARTIES INVOLVED.
I AM HERE TO ACT ON MISTER WAYNE'S BEHALF, AND MISTER WREN, AS A REALTOR IN THE DEAL, WILL REPRESENT YOU, MISTER D'URBERVILLE.
AS YOU KNOW, PAUL, THE INITIAL DOWN PAYMENT WILL BE TEN MILLION...
...WITH THE REMAINING BALANCE BEING DISTRIBUTED OVER THE NEXT TEN YEARS.
WHICH MAKES ME TEN TIMES READY TO BE DONE WITH THESE TIRESOME LEGALITIES.
SIGN HERE, PLEASE.
AND NOW, MISTER WREN, I NEED YOU TO WITNESS MISTER D'URBERVILLE'S SIGNATURE-- HERE.
THANKS SO MUCH, PAUL. I'D LIKE TO THINK YOU WON'T BE SORRY ABOUT THIS.
SORRY? HA! GOD, I'M OVERJOYED.
NO, THIS IS ONE DEAL WITH WHICH ALL PARTIES ARE WELL SATISFIED.

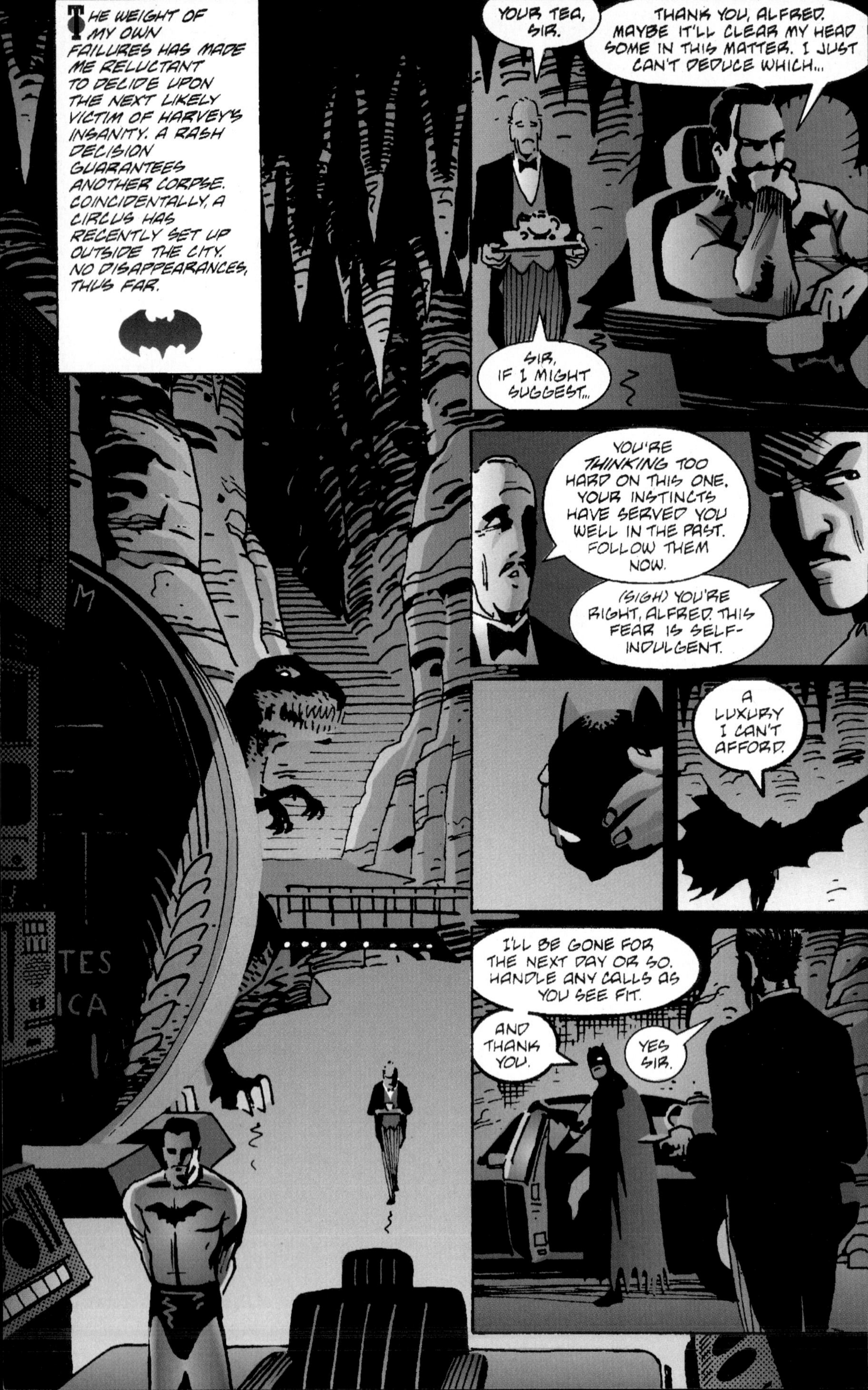
THE WEIGHT OF MY OWN FAILURES HAS MADE ME RELUCTANT TO DECIDE UPON THE NEXT LIKELY VICTIM OF HARVEY'S INSANITY. A RASH DECISION GUARANTEES ANOTHER CORPSE. COINCIDENTALLY, A CIRCUS HAS RECENTLY SET UP OUTSIDE THE CITY. NO DISAPPEARANCES, THUS FAR.
YOUR TEA, SIR.
THANK YOU, ALFRED. MAYBE IT'LL CLEAR MY HEAD SOME IN THIS MATTER. I JUST CAN'T DEDUCE WHICH...
SIR, IF I MIGHT SUGGEST...
YOU'RE THINKING TOO HARD ON THIS ONE. YOUR INSTINCTS HAVE SERVED YOU WELL IN THE PAST. FOLLOW THEM NOW.
(SIGH) YOU'RE RIGHT, ALFRED. THIS FEAR IS SELF-INDULGENT.
A LUXURY I CAN'T AFFORD.
I'LL BE GONE FOR THE NEXT DAY OR SO. HANDLE ANY CALLS AS YOU SEE FIT.
AND THANK YOU.
YES SIR.

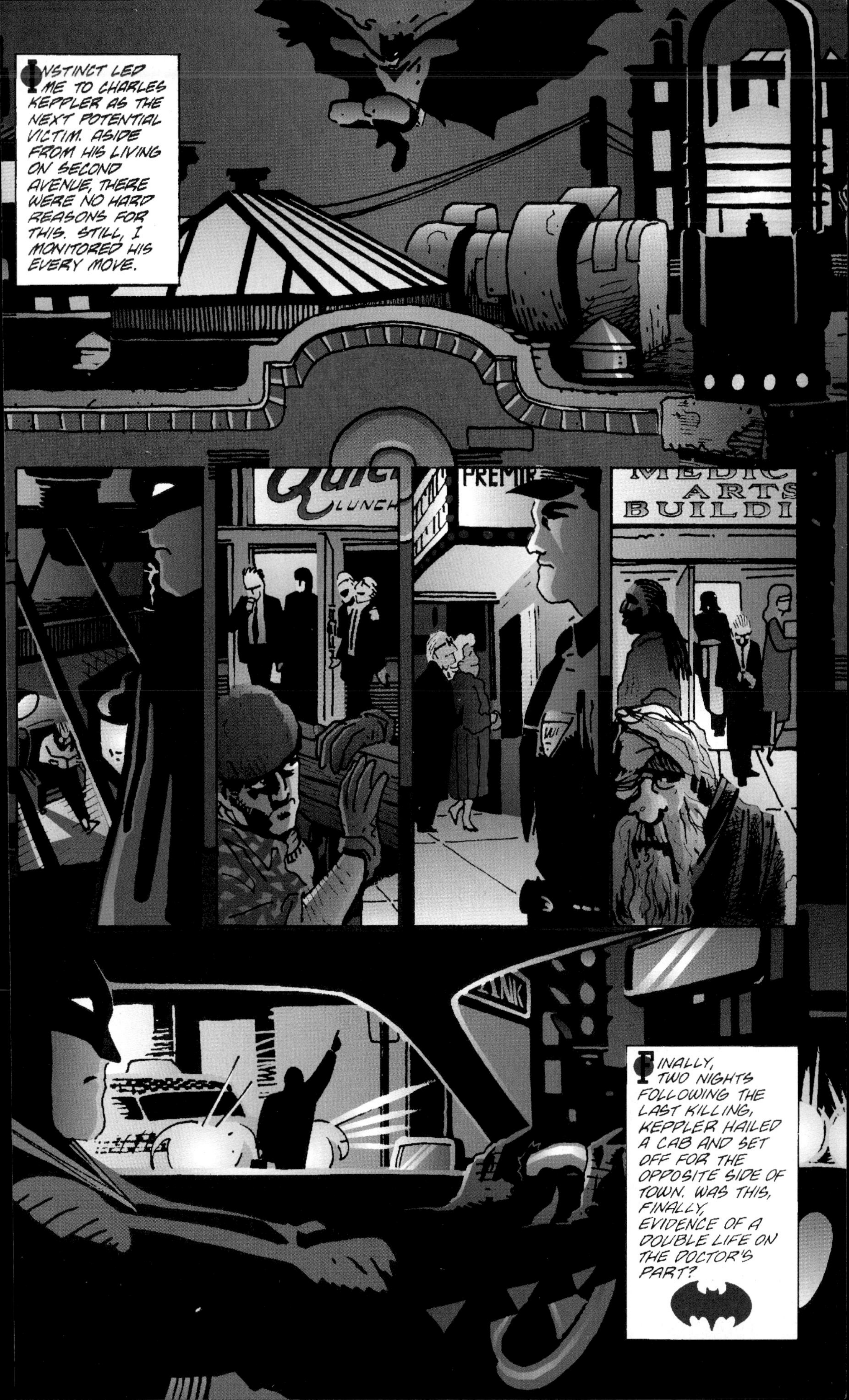
INSTINCT LED ME TO CHARLES KEPPLER AS THE NEXT POTENTIAL VICTIM. ASIDE FROM HIS LIVING ON SECOND AVENUE, THERE WERE NO HARD REASONS FOR THIS. STILL, I MONITORED HIS EVERY MOVE.
QUICK LUNCH
PREMIR
MEDIC ARTS BUILDI
FINALLY, TWO NIGHTS FOLLOWING THE LAST KILLING, KEPPLER HAILED A CAB AND SET OFF FOR THE OPPOSITE SIDE OF TOWN. WAS THIS, FINALLY, EVIDENCE OF A DOUBLE LIFE ON THE DOCTOR'S PART?

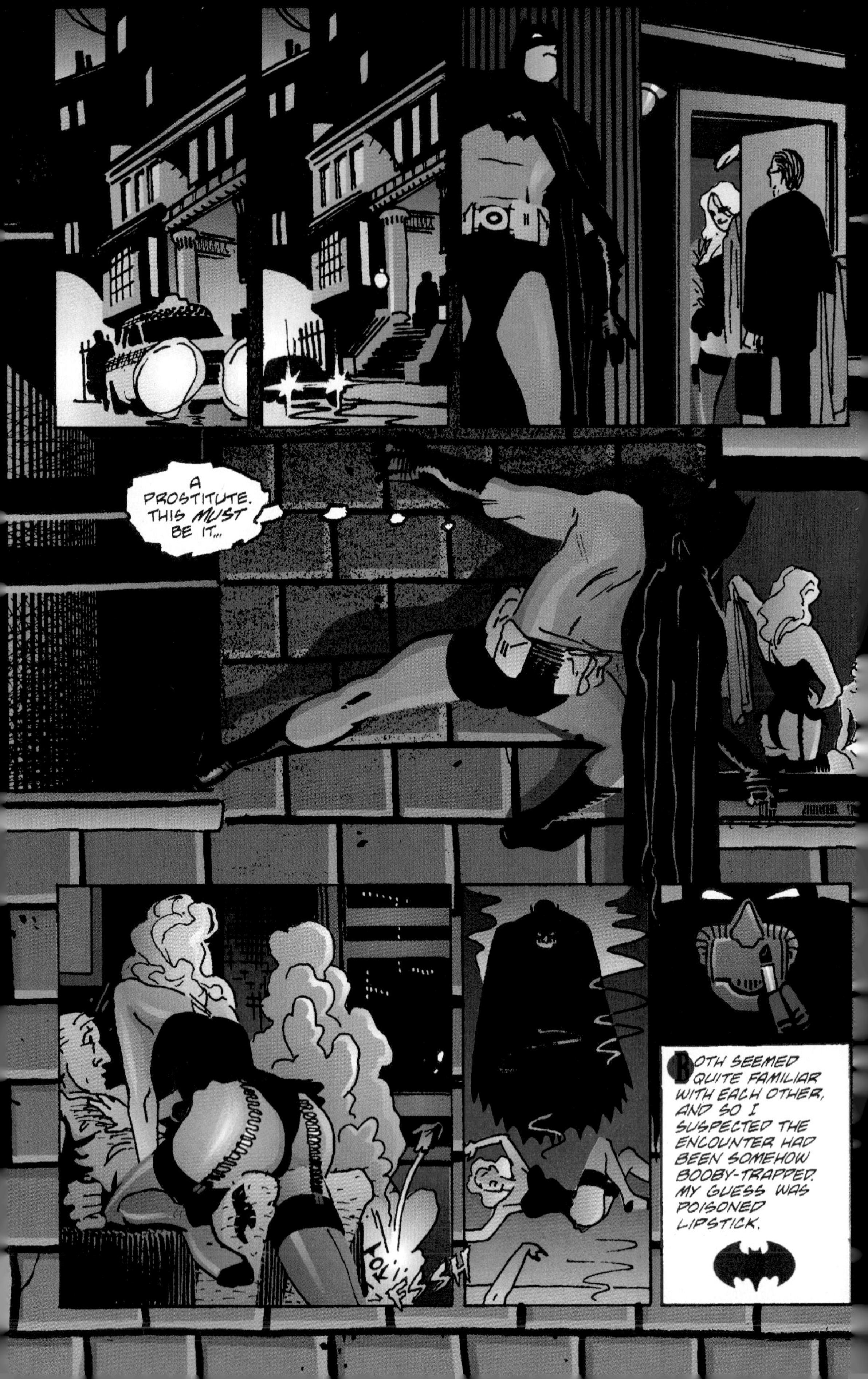
A PROSTITUTE. THIS MUST BE IT...
BOTH SEEMED QUITE FAMILIAR WITH EACH OTHER, AND SO I SUSPECTED THE ENCOUNTER HAD BEEN SOMEHOW BOOBY-TRAPPED. MY GUESS WAS POISONED LIPSTICK.

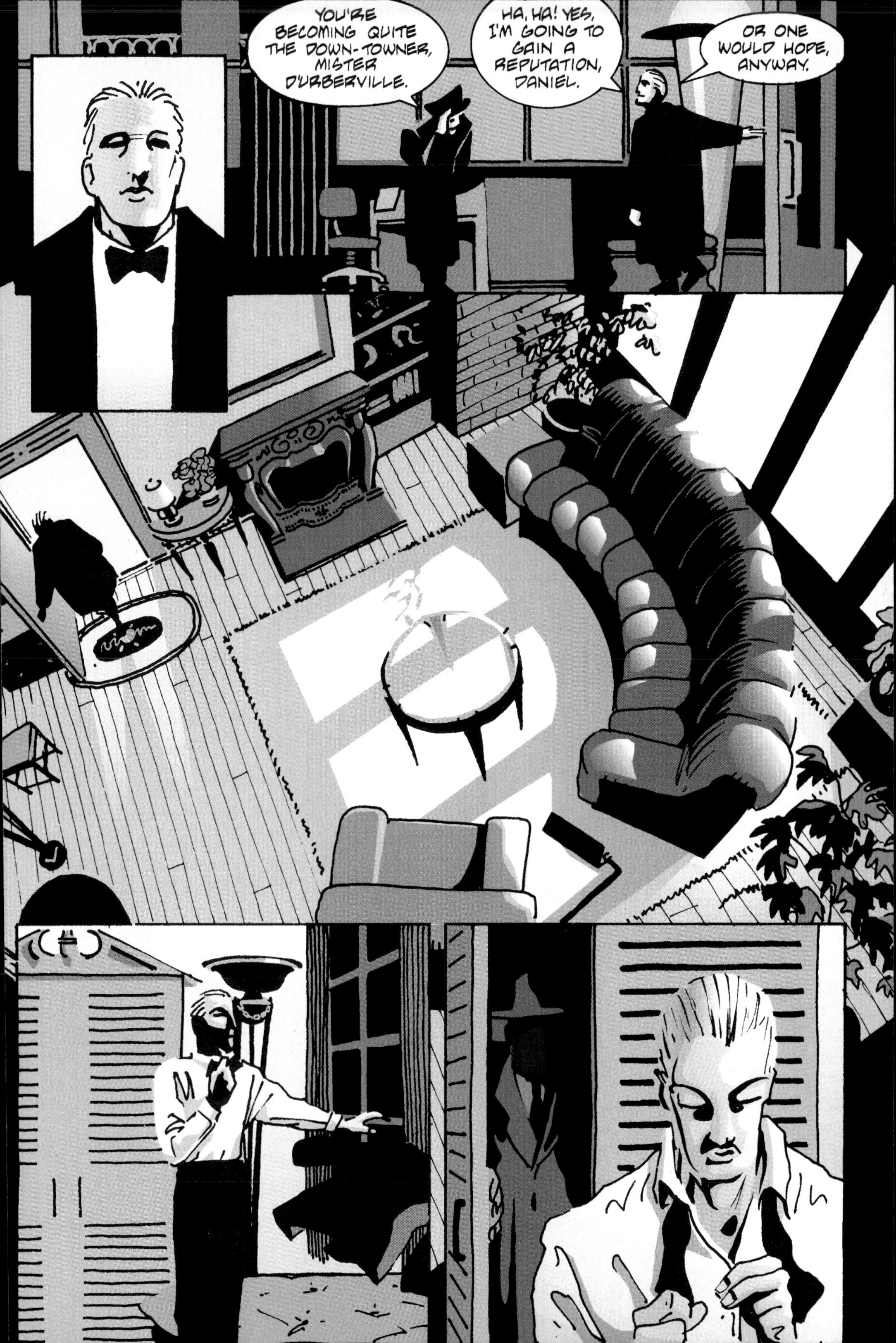
YOU'RE BECOMING QUITE THE DOWN-TOWNER, MISTER D'URBERVILLE.
HA, HA! YES, I'M GOING TO GAIN A REPUTATION, DANIEL.
OR ONE WOULD HOPE, ANYWAY.

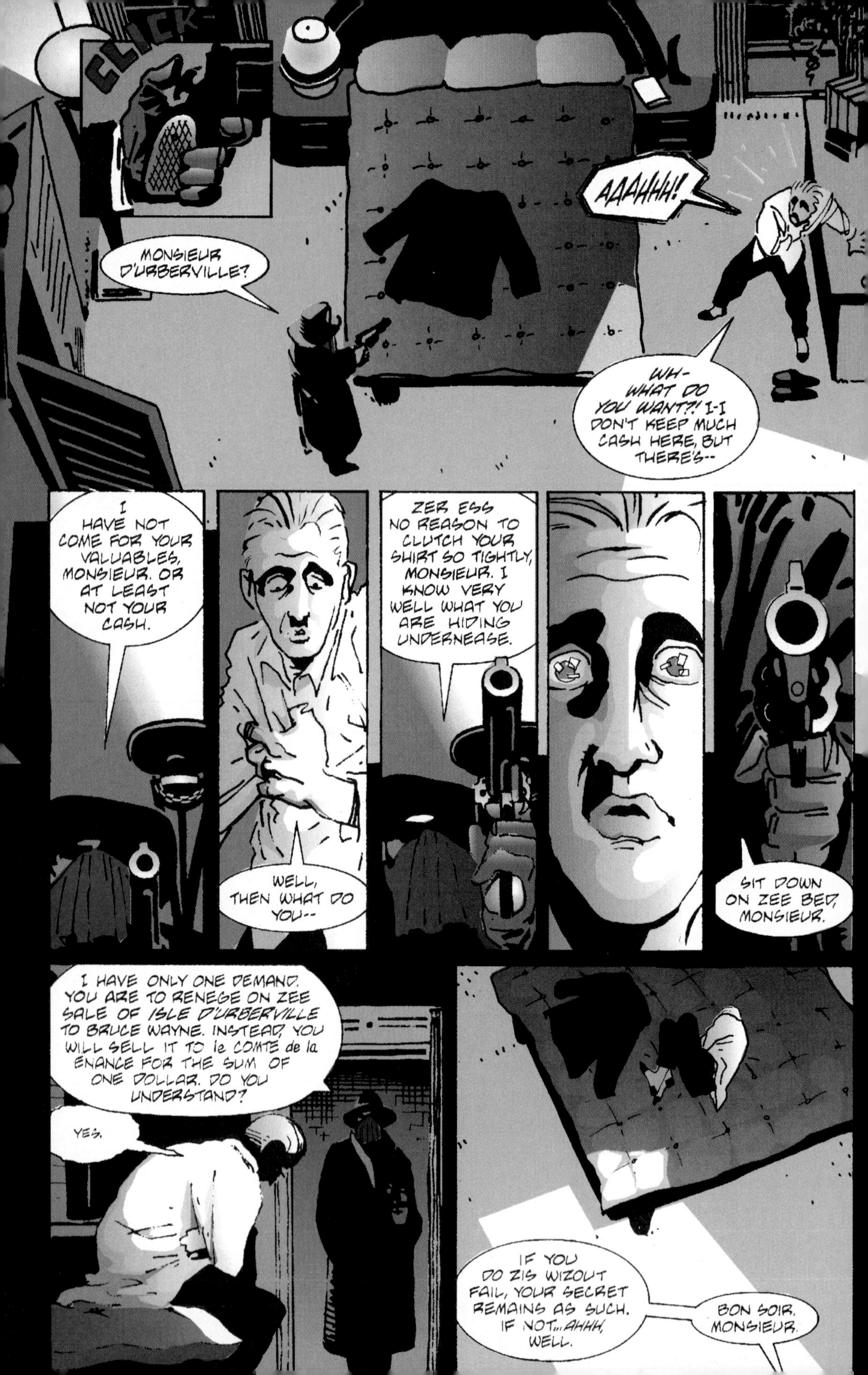
CLICK
MONSIEUR D'URBERVILLE?
AAAHHH!
WH- WHAT DO YOU WANT?! I-I DON'T KEEP MUCH CASH HERE, BUT THERE'S--
I HAVE NOT COME FOR YOUR VALUABLES, MONSIEUR. OR AT LEAST NOT YOUR CASH.
WELL, THEN WHAT DO YOU--
ZER ESS NO REASON TO CLUTCH YOUR SHIRT SO TIGHTLY, MONSIEUR. I KNOW VERY WELL WHAT YOU ARE HIDING UNDERNEASE.
SIT DOWN ON ZEE BED, MONSIEUR.
I HAVE ONLY ONE DEMAND. YOU ARE TO RENEGE ON ZEE SALE OF ISLE D'URBERVILLE TO BRUCE WAYNE. INSTEAD, YOU WILL SELL IT TO le COMTE de la ENANCE FOR THE SUM OF ONE DOLLAR. DO YOU UNDERSTAND?
YES.
IF YOU DO ZIS WIZOUT FAIL, YOUR SECRET REMAINS AS SUCH. IF NOT...AHHH, WELL.
BON SOIR, MONSIEUR.

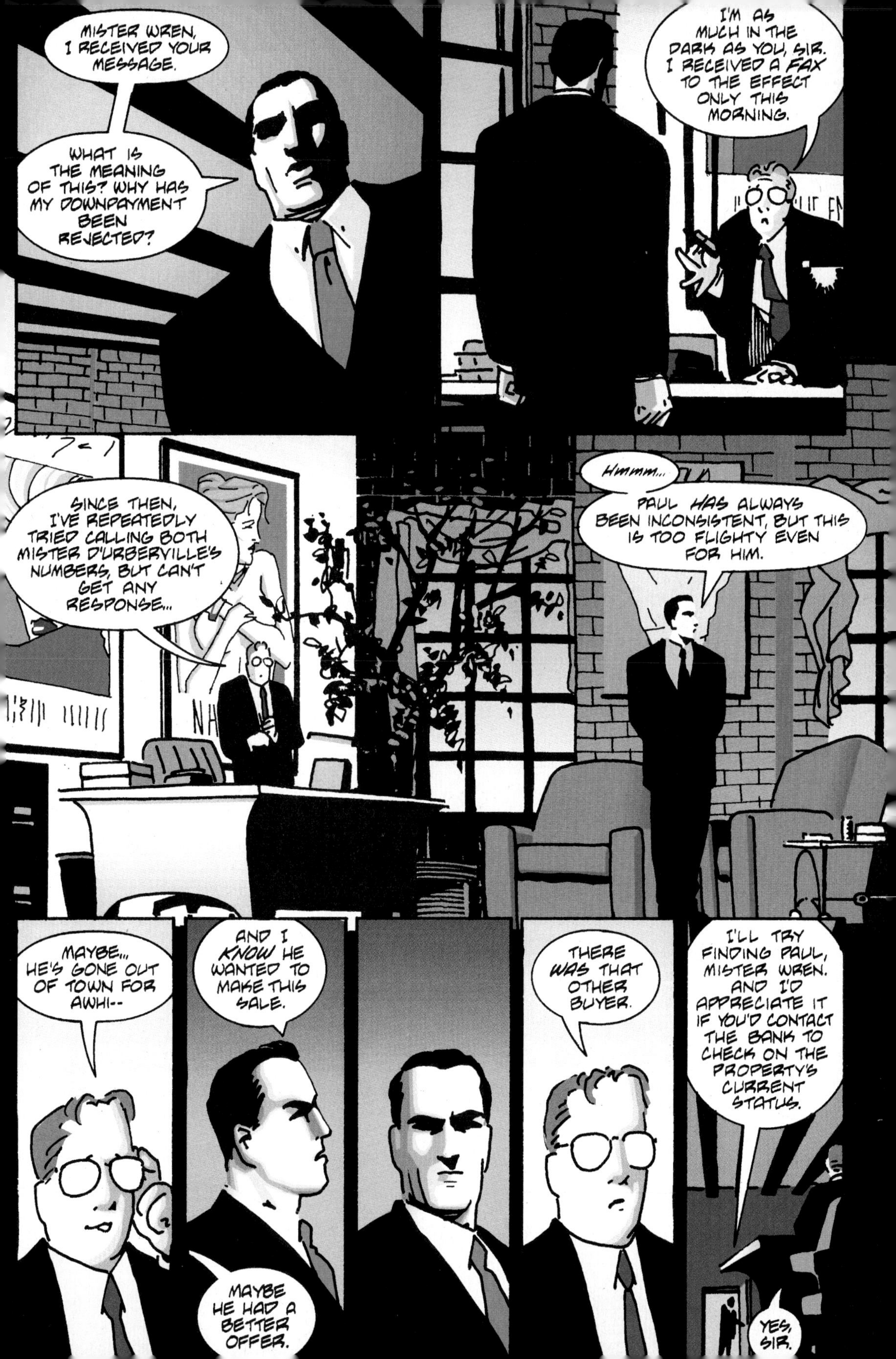
MISTER WREN, I RECEIVED YOUR MESSAGE.
WHAT IS THE MEANING OF THIS? WHY HAS MY DOWNPAYMENT BEEN REJECTED?
I'M AS MUCH IN THE DARK AS YOU, SIR. I RECEIVED A FAX TO THE EFFECT ONLY THIS MORNING.
SINCE THEN, I'VE REPEATEDLY TRIED CALLING BOTH MISTER D'URBERVILLE'S NUMBERS, BUT CAN'T GET ANY RESPONSE...
Hmmm...
PAUL HAS ALWAYS BEEN INCONSISTENT, BUT THIS IS TOO FLIGHTY EVEN FOR HIM.
MAYBE... HE'S GONE OUT OF TOWN FOR AWHI--
AND I KNOW HE WANTED TO MAKE THIS SALE.
MAYBE HE HAD A BETTER OFFER.
THERE WAS THAT OTHER BUYER.
I'LL TRY FINDING PAUL, MISTER WREN. AND I'D APPRECIATE IT IF YOU'D CONTACT THE BANK TO CHECK ON THE PROPERTY'S CURRENT STATUS.
YES, SIR.

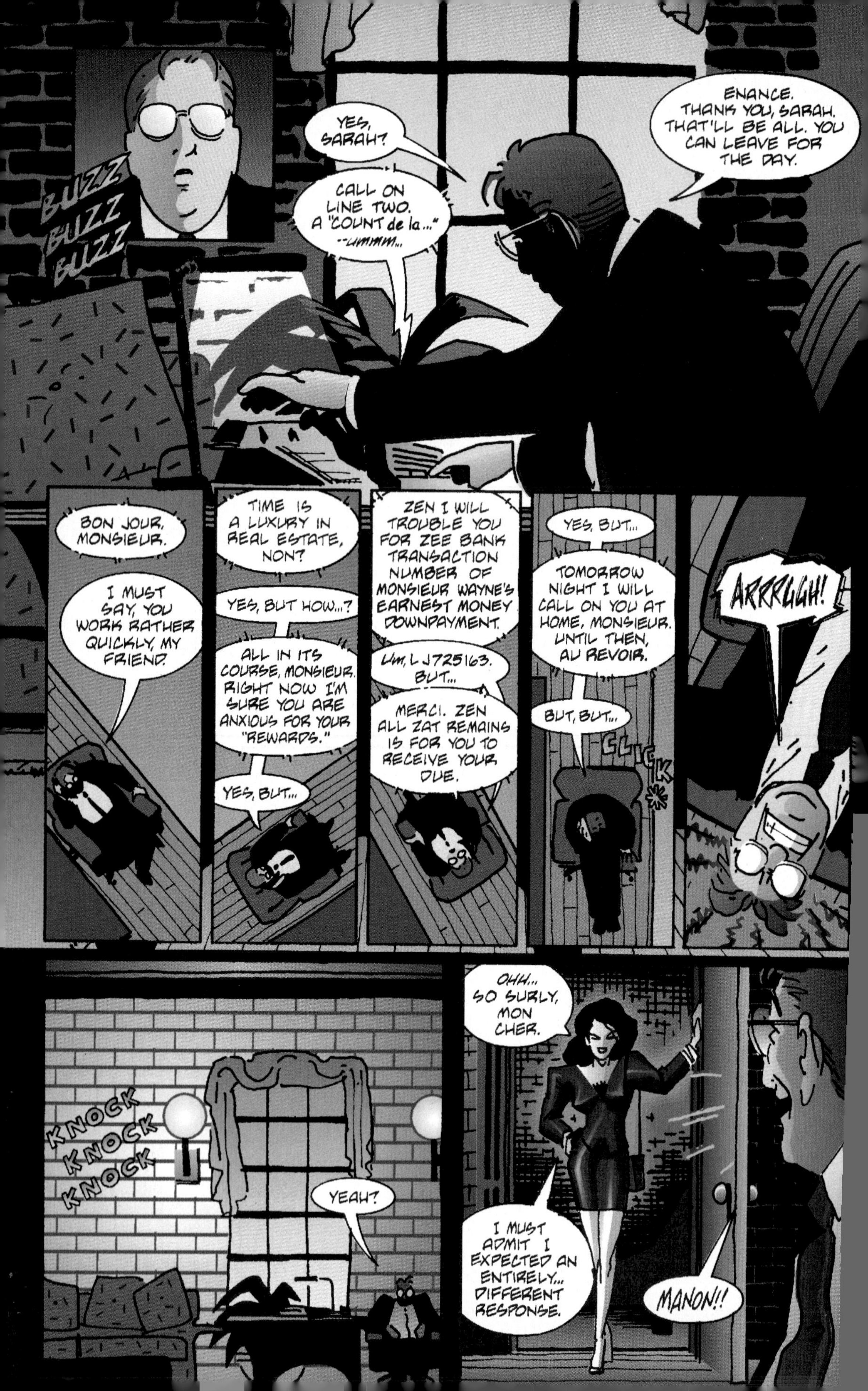
BUZZ BUZZ BUZZ
YES, SARAH?
CALL ON LINE TWO. A "COUNT de la..." --UMMMM...
ENANCE. THANK YOU, SARAH. THAT'LL BE ALL. YOU CAN LEAVE FOR THE DAY.
BON JOUR, MONSIEUR.
I MUST SAY, YOU WORK RATHER QUICKLY, MY FRIEND.
TIME IS A LUXURY IN REAL ESTATE, NON?
YES, BUT HOW...?
ALL IN ITS COURSE, MONSIEUR. RIGHT NOW I'M SURE YOU ARE ANXIOUS FOR YOUR "REWARDS."
YES, BUT...
ZEN I WILL TROUBLE YOU FOR ZEE BANK TRANSACTION NUMBER OF MONSIEUR WAYNE'S EARNEST MONEY DOWNPAYMENT.
Um, L J725163. BUT...
MERCI. ZEN ALL ZAT REMAINS IS FOR YOU TO RECEIVE YOUR DUE.
YES, BUT...
TOMORROW NIGHT I WILL CALL ON YOU AT HOME, MONSIEUR. UNTIL THEN, AU REVOIR.
BUT, BUT...
CLICK
ARRRGGH!
KNOCK KNOCK KNOCK
YEAH?
OHH... SO SURLY, MON CHER.
I MUST ADMIT I EXPECTED AN ENTIRELY... DIFFERENT RESPONSE.
MANON!!

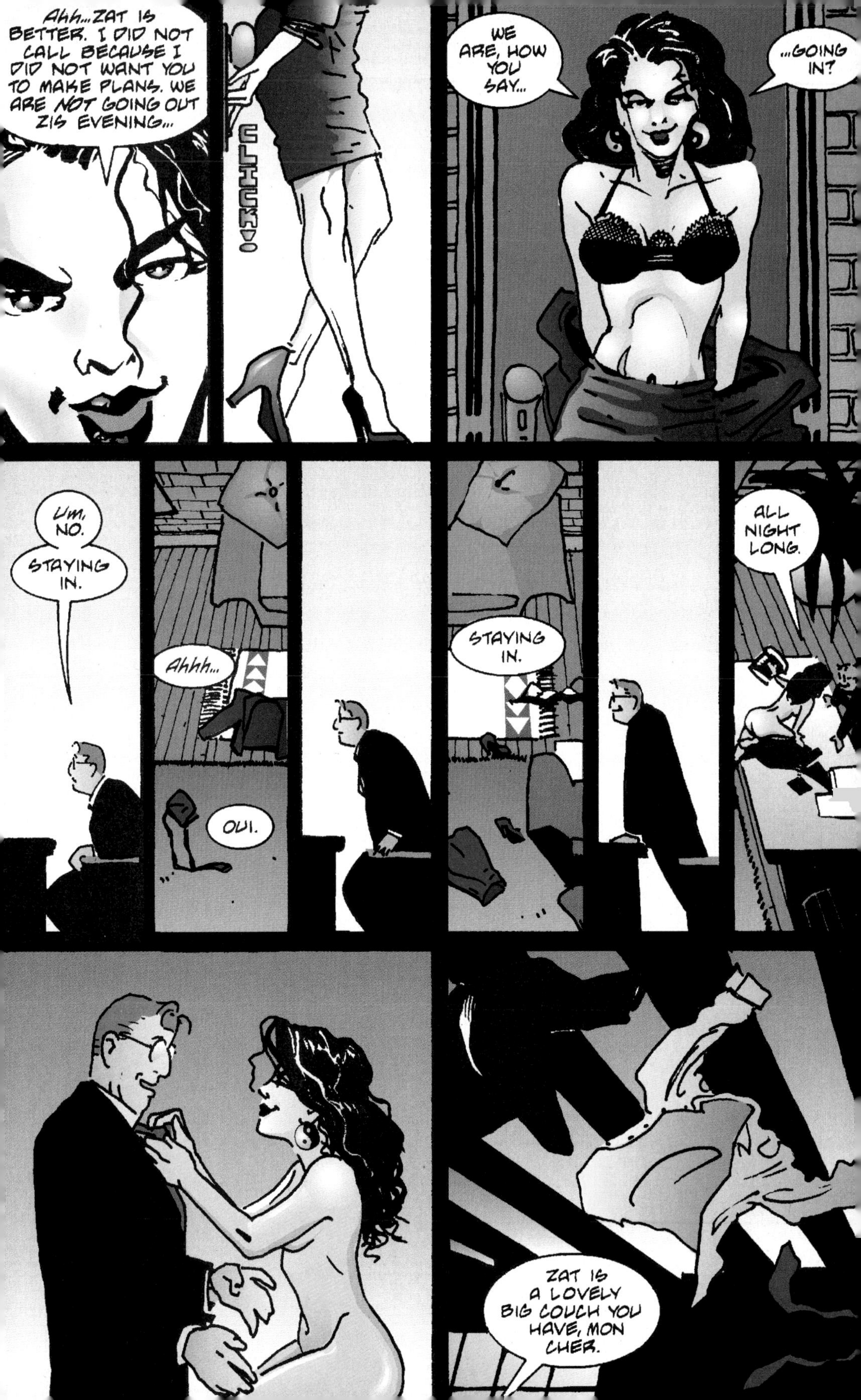
Ahh...ZAT IS BETTER. I DID NOT CALL BECAUSE I DID NOT WANT YOU TO MAKE PLANS. WE ARE *NOT* GOING OUT ZIS EVENING...
CLICK!
WE ARE, HOW YOU SAY...
...GOING IN?
Um, NO.
STAYING IN.
Ahhh...
OUI.
STAYING IN.
ALL NIGHT LONG.
ZAT IS A LOVELY BIG COUCH YOU HAVE, MON CHER.

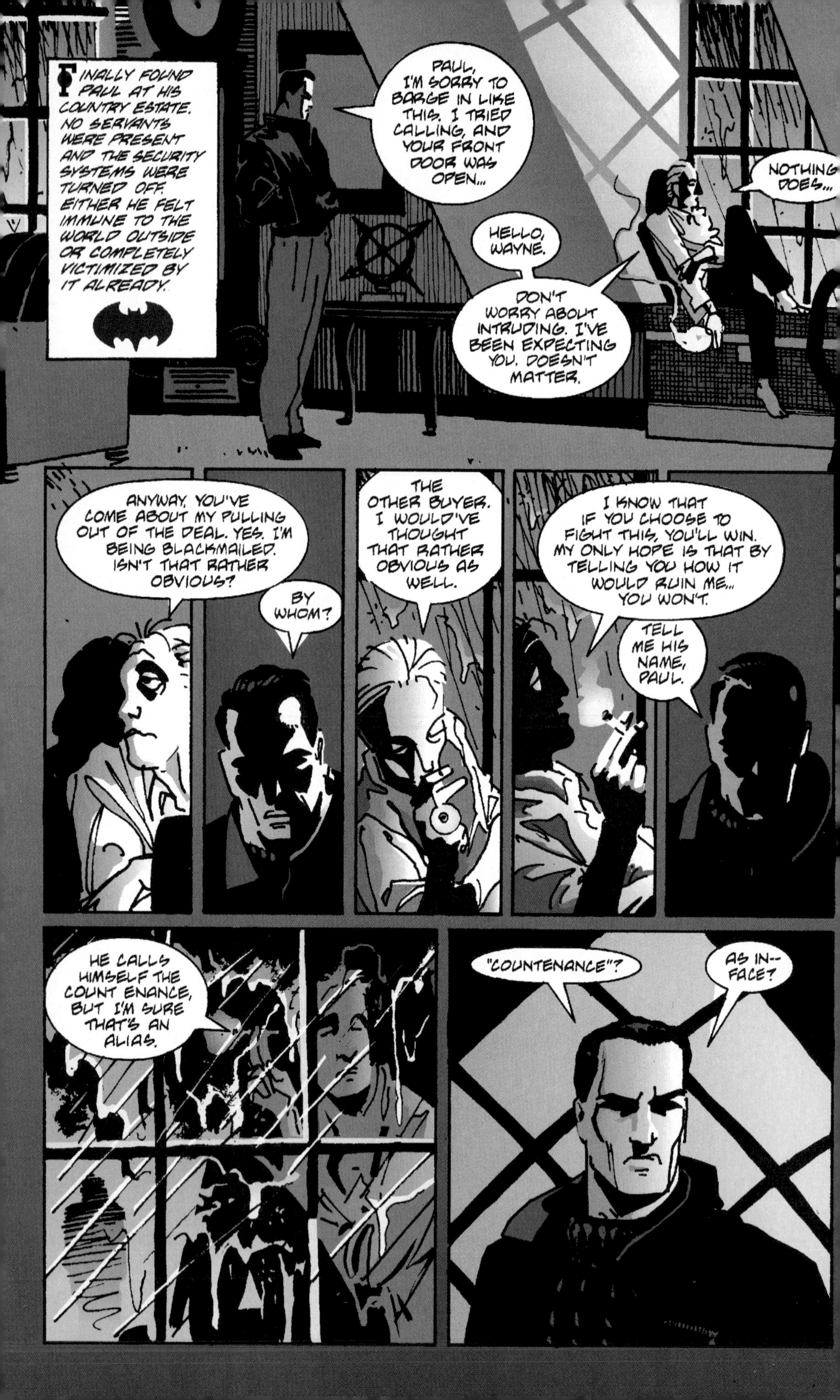
FINALLY FOUND PAUL AT HIS COUNTRY ESTATE. NO SERVANTS WERE PRESENT AND THE SECURITY SYSTEMS WERE TURNED OFF. EITHER HE FELT IMMUNE TO THE WORLD OUTSIDE OR COMPLETELY VICTIMIZED BY IT ALREADY.
PAUL, I'M SORRY TO BARGE IN LIKE THIS. I TRIED CALLING, AND YOUR FRONT DOOR WAS OPEN...
NOTHING DOES...
HELLO, WAYNE.
DON'T WORRY ABOUT INTRUDING. I'VE BEEN EXPECTING YOU. DOESN'T MATTER.
ANYWAY, YOU'VE COME ABOUT MY PULLING OUT OF THE DEAL. YES. I'M BEING BLACKMAILED. ISN'T THAT RATHER OBVIOUS?
BY WHOM?
THE OTHER BUYER. I WOULD'VE THOUGHT THAT RATHER OBVIOUS AS WELL.
I KNOW THAT IF YOU CHOOSE TO FIGHT THIS, YOU'LL WIN. MY ONLY HOPE IS THAT BY TELLING YOU HOW IT WOULD RUIN ME... YOU WON'T.
TELL ME HIS NAME, PAUL.
HE CALLS HIMSELF THE COUNT ENANCE, BUT I'M SURE THAT'S AN ALIAS.
"COUNTENANCE"?
AS IN-- FACE?

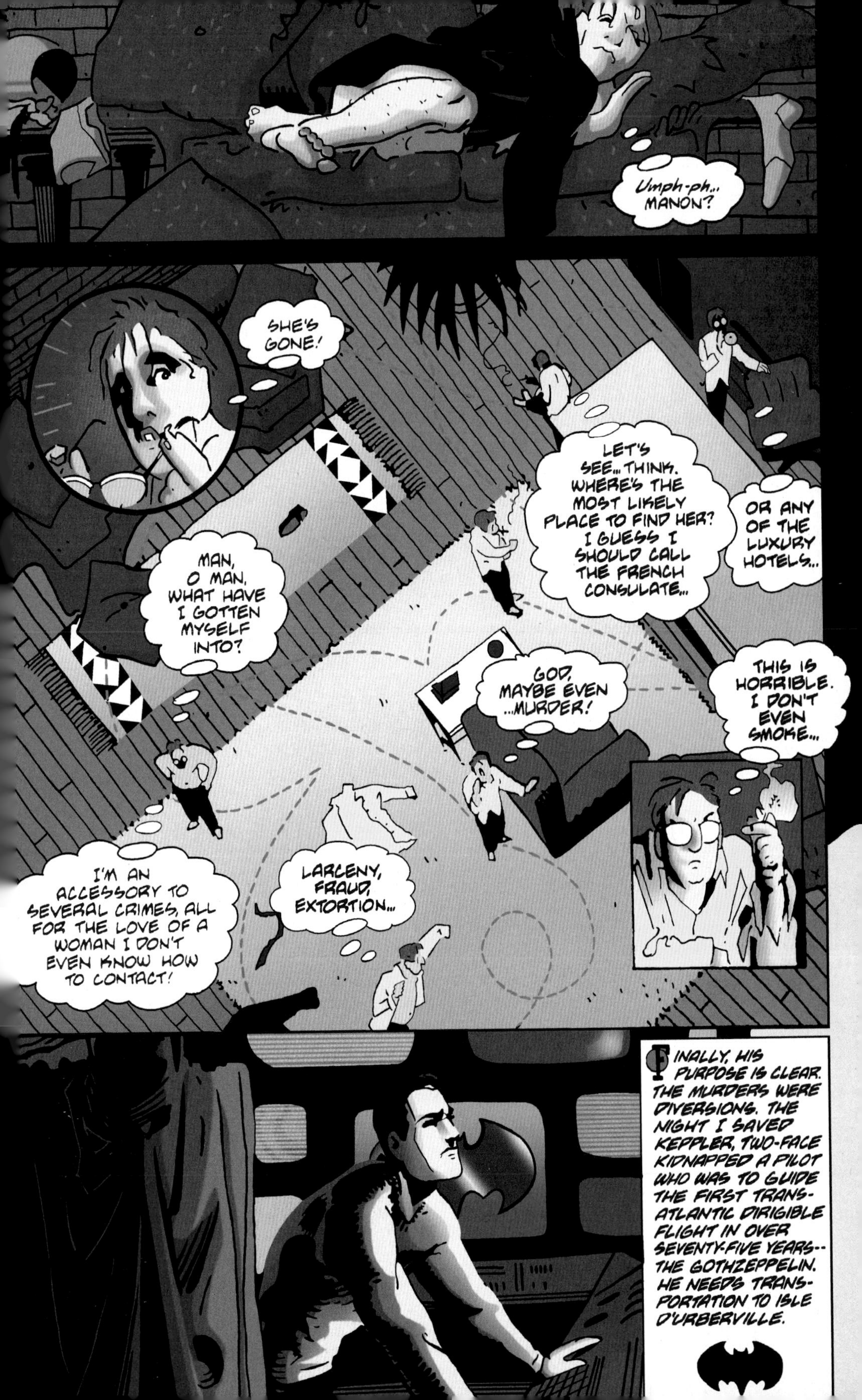
Umph-ph... MANON?
SHE'S GONE!
LET'S SEE... THINK. WHERE'S THE MOST LIKELY PLACE TO FIND HER? I GUESS I SHOULD CALL THE FRENCH CONSULATE...
OR ANY OF THE LUXURY HOTELS...
MAN, O MAN, WHAT HAVE I GOTTEN MYSELF INTO?
GOD, MAYBE EVEN ...MURDER!
THIS IS HORRIBLE. I DON'T EVEN SMOKE...
I'M AN ACCESSORY TO SEVERAL CRIMES, ALL FOR THE LOVE OF A WOMAN I DON'T EVEN KNOW HOW TO CONTACT!
LARCENY, FRAUD, EXTORTION...
FINALLY, HIS PURPOSE IS CLEAR. THE MURDERS WERE DIVERSIONS. THE NIGHT I SAVED KEPPLER, TWO-FACE KIDNAPPED A PILOT WHO WAS TO GUIDE THE FIRST TRANS-ATLANTIC DIRIGIBLE FLIGHT IN OVER SEVENTY-FIVE YEARS-- THE GOTHZEPPELIN. HE NEEDS TRANS-PORTATION TO ISLE D'URBERVILLE.

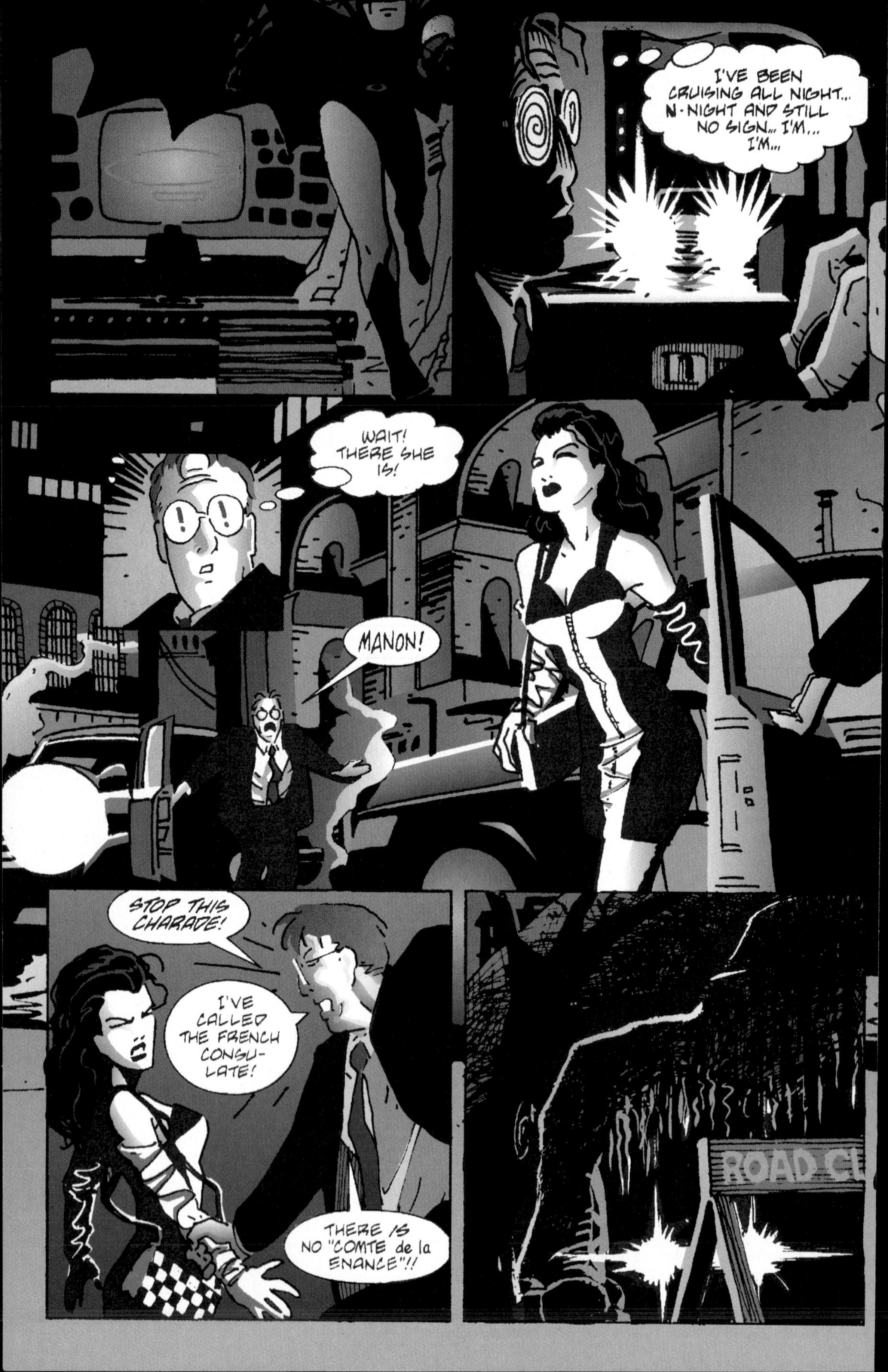
I'VE BEEN CRUISING ALL NIGHT... N-NIGHT AND STILL NO SIGN... I'M... I'M...
WAIT! THERE SHE IS!
MANON!
STOP THIS CHARADE!
I'VE CALLED THE FRENCH CONSU-LATE!
THERE IS NO "COMTE de la ENANCE"!!
ROAD CL

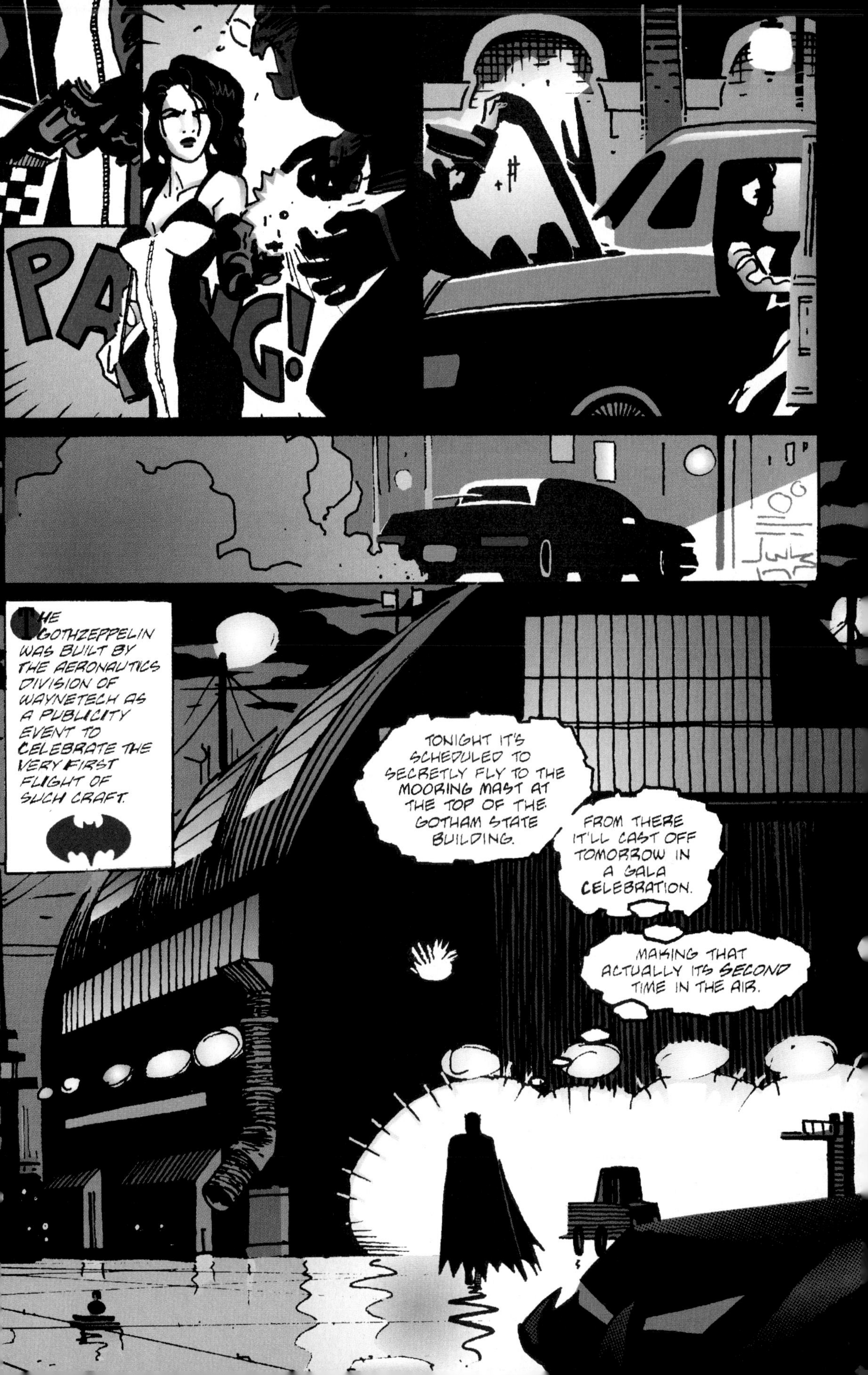
PANG!
THE GOTHZEPPELIN WAS BUILT BY THE AERONAUTICS DIVISION OF WAYNETECH AS A PUBLICITY EVENT TO CELEBRATE THE VERY FIRST FLIGHT OF SUCH CRAFT.
TONIGHT IT'S SCHEDULED TO SECRETLY FLY TO THE MOORING MAST AT THE TOP OF THE GOTHAM STATE BUILDING.
FROM THERE IT'LL CAST OFF TOMORROW IN A GALA CELEBRATION.
MAKING THAT ACTUALLY ITS SECOND TIME IN THE AIR.

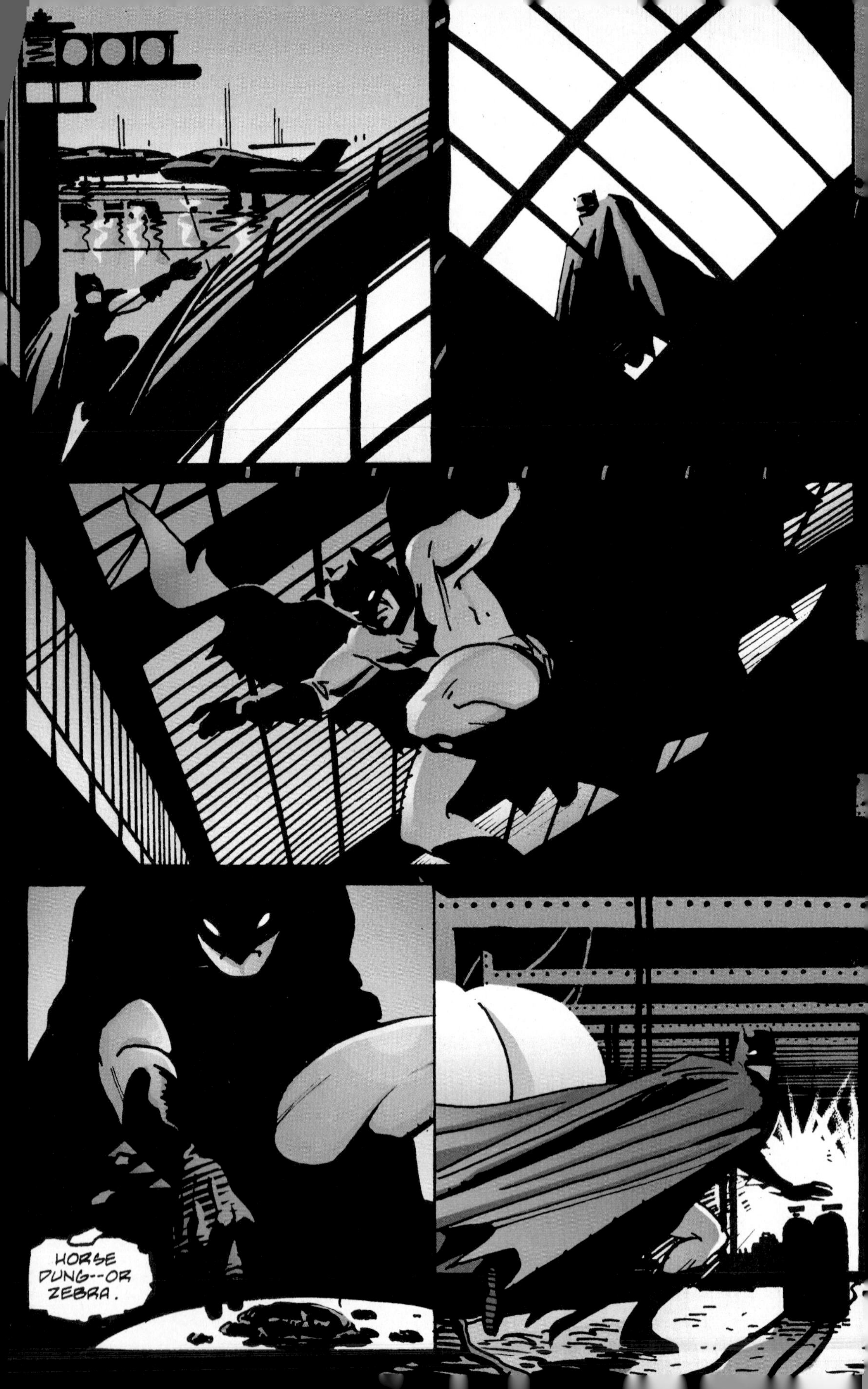
HORSE DUNG--OR ZEBRA.

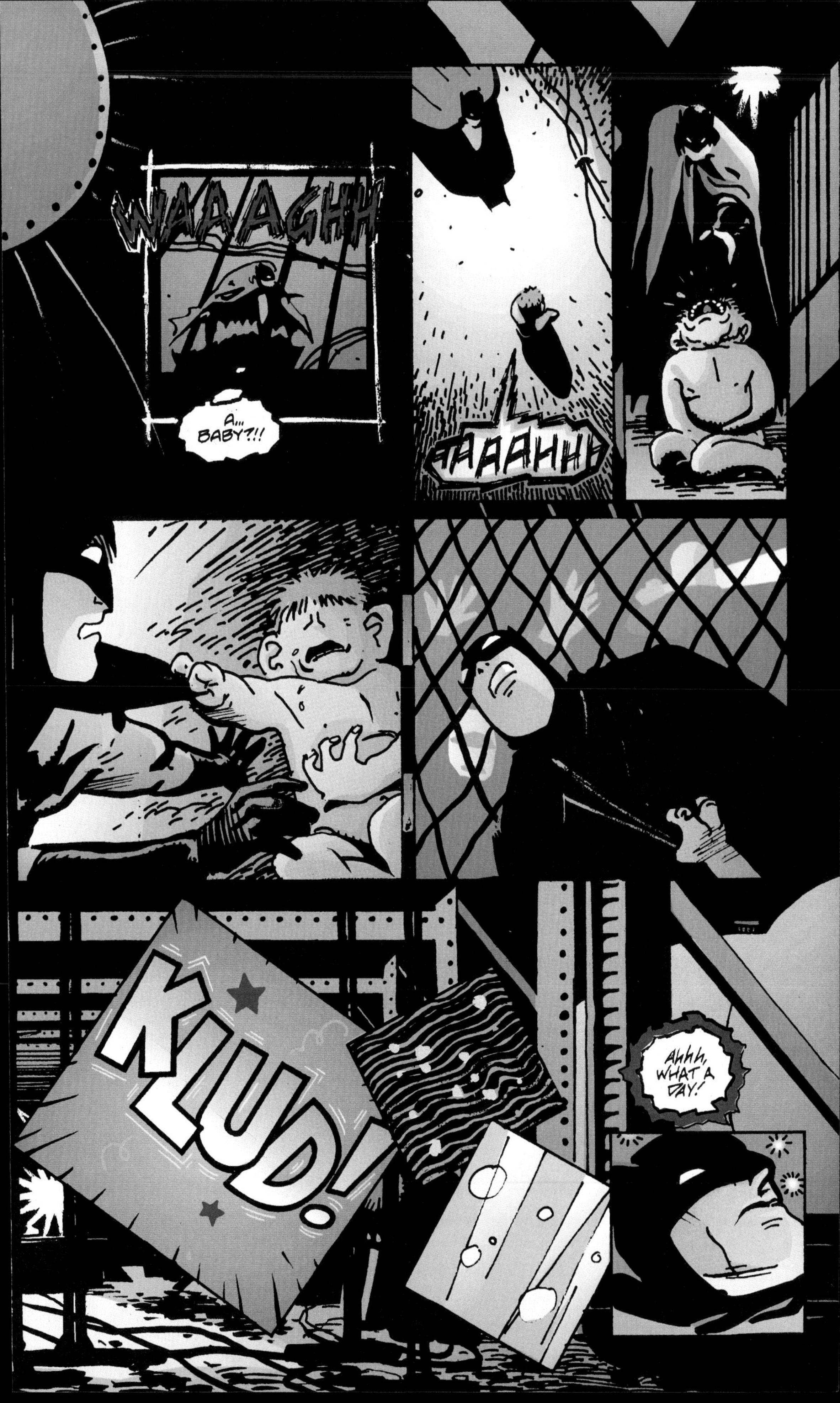
WAAAGHH
A... BABY?!!
AAAAHHH
KLUD!
Ahhh, WHAT A DAY!

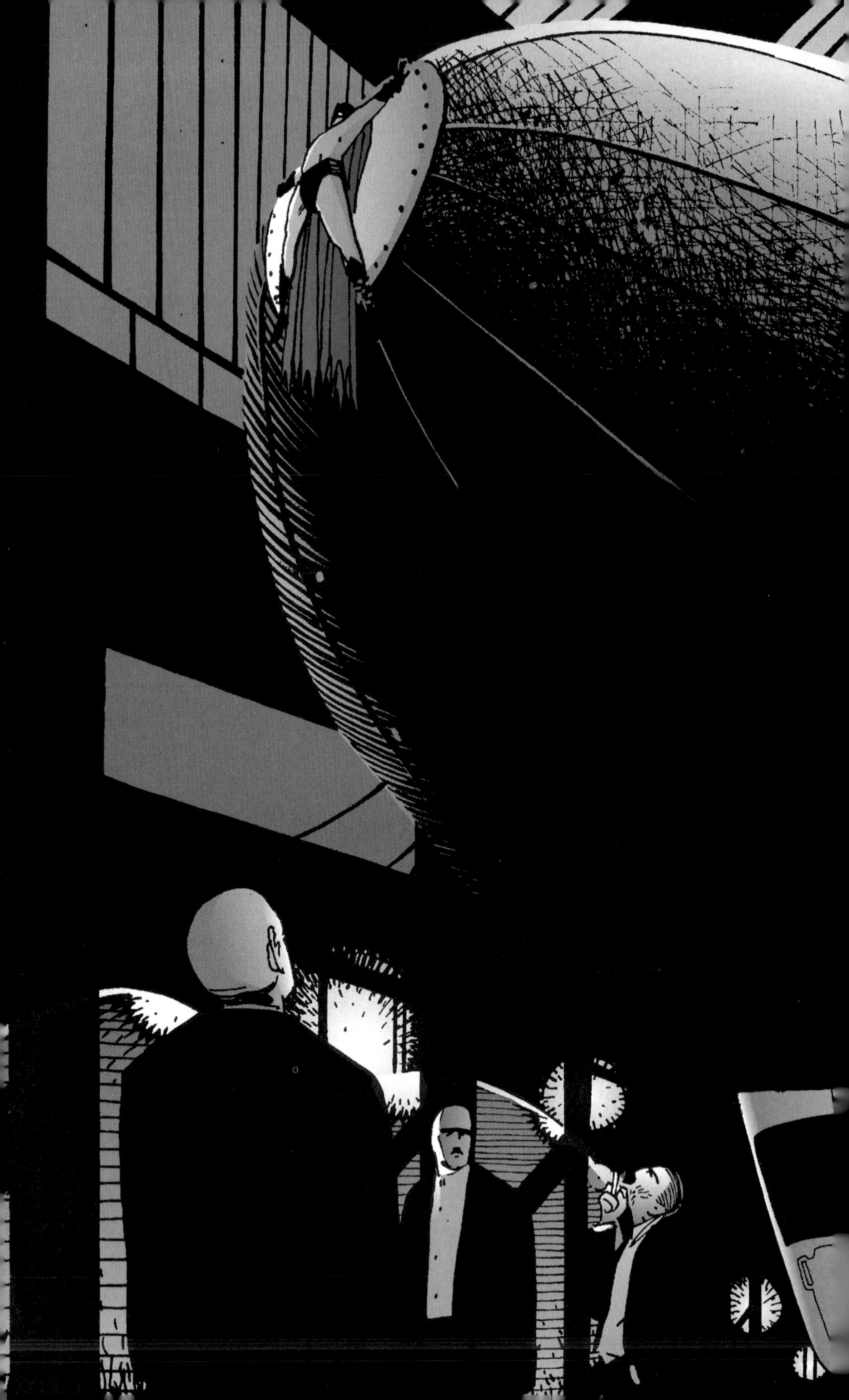

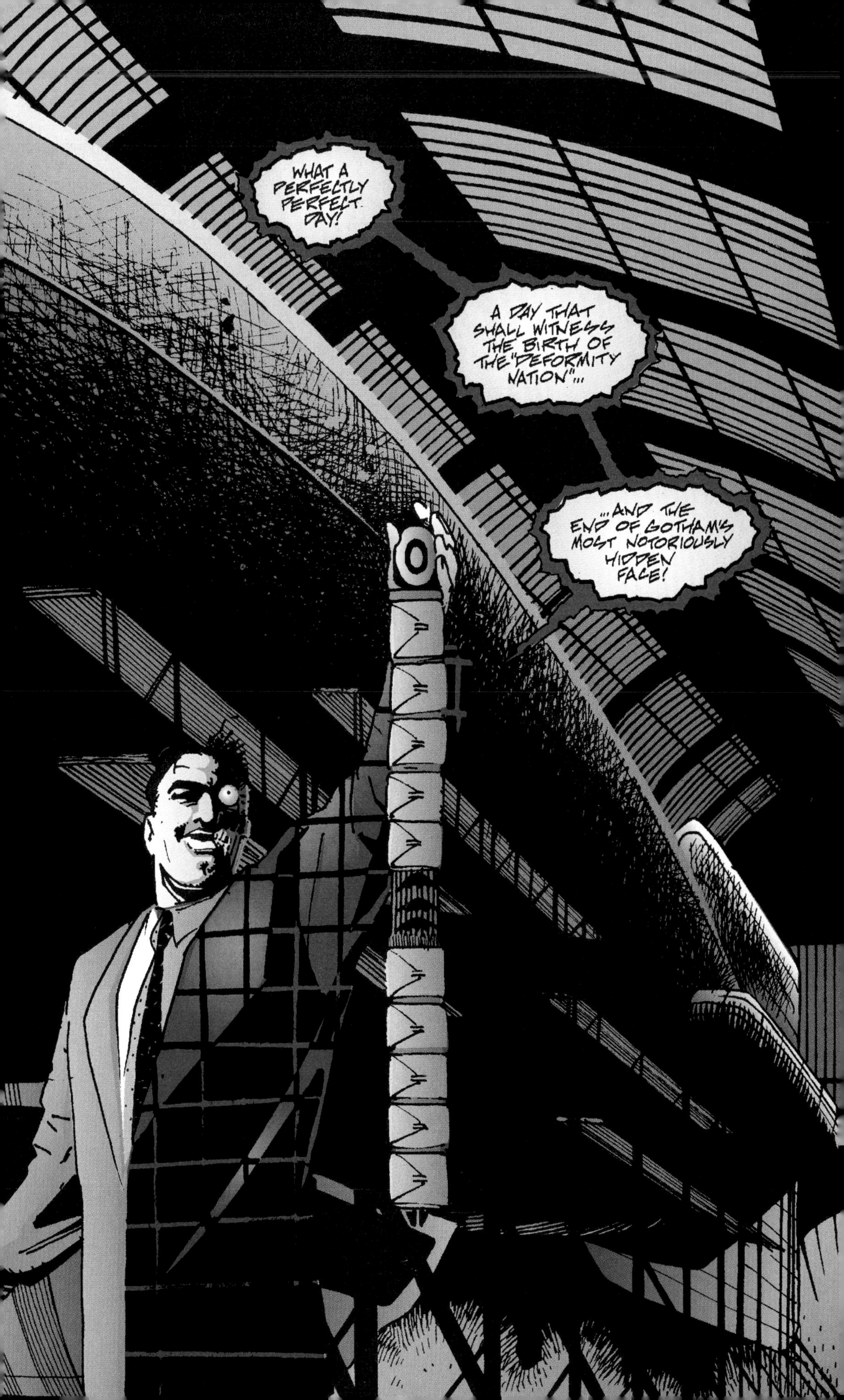
WHAT A PERFECTLY PERFECT DAY!
A DAY THAT SHALL WITNESS THE BIRTH OF THE "DEFORMITY NATION"...
...AND THE END OF GOTHAM'S MOST NOTORIOUSLY HIDDEN FACE!

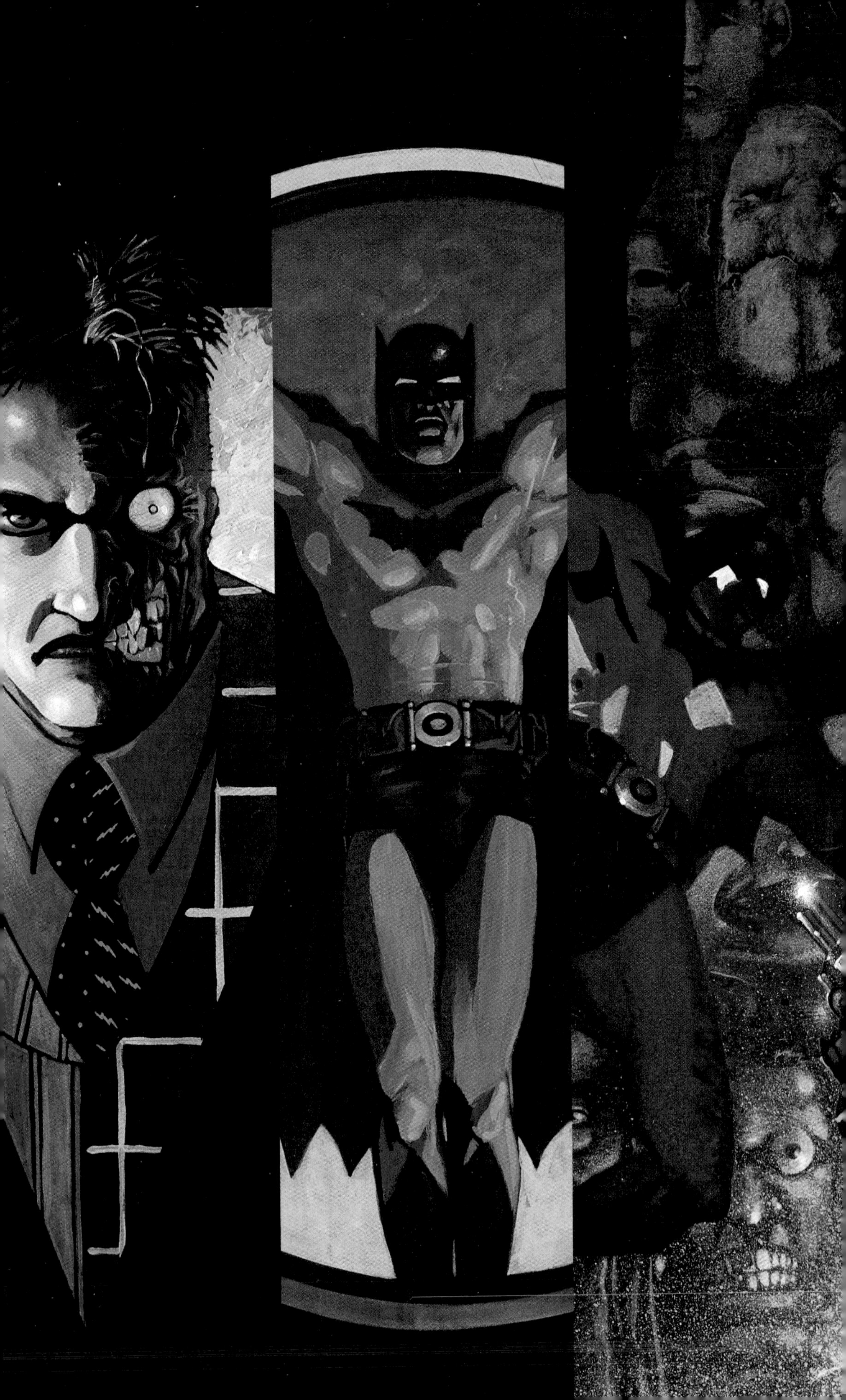

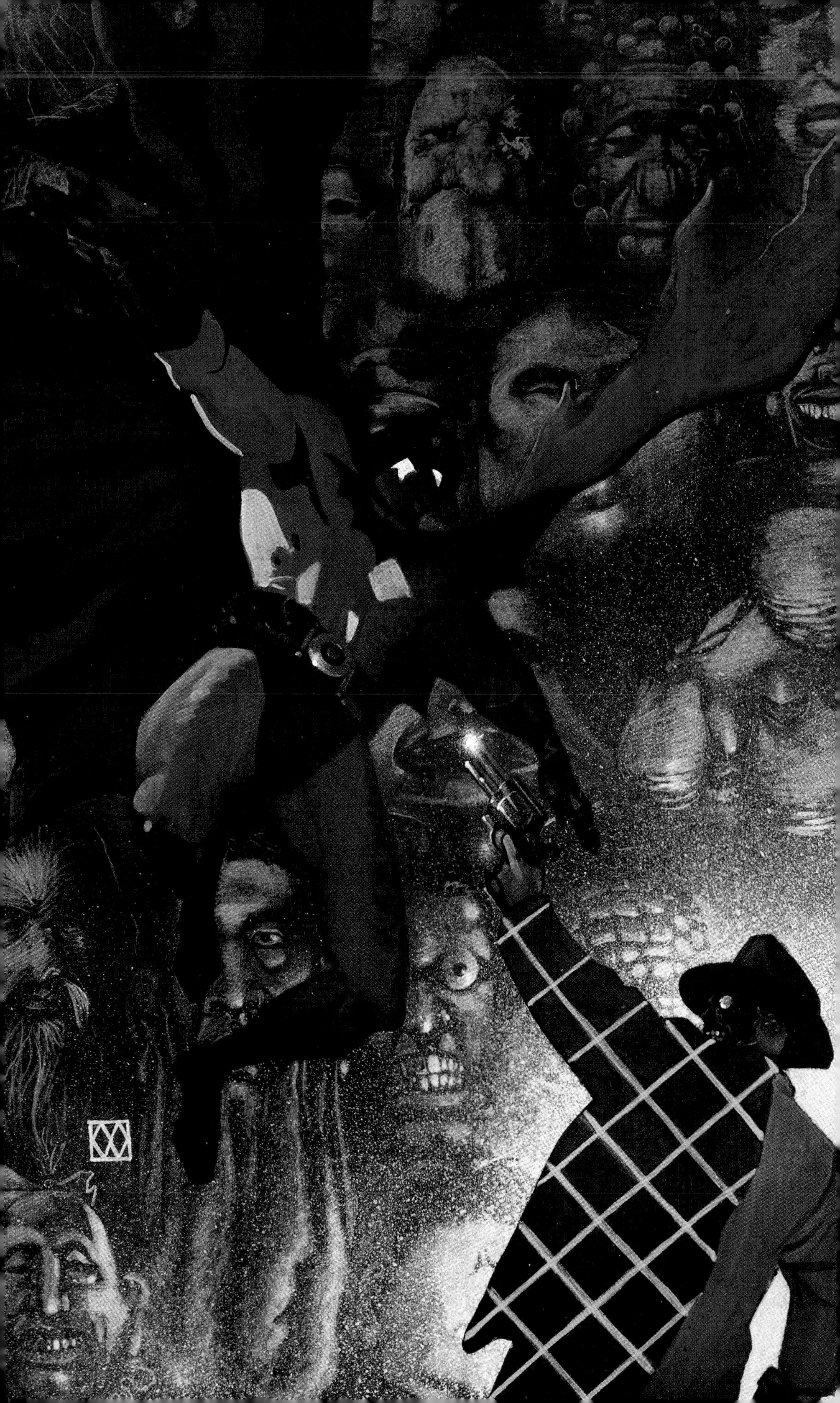

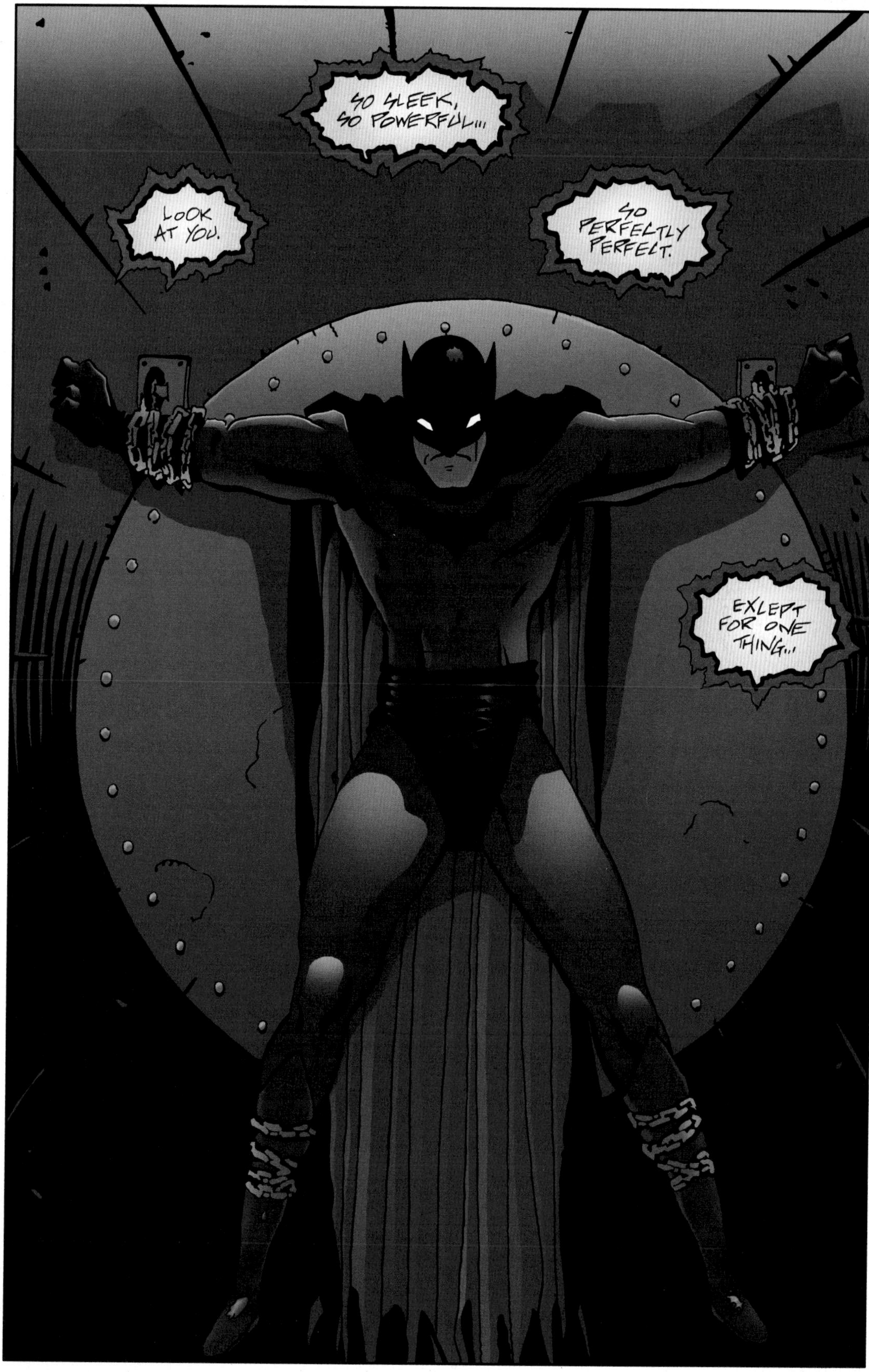
LOOK AT YOU.
SO SLEEK, SO POWERFUL...
SO PERFECTLY PERFECT.
EXCEPT FOR ONE THING...

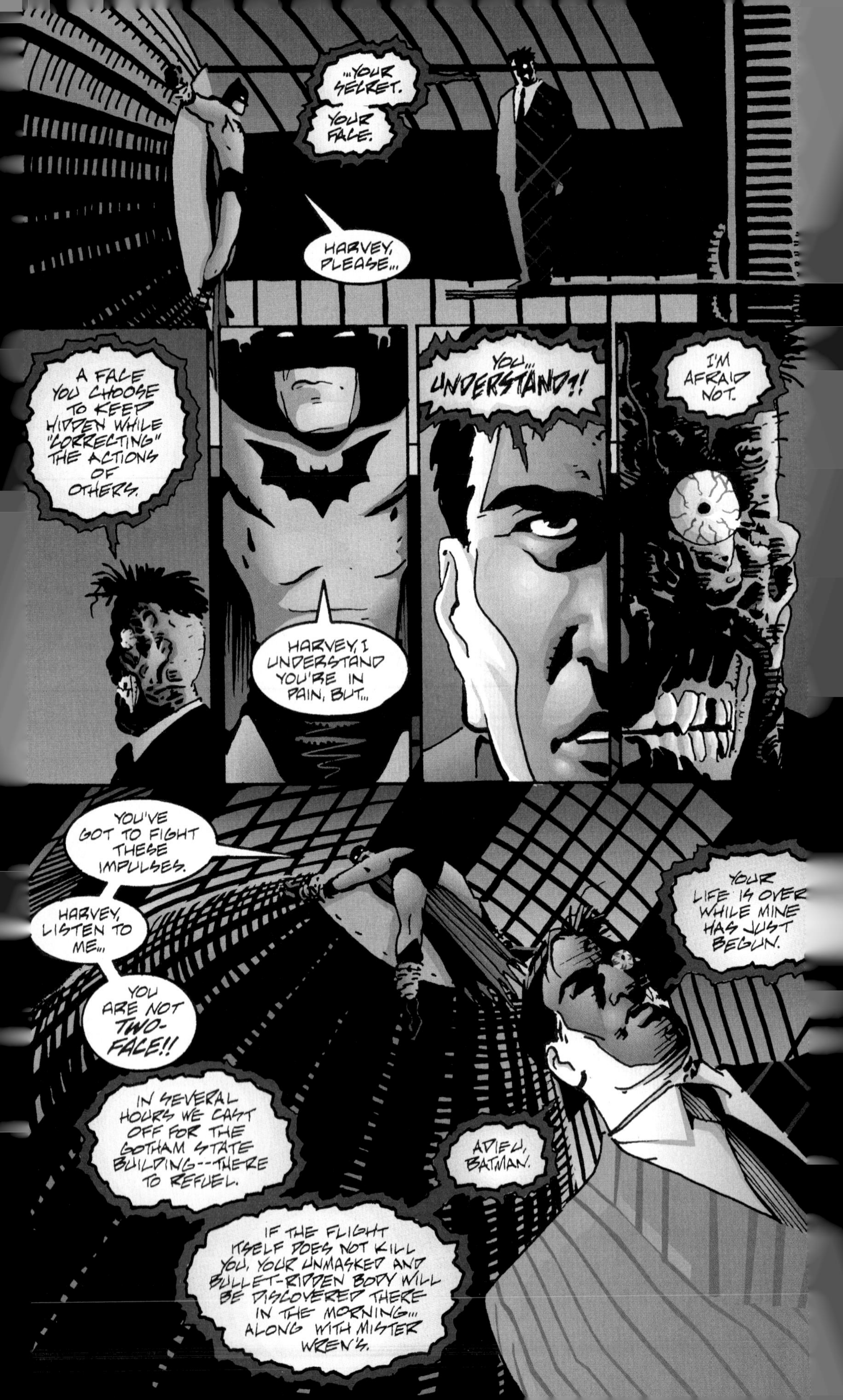
...YOUR SECRET.
YOUR FACE.
HARVEY, PLEASE...
A FACE YOU CHOOSE TO KEEP HIDDEN WHILE "CORRECTING" THE ACTIONS OF OTHERS.
HARVEY, I UNDERSTAND YOU'RE IN PAIN, BUT...
YOU... UNDERSTAND?!
I'M AFRAID NOT.
YOU'VE GOT TO FIGHT THESE IMPULSES.
HARVEY, LISTEN TO ME...
YOU ARE NOT TWO-FACE!!
YOUR LIFE IS OVER WHILE MINE HAS JUST BEGUN.
IN SEVERAL HOURS WE CAST OFF FOR THE GOTHAM STATE BUILDING--THERE TO REFUEL.
ADIEU, BATMAN.
IF THE FLIGHT ITSELF DOES NOT KILL YOU, YOUR UNMASKED AND BULLET-RIDDEN BODY WILL BE DISCOVERED THERE IN THE MORNING... ALONG WITH MISTER WREN'S.

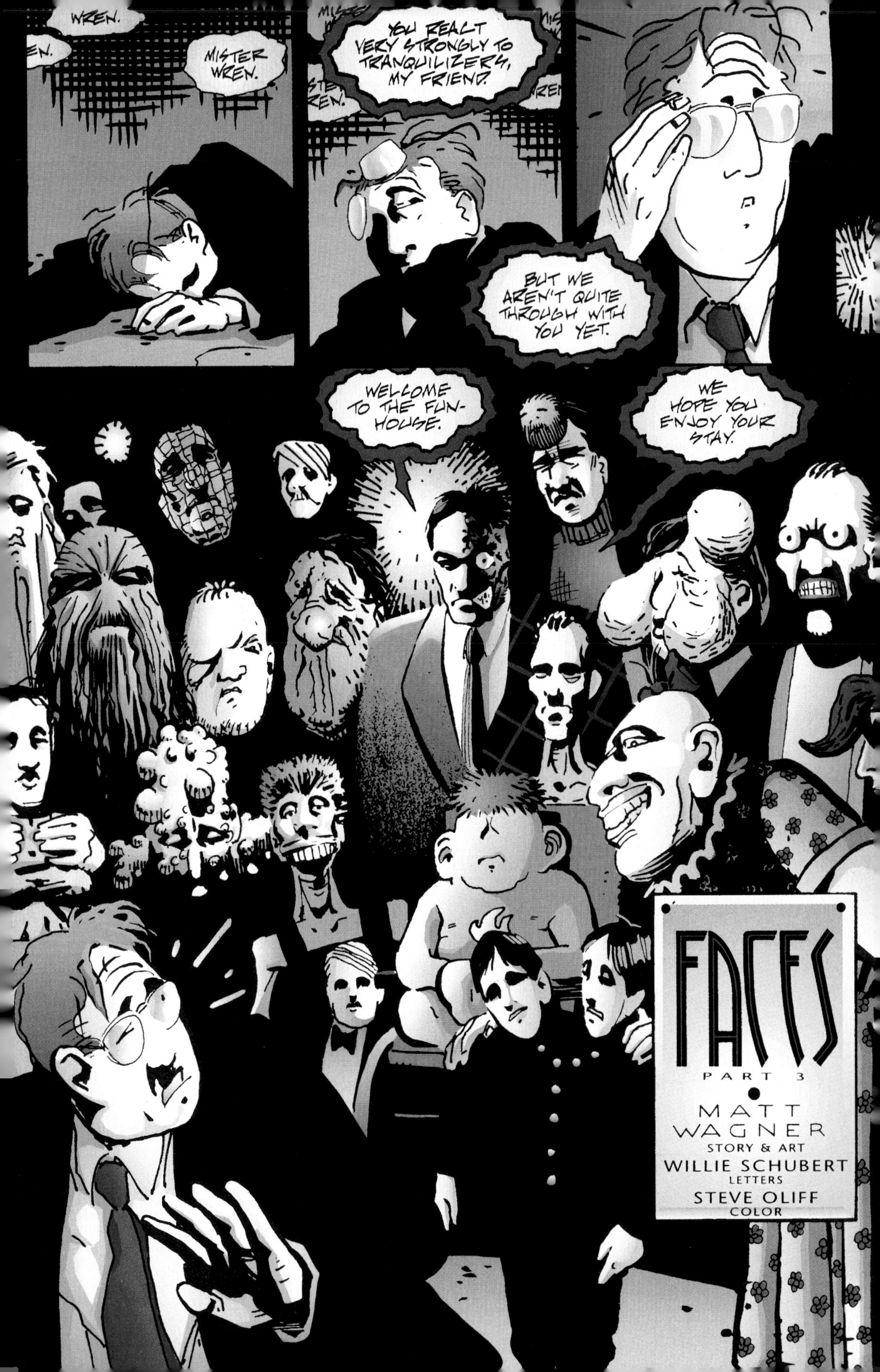
WREN.
MISTER WREN.
YOU REACT VERY STRONGLY TO TRANQUILIZERS, MY FRIEND.
BUT WE AREN'T QUITE THROUGH WITH YOU YET.
WELCOME TO THE FUN-HOUSE.
WE HOPE YOU ENJOY YOUR STAY.
FACES
PART 3
MATT WAGNER
STORY & ART
WILLIE SCHUBERT
LETTERS
STEVE OLIFF
COLOR

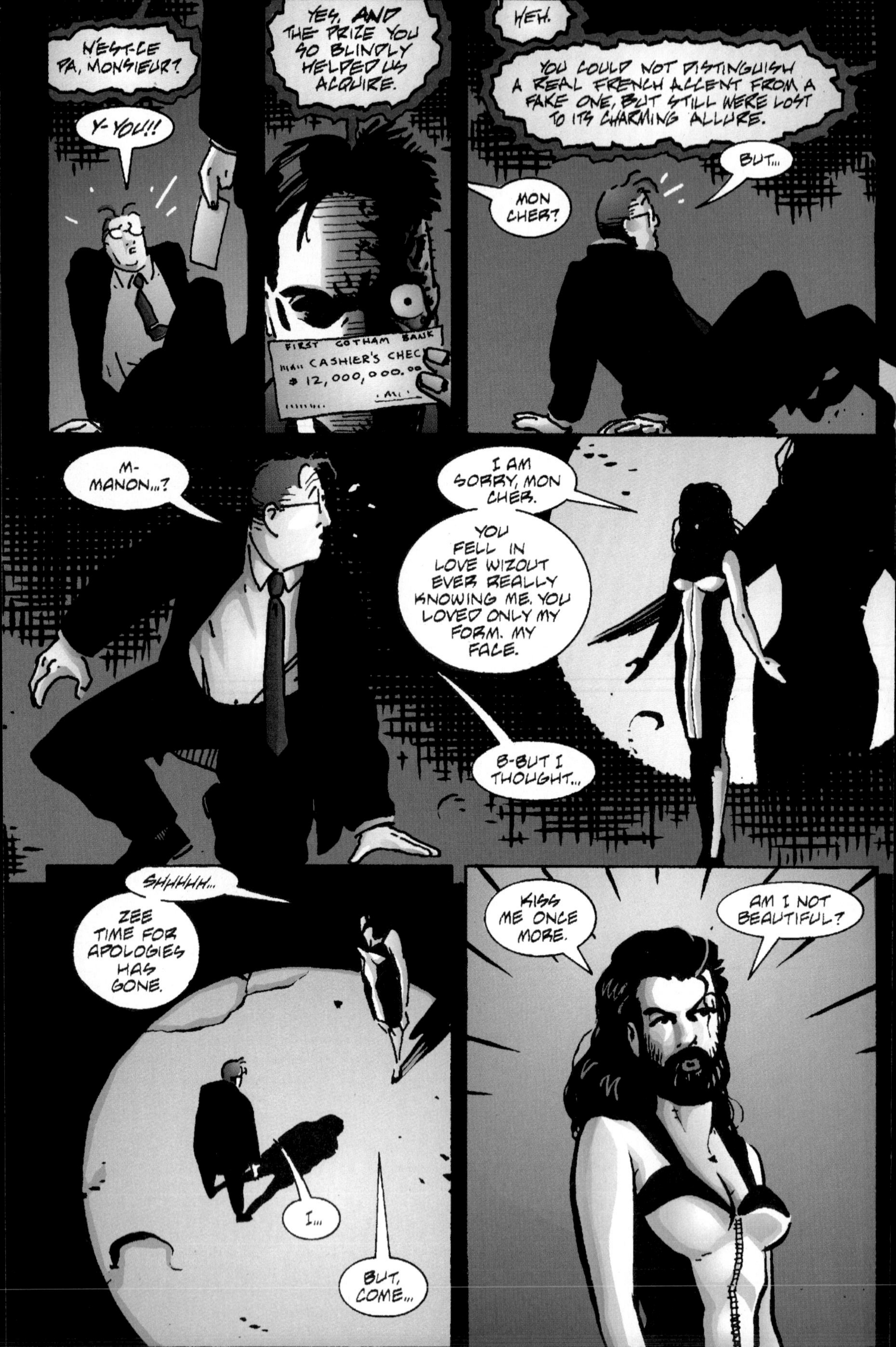
N'EST-CE PA, MONSIEUR?
Y-YOU!!
YES, AND THE PRIZE YOU SO BLINDLY HELPED US ACQUIRE.
FIRST GOTHAM BANK
CASHIER'S CHEC
$ 12,000,000.00
HEH.
YOU COULD NOT DISTINGUISH A REAL FRENCH ACCENT FROM A FAKE ONE, BUT STILL WERE LOST TO ITS CHARMING ALLURE.
BUT...
MON CHER?
M-MANON...?
I AM SORRY, MON CHER.
YOU FELL IN LOVE WIZOUT EVER REALLY KNOWING ME. YOU LOVED ONLY MY FORM. MY FACE.
B-BUT I THOUGHT...
SHHHHH...
ZEE TIME FOR APOLOGIES HAS GONE.
I...
BUT, COME...
KISS ME ONCE MORE.
AM I NOT BEAUTIFUL?

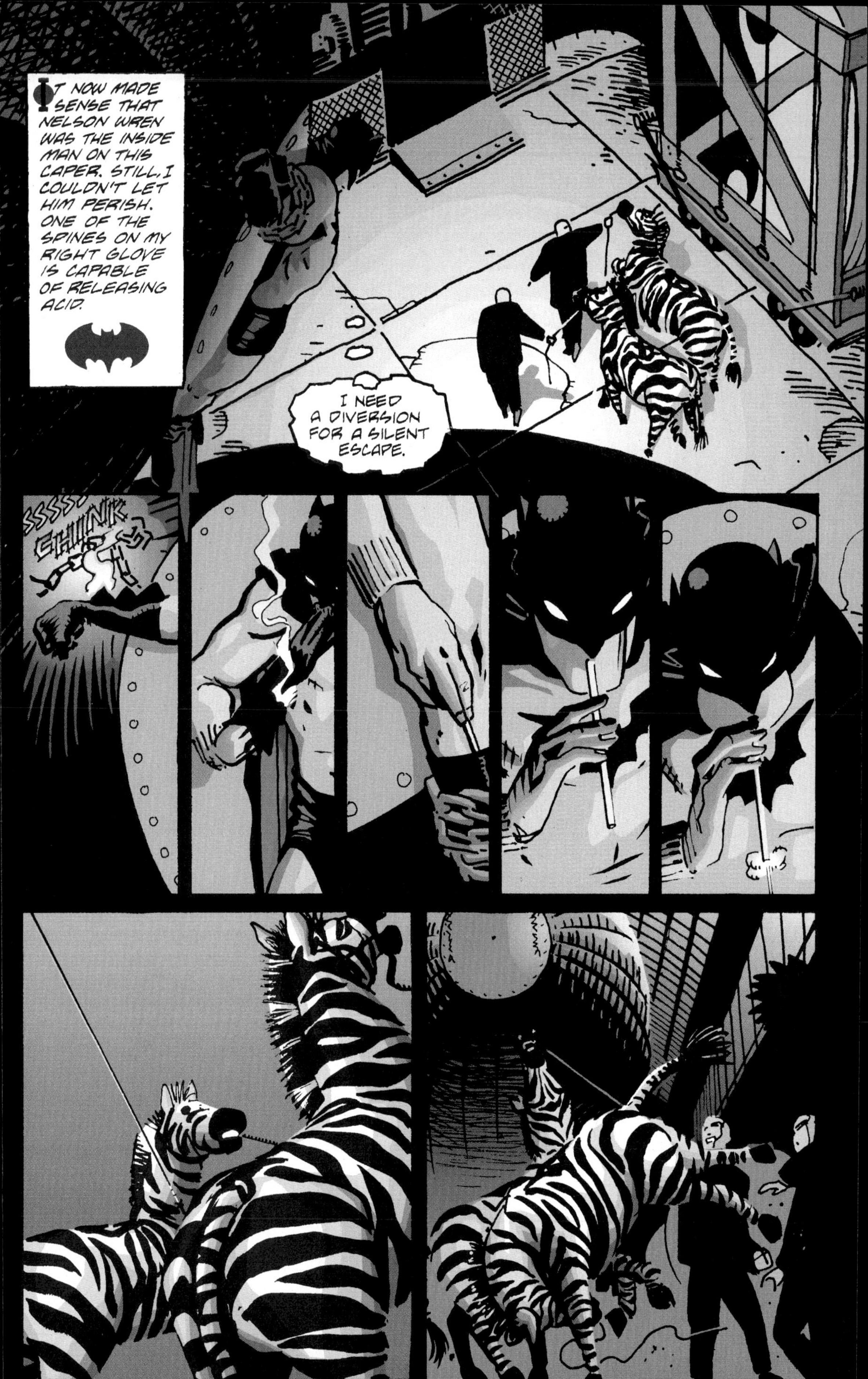
IT NOW MADE SENSE THAT NELSON WREN WAS THE INSIDE MAN ON THIS CAPER. STILL, I COULDN'T LET HIM PERISH. ONE OF THE SPINES ON MY RIGHT GLOVE IS CAPABLE OF RELEASING ACID.
I NEED A DIVERSION FOR A SILENT ESCAPE.
SSSSS
CHUNK

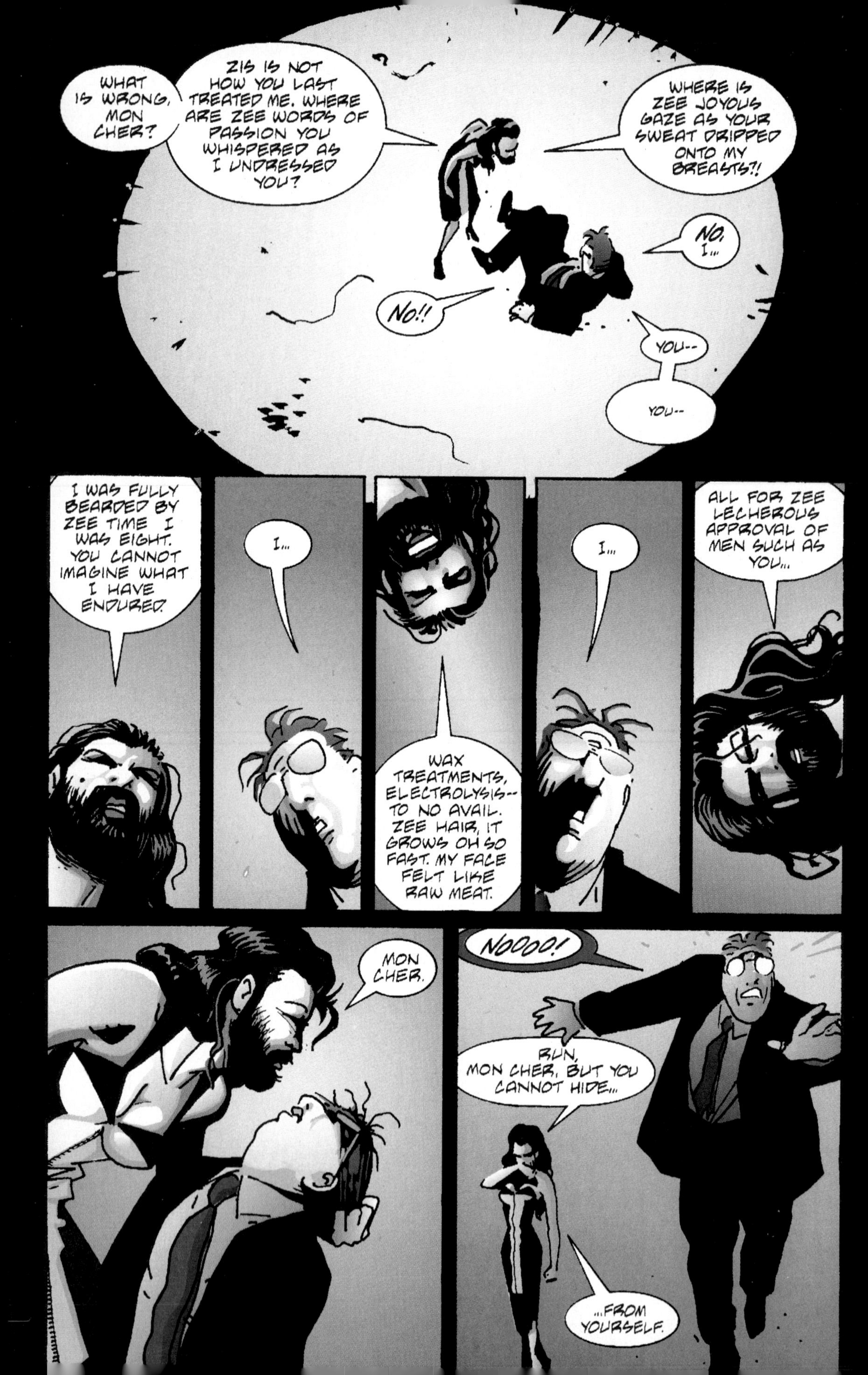
WHAT IS WRONG, MON CHER?
ZIS IS NOT HOW YOU LAST TREATED ME. WHERE ARE ZEE WORDS OF PASSION YOU WHISPERED AS I UNDRESSED YOU?
WHERE IS ZEE JOYOUS GAZE AS YOUR SWEAT DRIPPED ONTO MY BREASTS?!
NO. I...
NO!!
YOU--
YOU--
I WAS FULLY BEARDED BY ZEE TIME I WAS EIGHT. YOU CANNOT IMAGINE WHAT I HAVE ENDURED.
I...
WAX TREATMENTS, ELECTROLYSIS-- TO NO AVAIL. ZEE HAIR, IT GROWS OH SO FAST. MY FACE FELT LIKE RAW MEAT.
I...
ALL FOR ZEE LECHEROUS APPROVAL OF MEN SUCH AS YOU...
MON CHER.
NOOOO!
RUN, MON CHER, BUT YOU CANNOT HIDE...
...FROM YOURSELF.

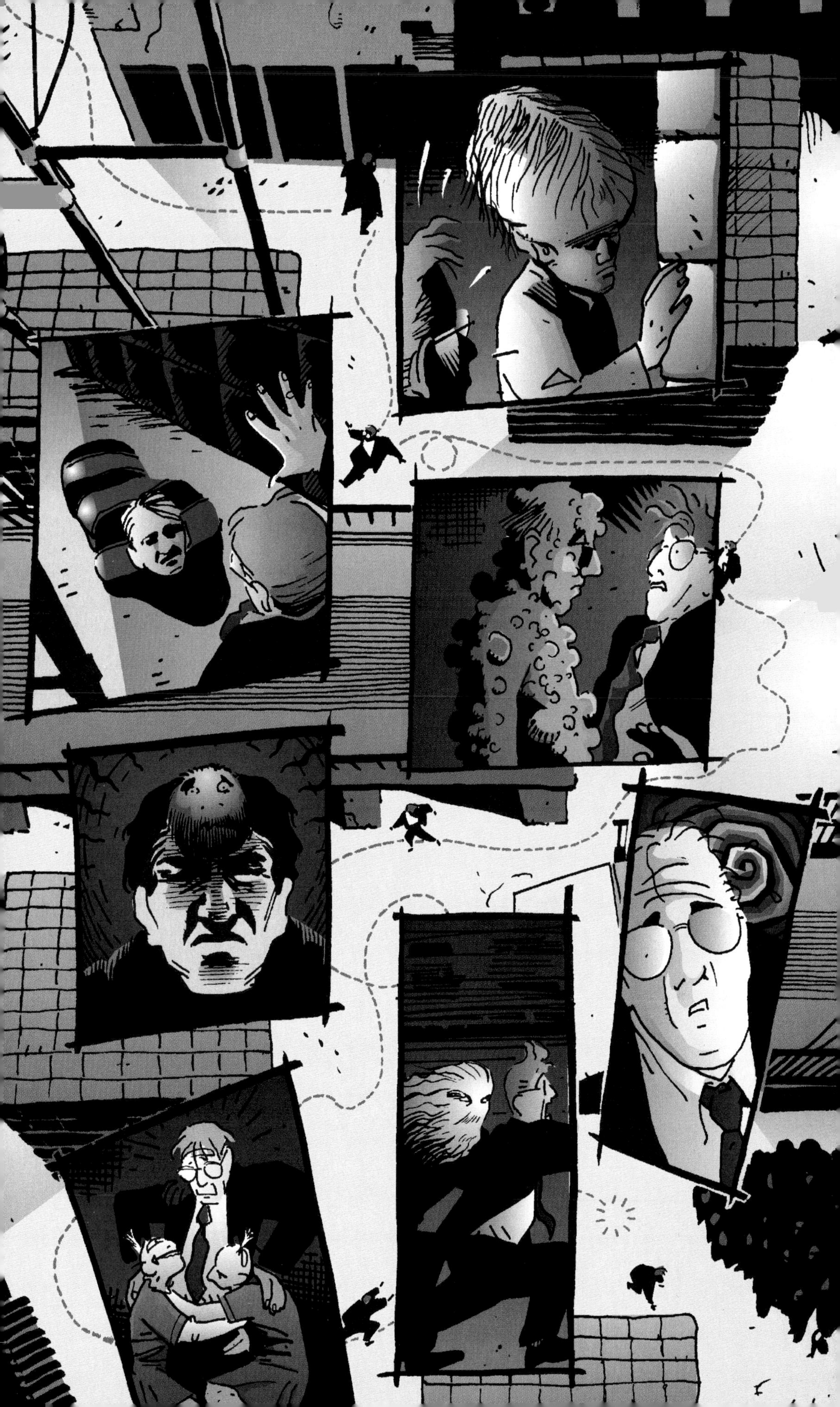

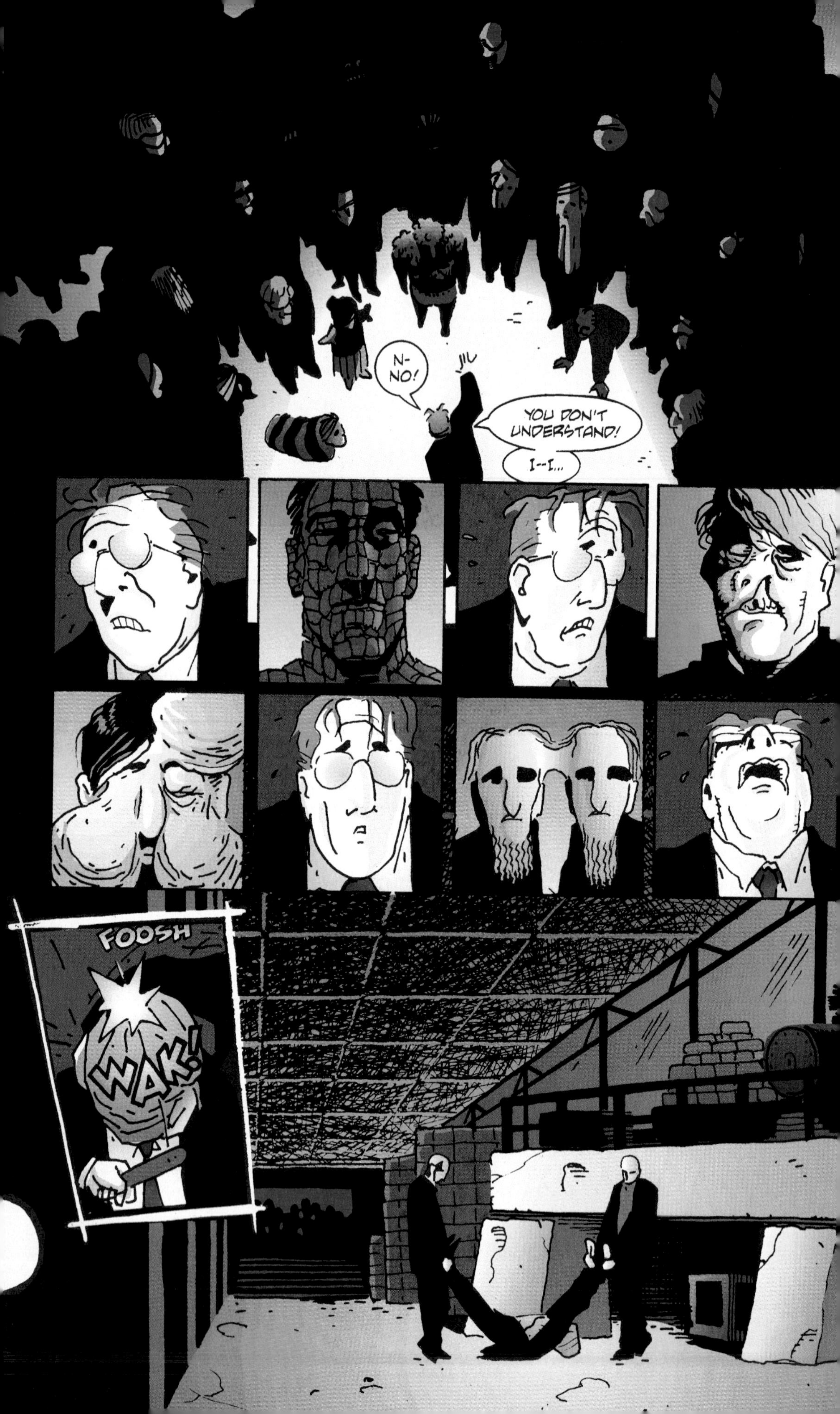
N-NO!
YOU DON'T UNDERSTAND!
I--I...
FOOSH
WAK!

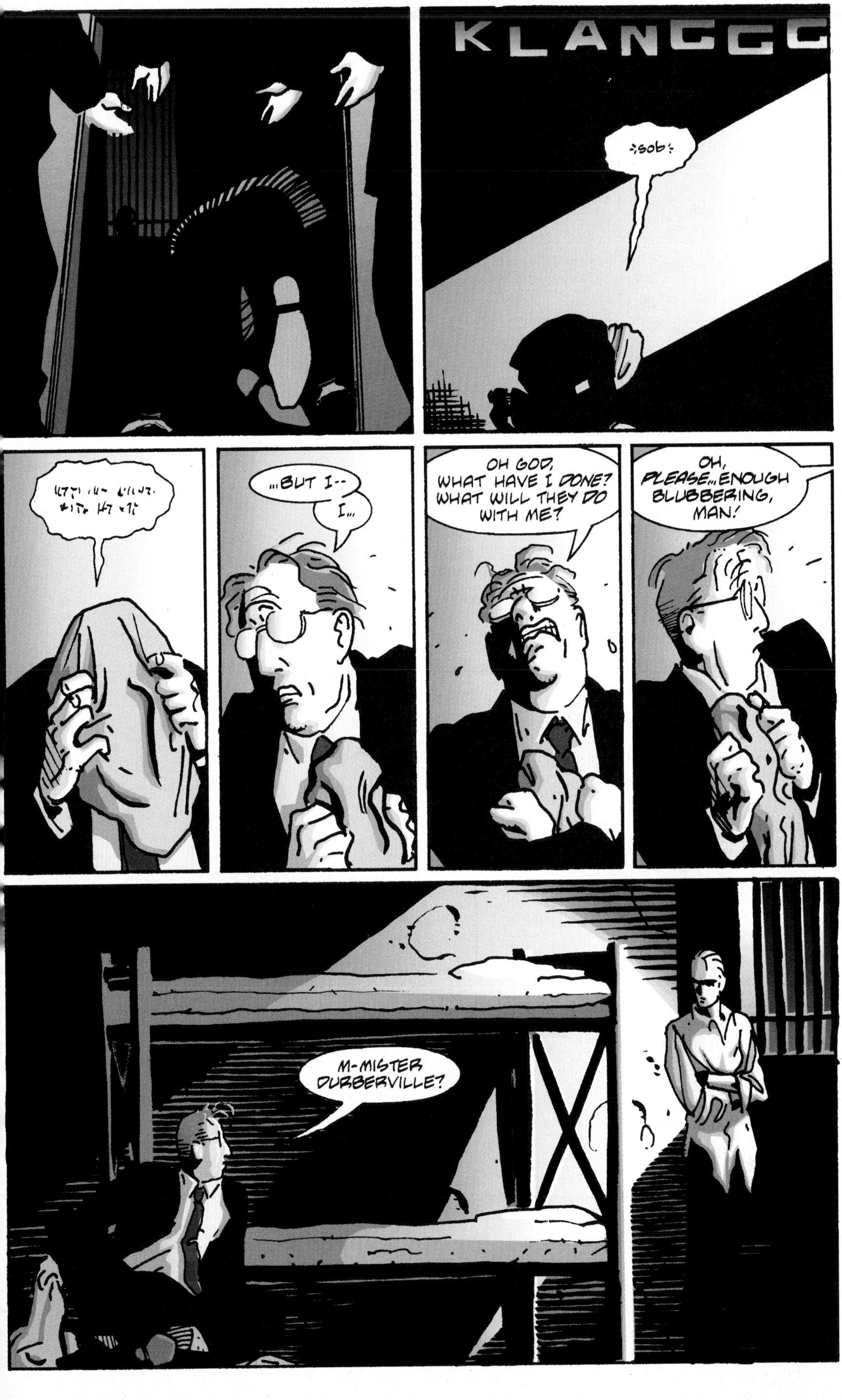
KLANGGG
sob
...BUT I--
I...
OH GOD, WHAT HAVE I DONE? WHAT WILL THEY DO WITH ME?
OH, PLEASE...ENOUGH BLUBBERING, MAN!
M-MISTER DURBERVILLE?

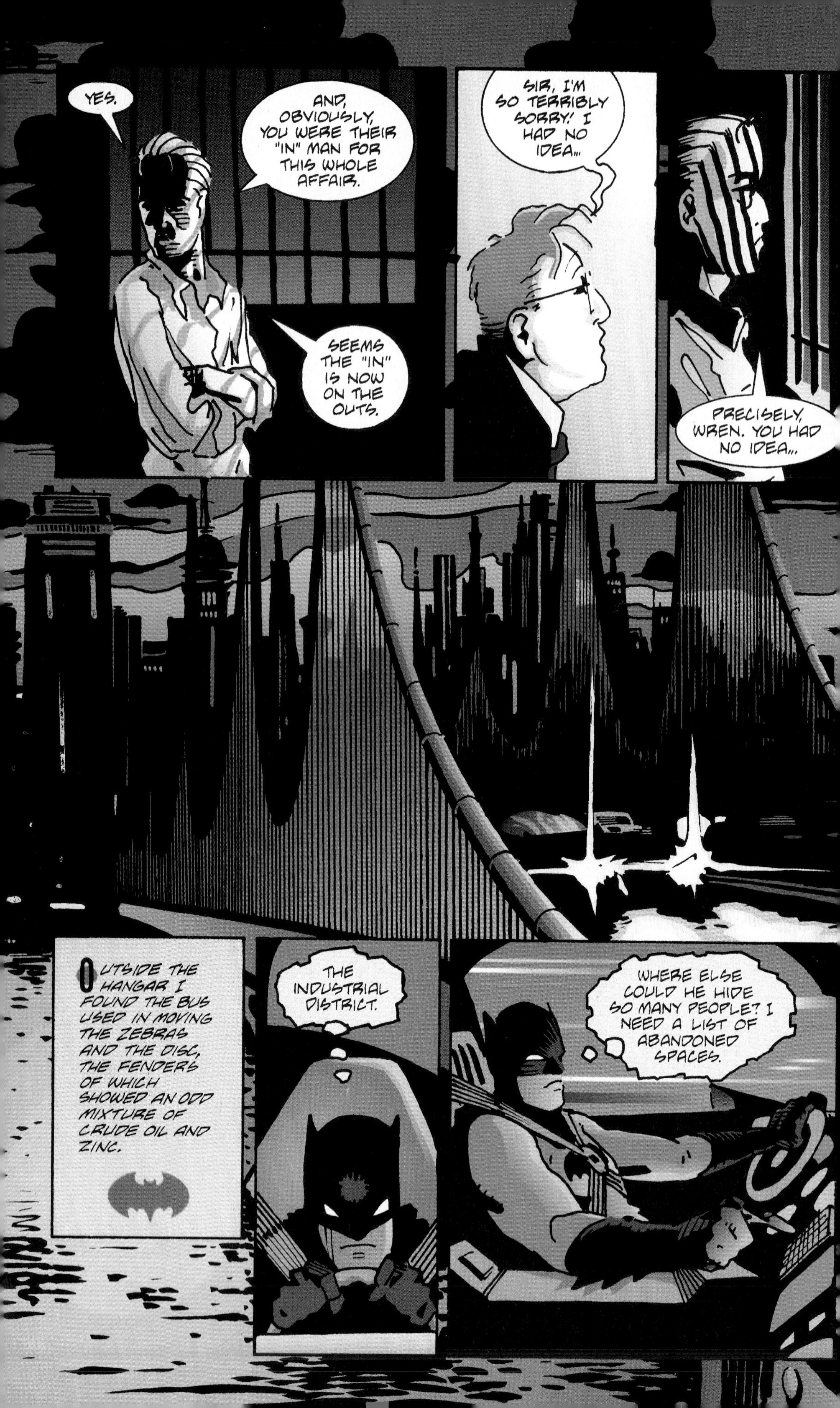
YES.
AND, OBVIOUSLY, YOU WERE THEIR "IN" MAN FOR THIS WHOLE AFFAIR.
SEEMS THE "IN" IS NOW ON THE OUTS.
SIR, I'M SO TERRIBLY SORRY! I HAD NO IDEA...
PRECISELY, WREN. YOU HAD NO IDEA...
OUTSIDE THE HANGAR I FOUND THE BUS USED IN MOVING THE ZEBRAS AND THE DISC, THE FENDERS OF WHICH SHOWED AN ODD MIXTURE OF CRUDE OIL AND ZINC.
THE INDUSTRIAL DISTRICT.
WHERE ELSE COULD HE HIDE SO MANY PEOPLE? I NEED A LIST OF ABANDONED SPACES.

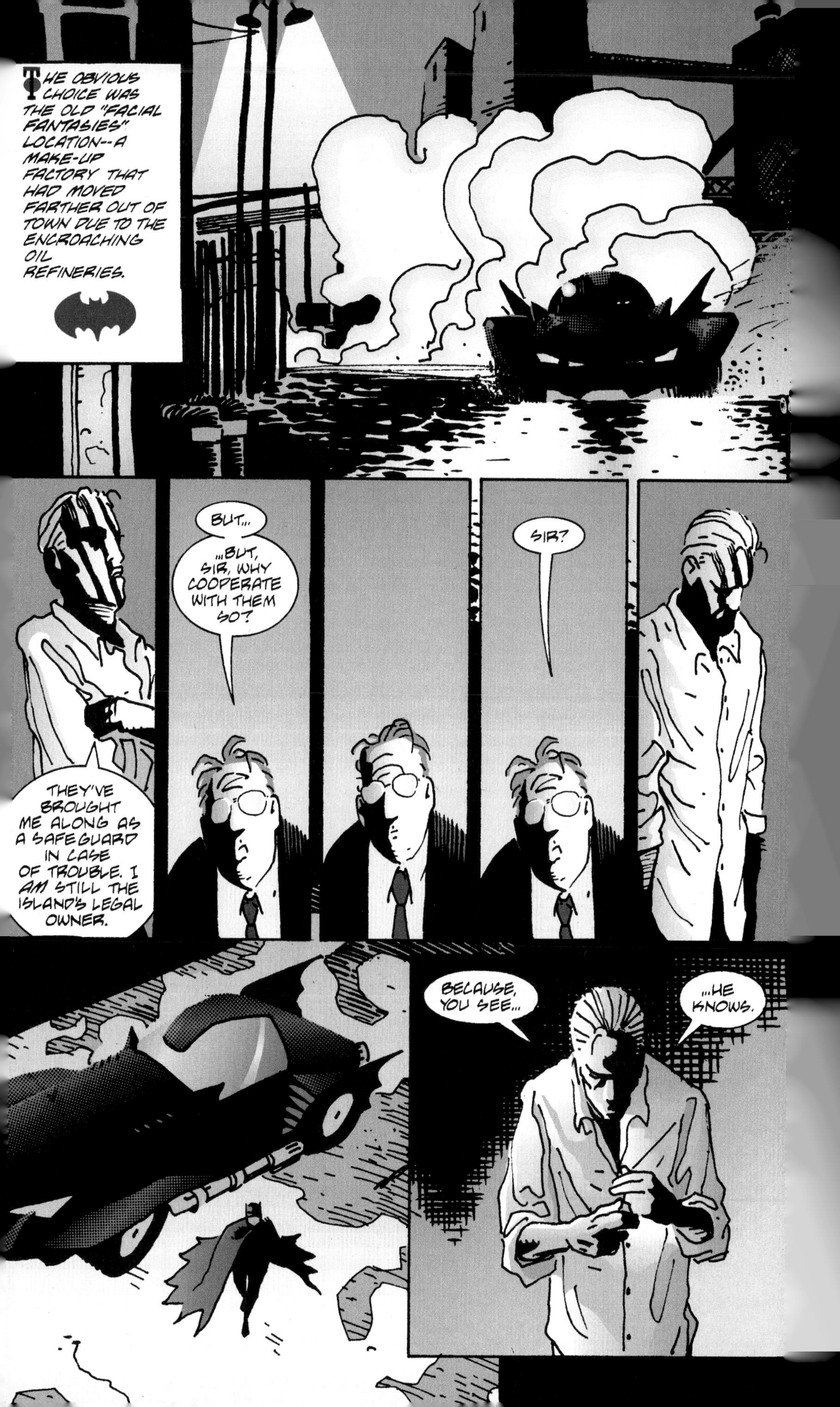
THE OBVIOUS CHOICE WAS THE OLD "FACIAL FANTASIES" LOCATION--A MAKE-UP FACTORY THAT HAD MOVED FARTHER OUT OF TOWN DUE TO THE ENCROACHING OIL REFINERIES.
BUT...
...BUT, SIR, WHY COOPERATE WITH THEM SO?
SIR?
THEY'VE BROUGHT ME ALONG AS A SAFEGUARD IN CASE OF TROUBLE. I AM STILL THE ISLAND'S LEGAL OWNER.
BECAUSE, YOU SEE...
...HE KNOWS.

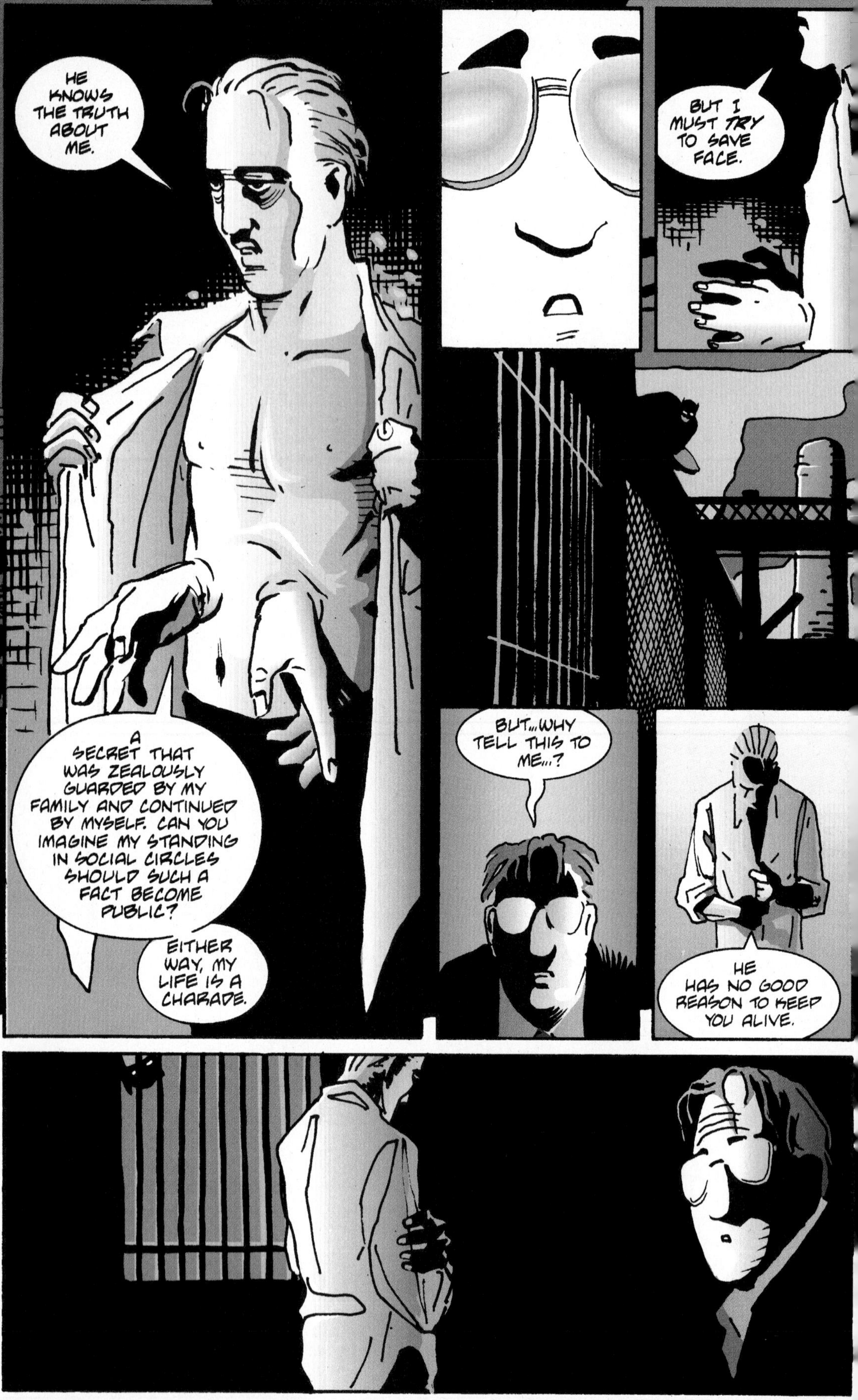
HE KNOWS THE TRUTH ABOUT ME.
A SECRET THAT WAS ZEALOUSLY GUARDED BY MY FAMILY AND CONTINUED BY MYSELF. CAN YOU IMAGINE MY STANDING IN SOCIAL CIRCLES SHOULD SUCH A FACT BECOME PUBLIC?
EITHER WAY, MY LIFE IS A CHARADE.
BUT I MUST TRY TO SAVE FACE.
BUT...WHY TELL THIS TO ME...?
HE HAS NO GOOD REASON TO KEEP YOU ALIVE.

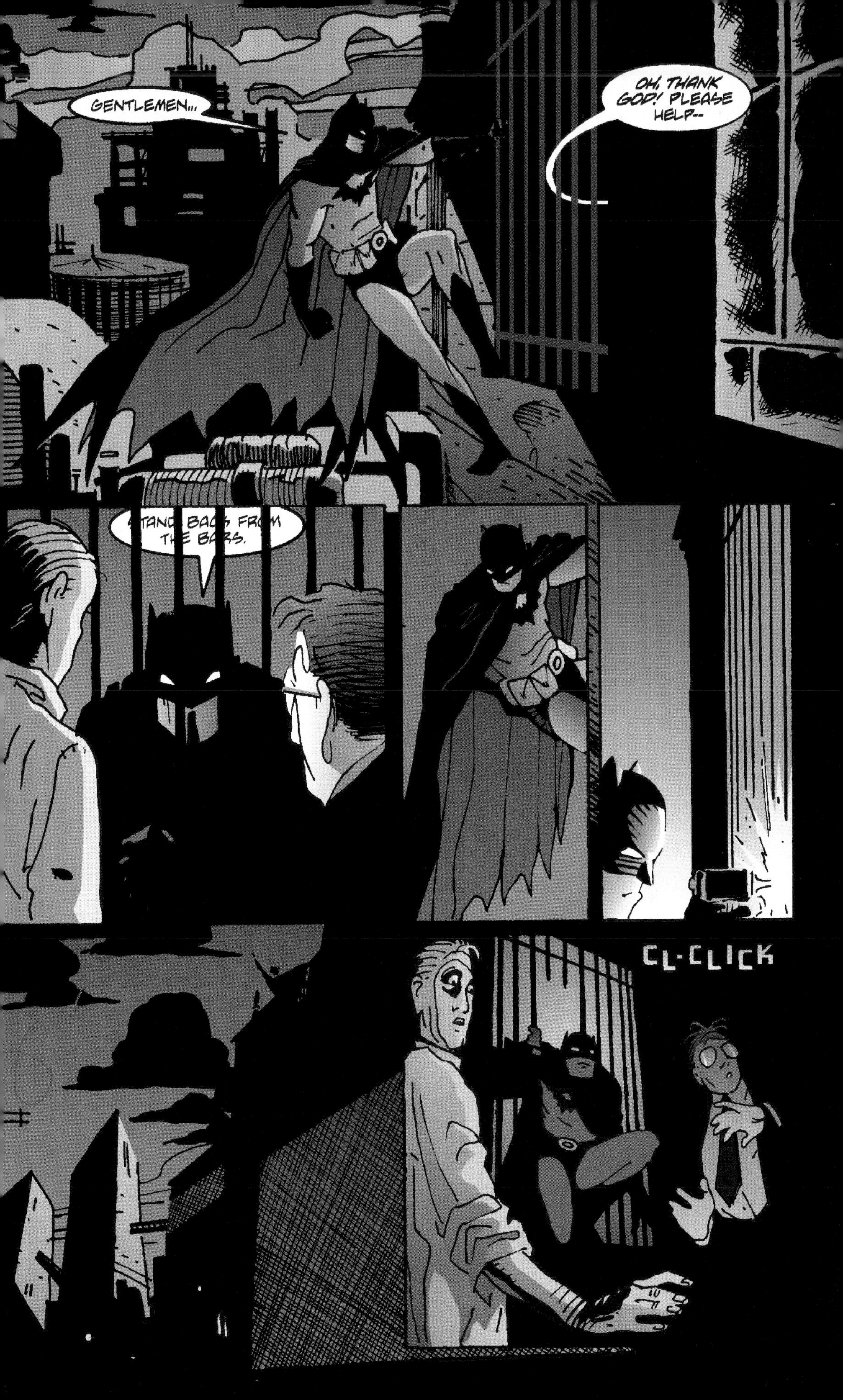
GENTLEMEN...
OH, THANK GOD! PLEASE HELP--
STAND BACK FROM THE BARS.
CL-CLICK

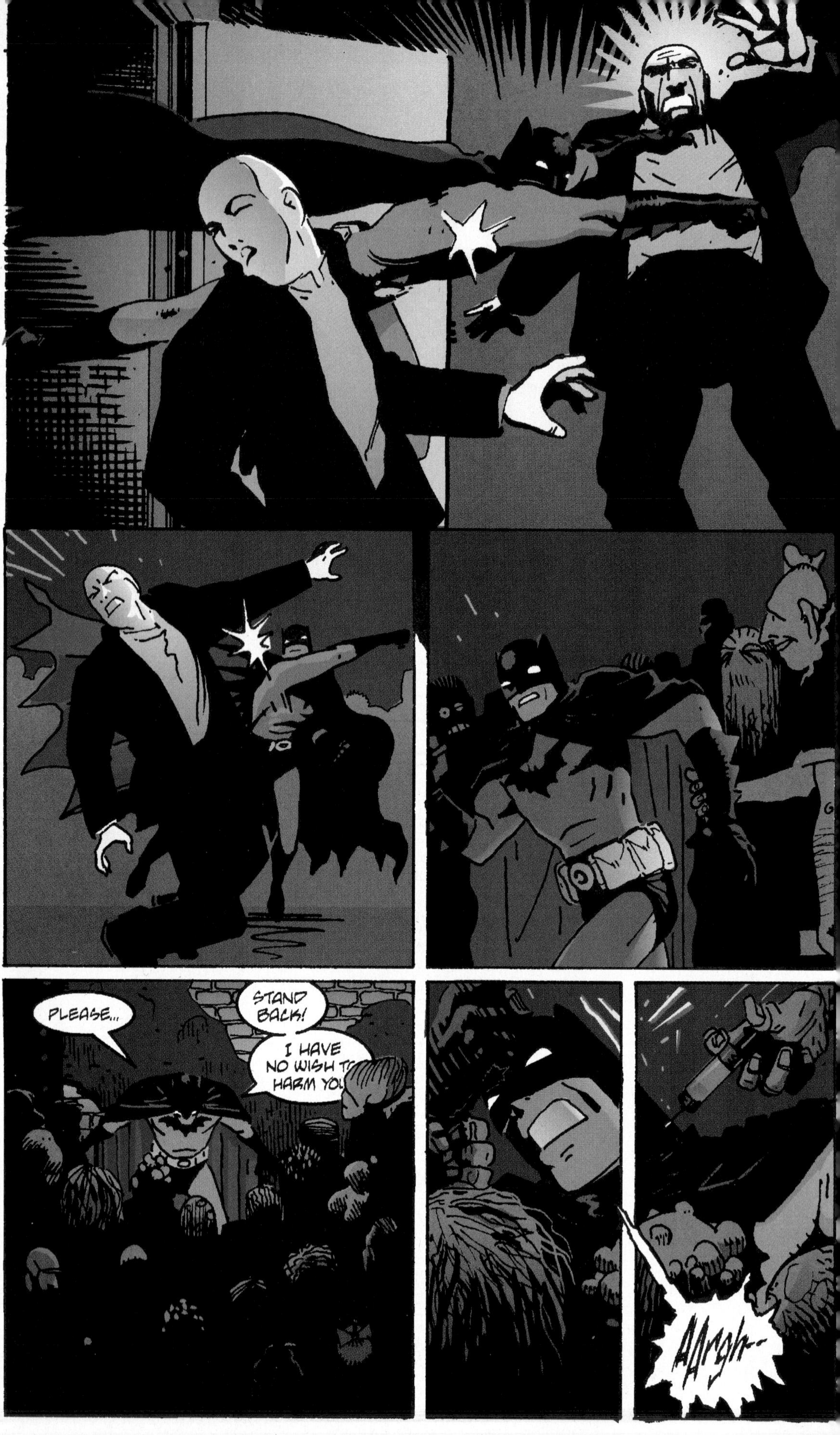
PLEASE...
STAND BACK!
I HAVE NO WISH T HARM YO
AArgh-

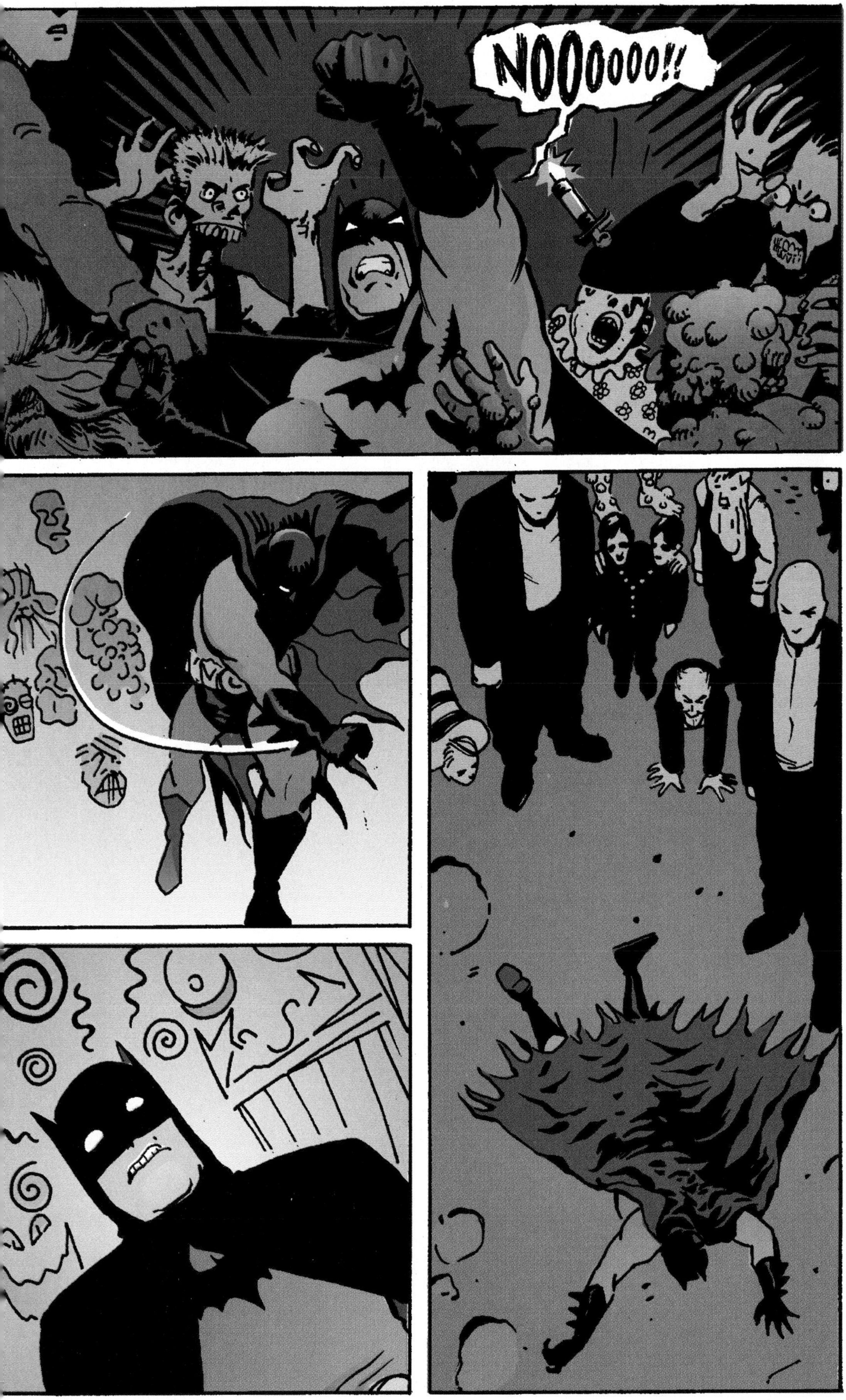
NOOOOOO!!

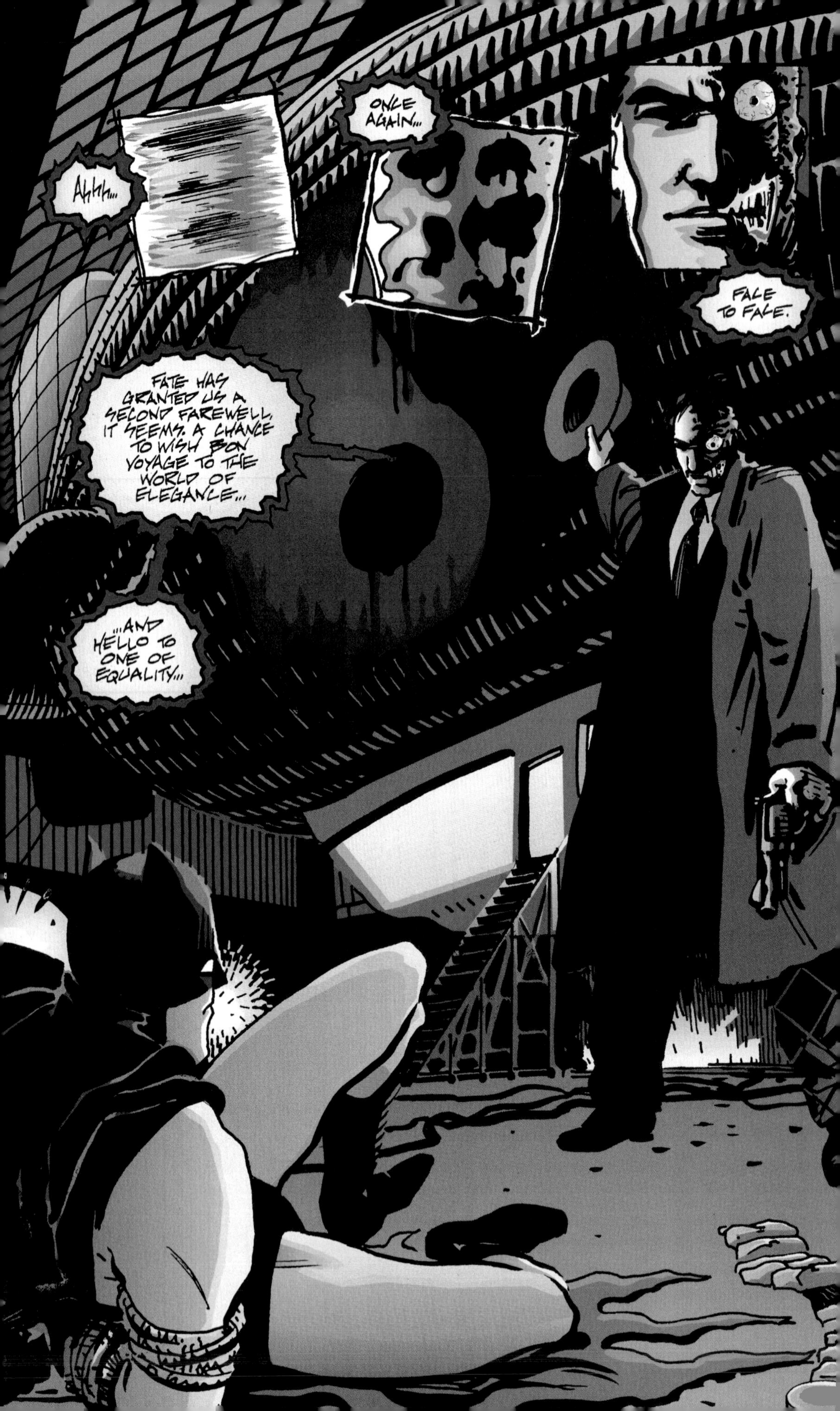

AHHH...
ONCE AGAIN...
FACE TO FACE.
FATE HAS GRANTED US A SECOND FAREWELL, IT SEEMS. A CHANCE TO WISH BON VOYAGE TO THE WORLD OF ELEGANCE...
...AND HELLO TO ONE OF EQUALITY...

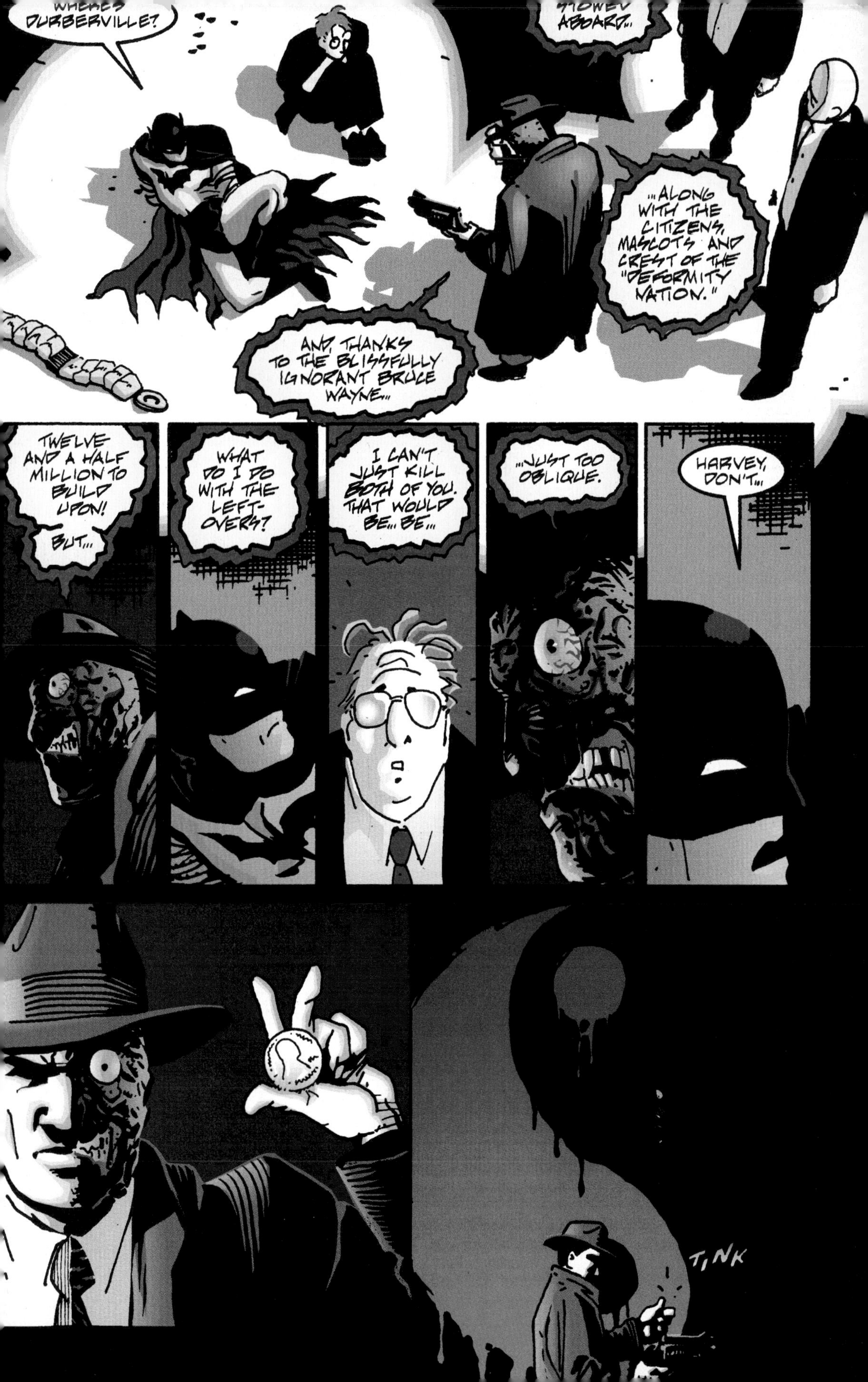

DURBERVILLE?
ABOARD...
...ALONG WITH THE CITIZENS, MASCOTS AND CREST OF THE "DEFORMITY NATION."
AND, THANKS TO THE BLISSFULLY IGNORANT BRUCE WAYNE...
TWELVE AND A HALF MILLION TO BUILD UPON! BUT...
WHAT DO I DO WITH THE LEFT-OVERS?
I CAN'T JUST KILL BOTH OF YOU. THAT WOULD BE... BE...
...JUST TOO OBLIQUE.
HARVEY, DON'T...
TINK

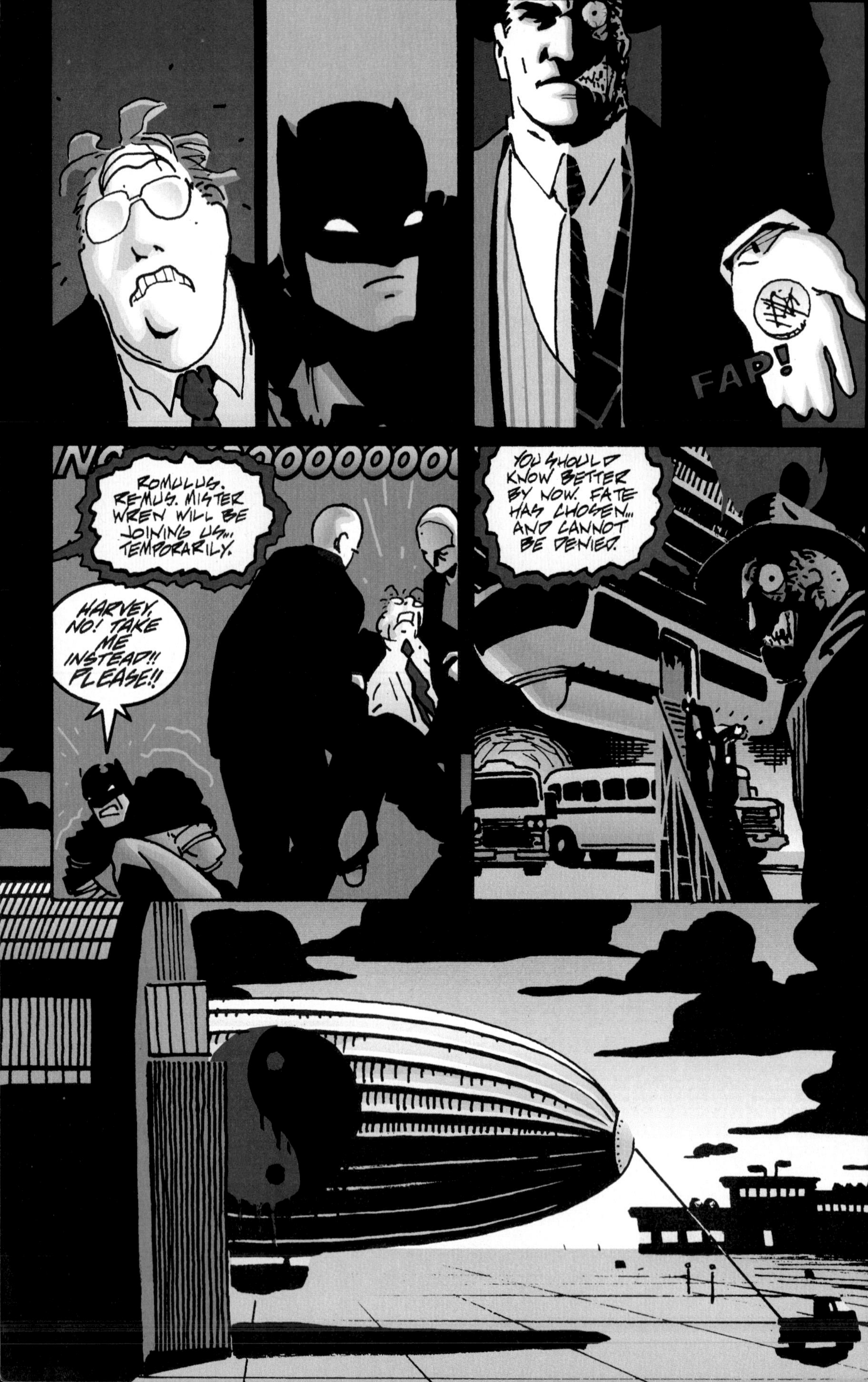
FAP!
NOOOOOOOOOO
ROMULUS. REMUS. MISTER WREN WILL BE JOINING US... TEMPORARILY.
HARVEY, NO! TAKE ME INSTEAD!! PLEASE!!
YOU SHOULD KNOW BETTER BY NOW. FATE HAS CHOSEN... AND CANNOT BE DENIED.

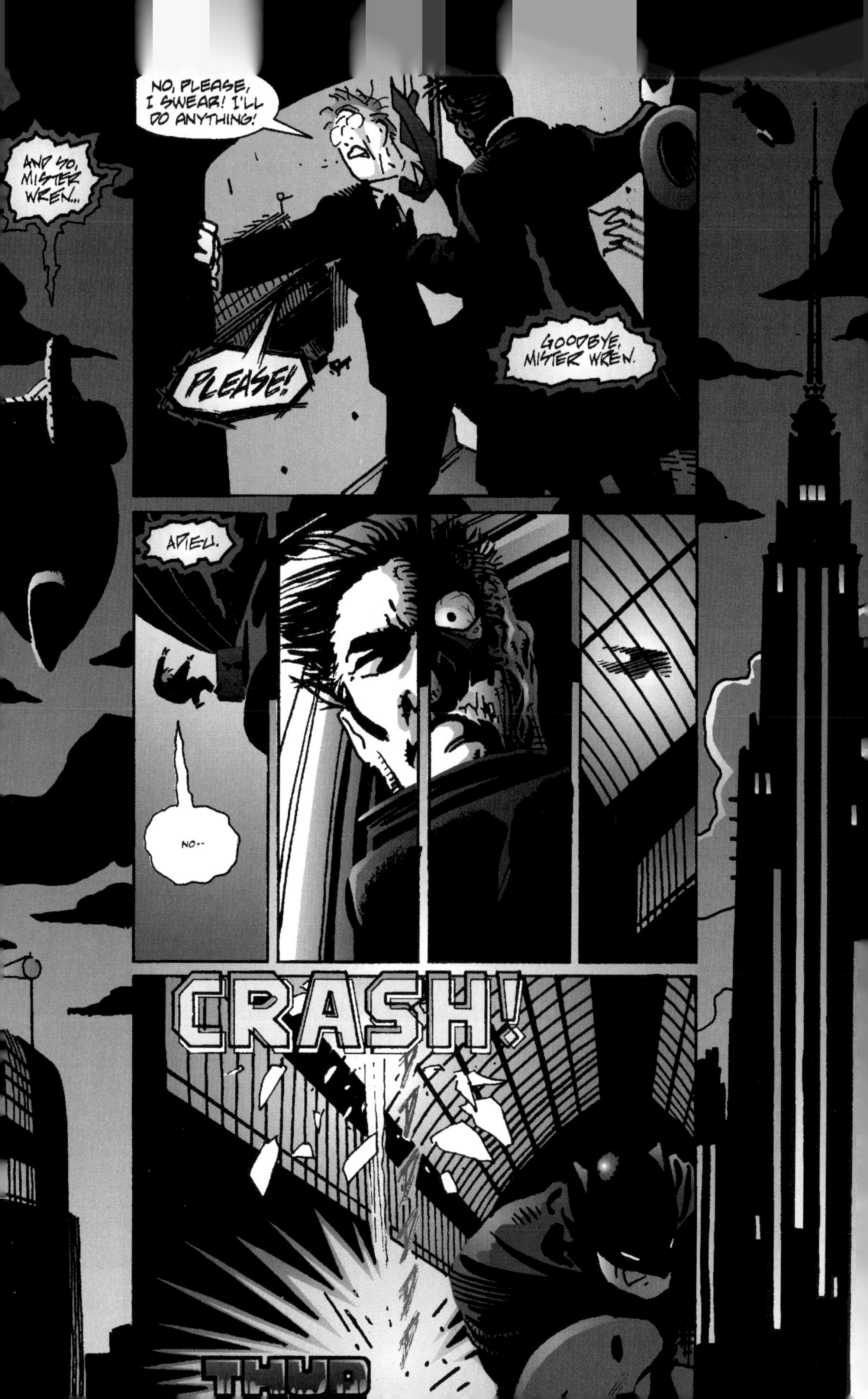
AND SO, MISTER WREN...
NO, PLEASE, I SWEAR! I'LL DO ANYTHING!
PLEASE!
GOODBYE, MISTER WREN.
ADIEU.
NO--
CRASH!
THUD

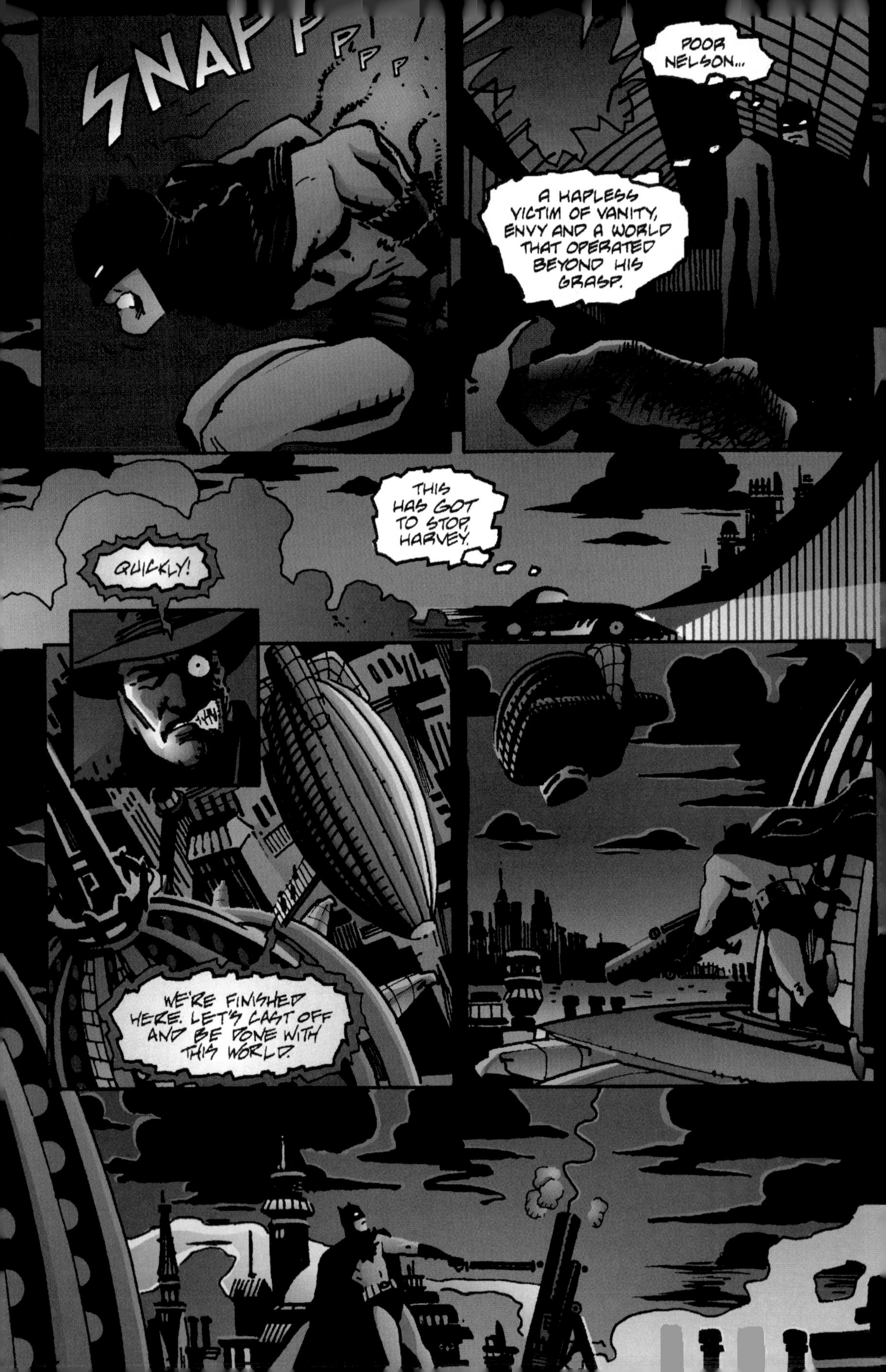
SNAPPPPP
POOR NELSON...
A HAPLESS VICTIM OF VANITY, ENVY AND A WORLD THAT OPERATED BEYOND HIS GRASP.
THIS HAS GOT TO STOP, HARVEY.
QUICKLY!
WE'RE FINISHED HERE. LET'S CAST OFF AND BE DONE WITH THIS WORLD.

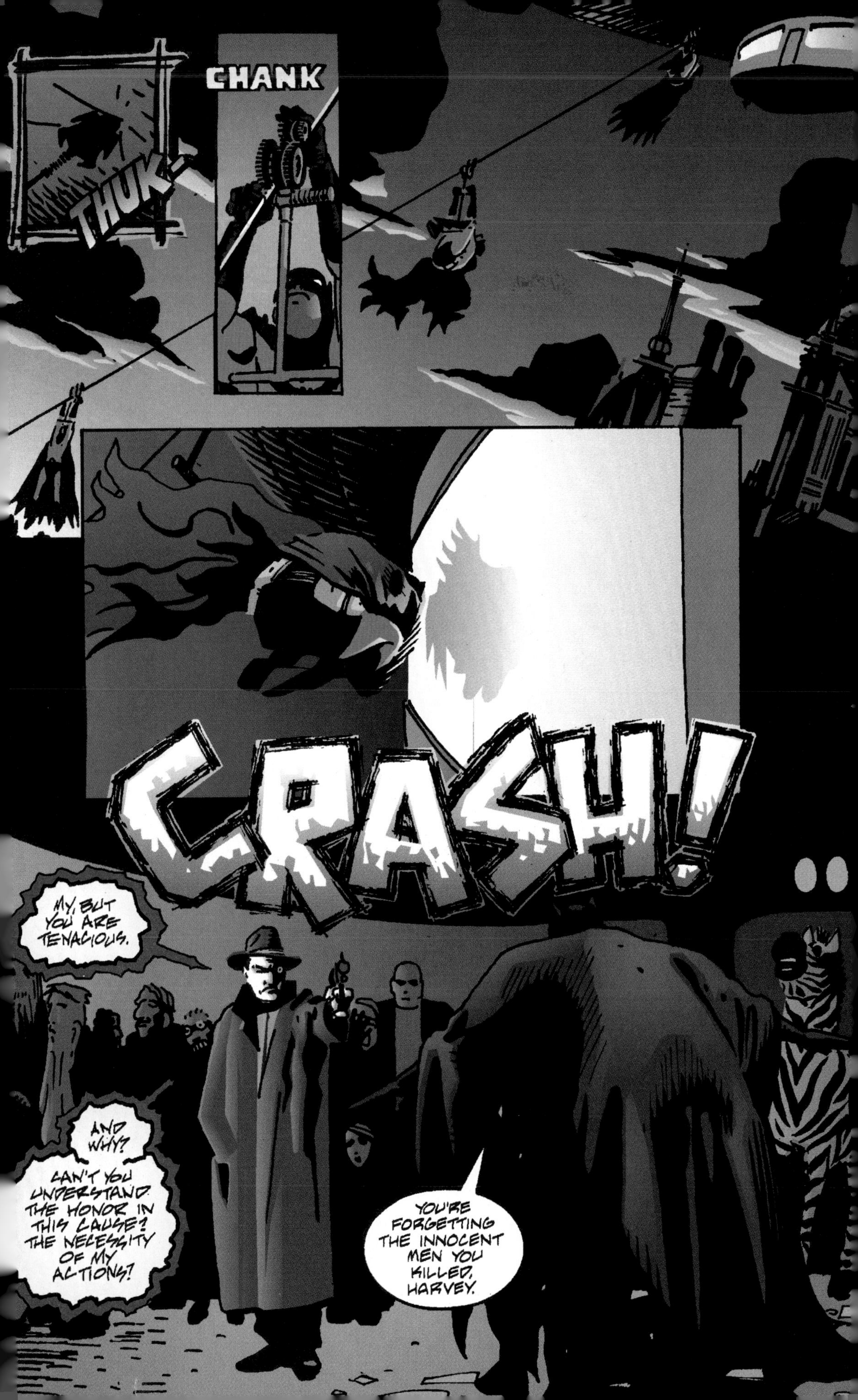
THUK
CHANK
CRASH!
MY, BUT YOU ARE TENACIOUS.
AND WHY?
CAN'T YOU UNDERSTAND THE HONOR IN THIS CAUSE? THE NECESSITY OF MY ACTIONS?
YOU'RE FORGETTING THE INNOCENT MEN YOU KILLED, HARVEY.

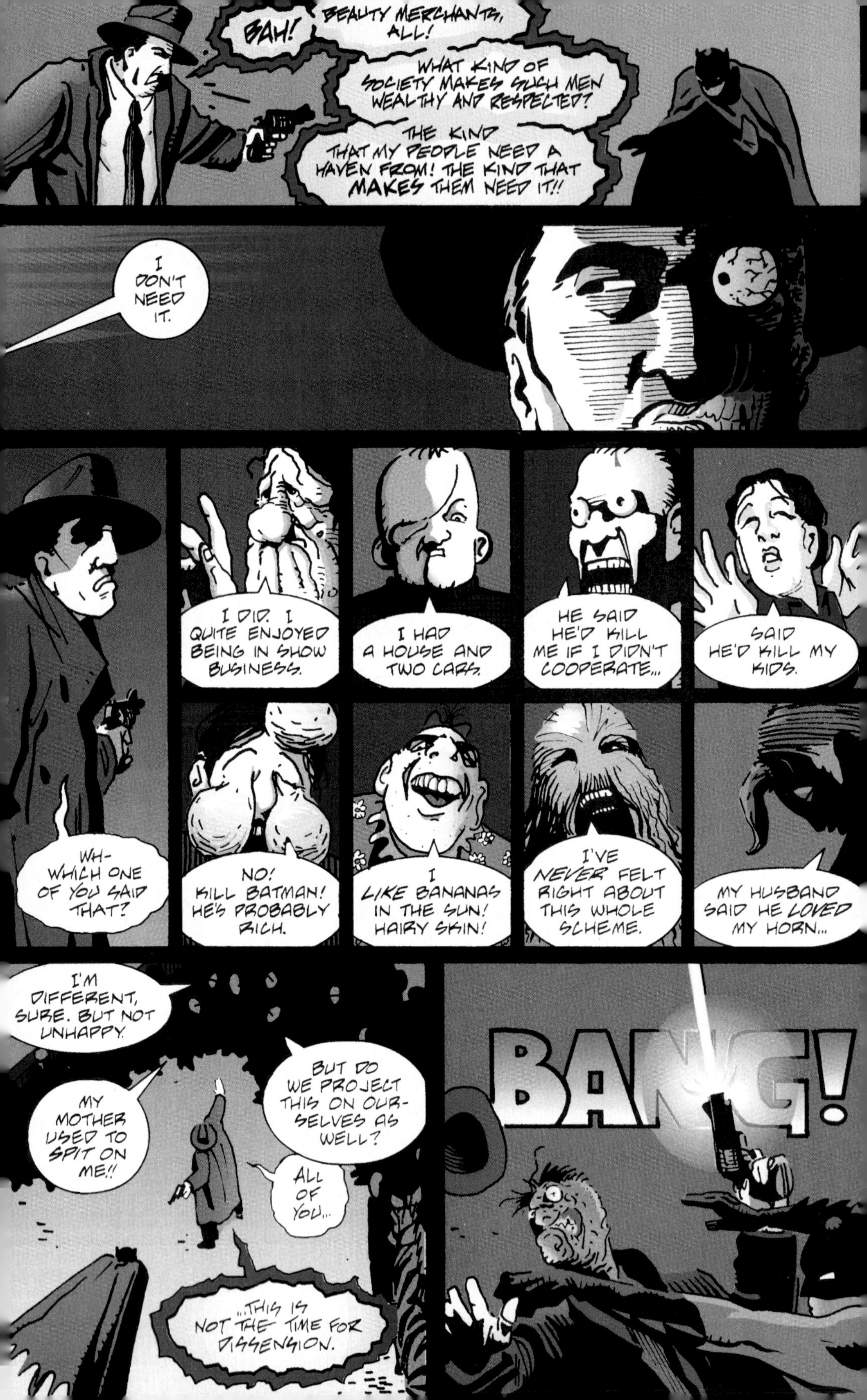
BAH!
BEAUTY MERCHANTS, ALL!
WHAT KIND OF SOCIETY MAKES SUCH MEN WEALTHY AND RESPECTED?
THE KIND THAT MY PEOPLE NEED A HAVEN FROM! THE KIND THAT MAKES THEM NEED IT!!
I DON'T NEED IT.
I DID. I QUITE ENJOYED BEING IN SHOW BUSINESS.
I HAD A HOUSE AND TWO CARS.
HE SAID HE'D KILL ME IF I DIDN'T COOPERATE...
SAID HE'D KILL MY KIDS.
WH-WHICH ONE OF YOU SAID THAT?
NO! KILL BATMAN! HE'S PROBABLY RICH.
I LIKE BANANAS IN THE SUN! HAIRY SKIN!
I'VE NEVER FELT RIGHT ABOUT THIS WHOLE SCHEME.
MY HUSBAND SAID HE LOVED MY HORN...
I'M DIFFERENT, SURE. BUT NOT UNHAPPY.
MY MOTHER USED TO SPIT ON ME!!
BUT DO WE PROJECT THIS ON OURSELVES AS WELL?
ALL OF YOU...
...THIS IS NOT THE TIME FOR DISSENSION.
BANG!

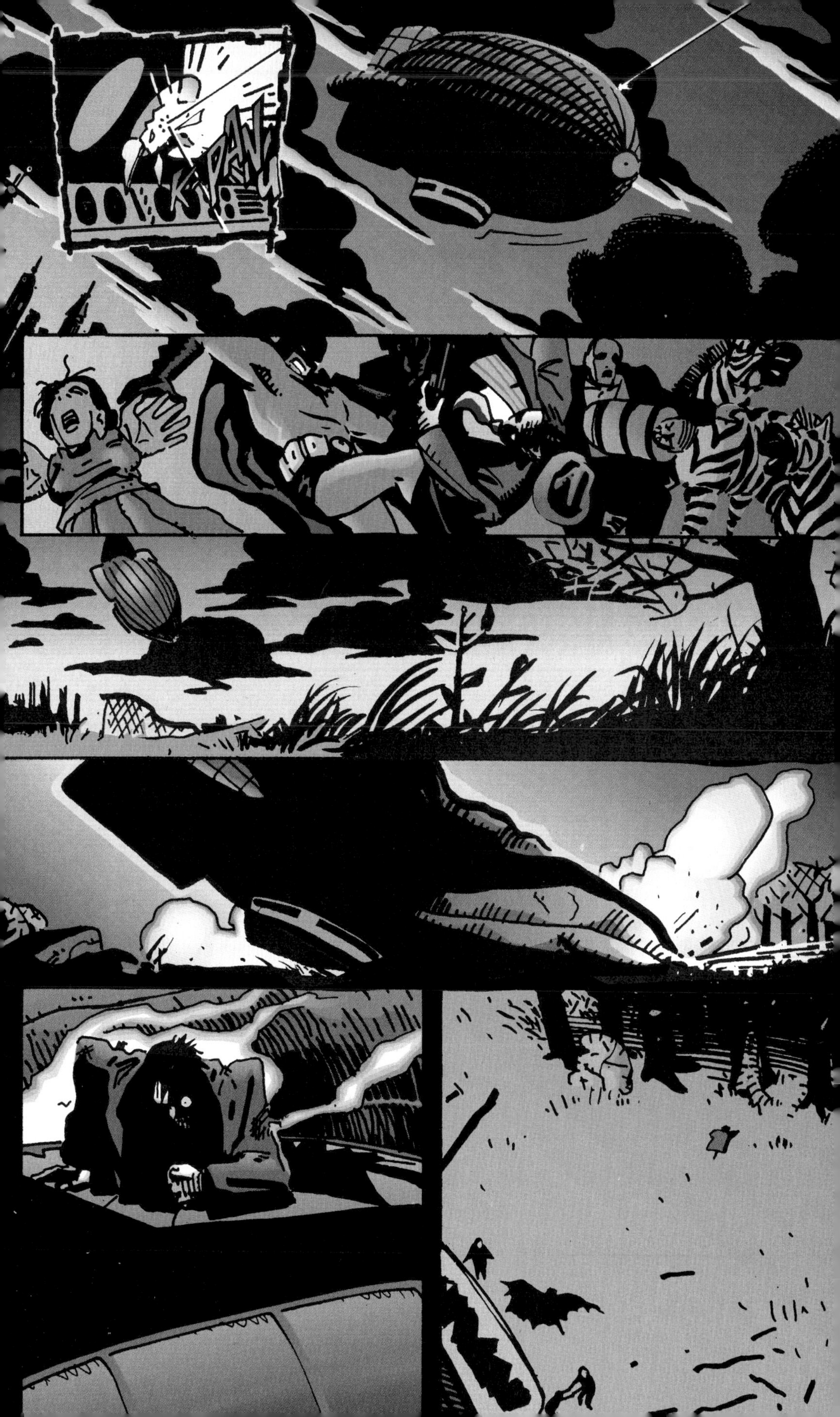
KSPANG

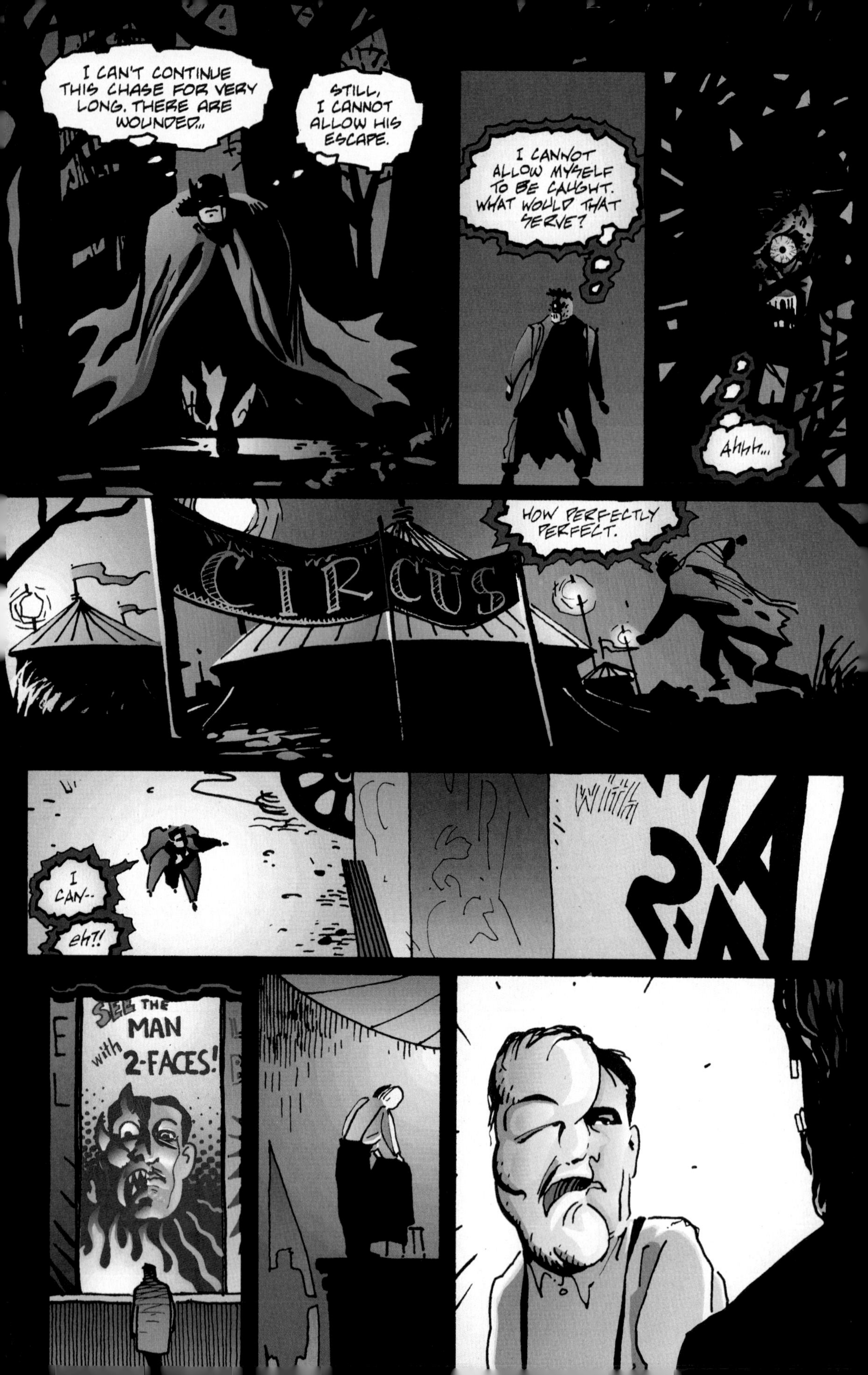
I CAN'T CONTINUE THIS CHASE FOR VERY LONG. THERE ARE WOUNDED...
STILL, I CANNOT ALLOW HIS ESCAPE.
I CANNOT ALLOW MYSELF TO BE CAUGHT. WHAT WOULD THAT SERVE?
Ahhh...
CIRCUS
HOW PERFECTLY PERFECT.
I CAN--
eh?!
SEE THE MAN with 2-FACES!

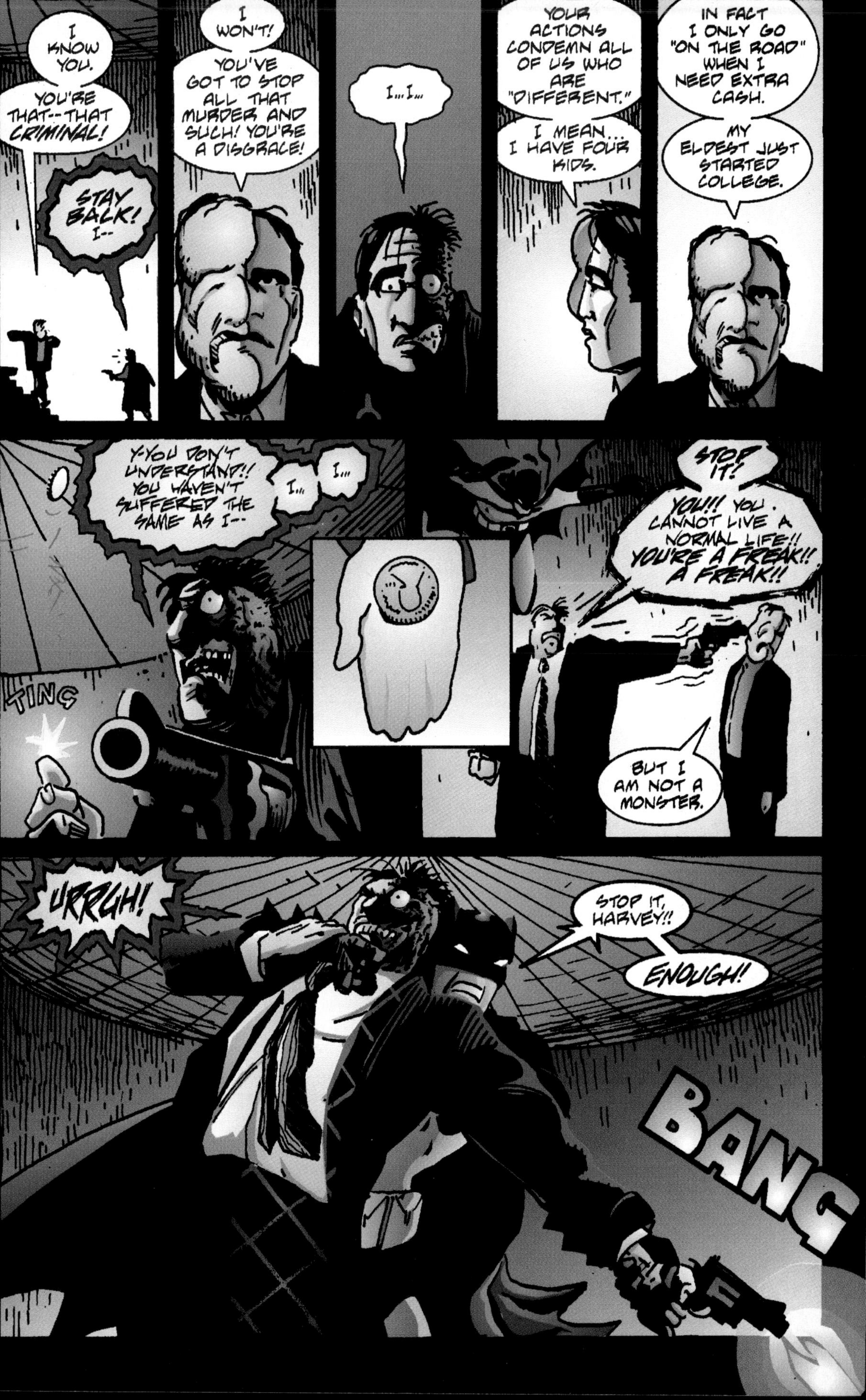
I KNOW YOU.
YOU'RE THAT--THAT CRIMINAL!
STAY BACK! I--
I WON'T!
YOU'VE GOT TO STOP ALL THAT MURDER AND SUCH! YOU'RE A DISGRACE!
I...I...
YOUR ACTIONS CONDEMN ALL OF US WHO ARE "DIFFERENT."
I MEAN... I HAVE FOUR KIDS.
IN FACT I ONLY GO "ON THE ROAD" WHEN I NEED EXTRA CASH.
MY ELDEST JUST STARTED COLLEGE.
Y-YOU DON'T UNDERSTAND!! YOU HAVEN'T SUFFERED THE SAME AS I--
I...
I...
TING
STOP IT!
YOU!! YOU CANNOT LIVE A NORMAL LIFE!! YOU'RE A FREAK!! A FREAK!!
BUT I AM NOT A MONSTER.
URRGH!
STOP IT, HARVEY!!
ENOUGH!
BANG

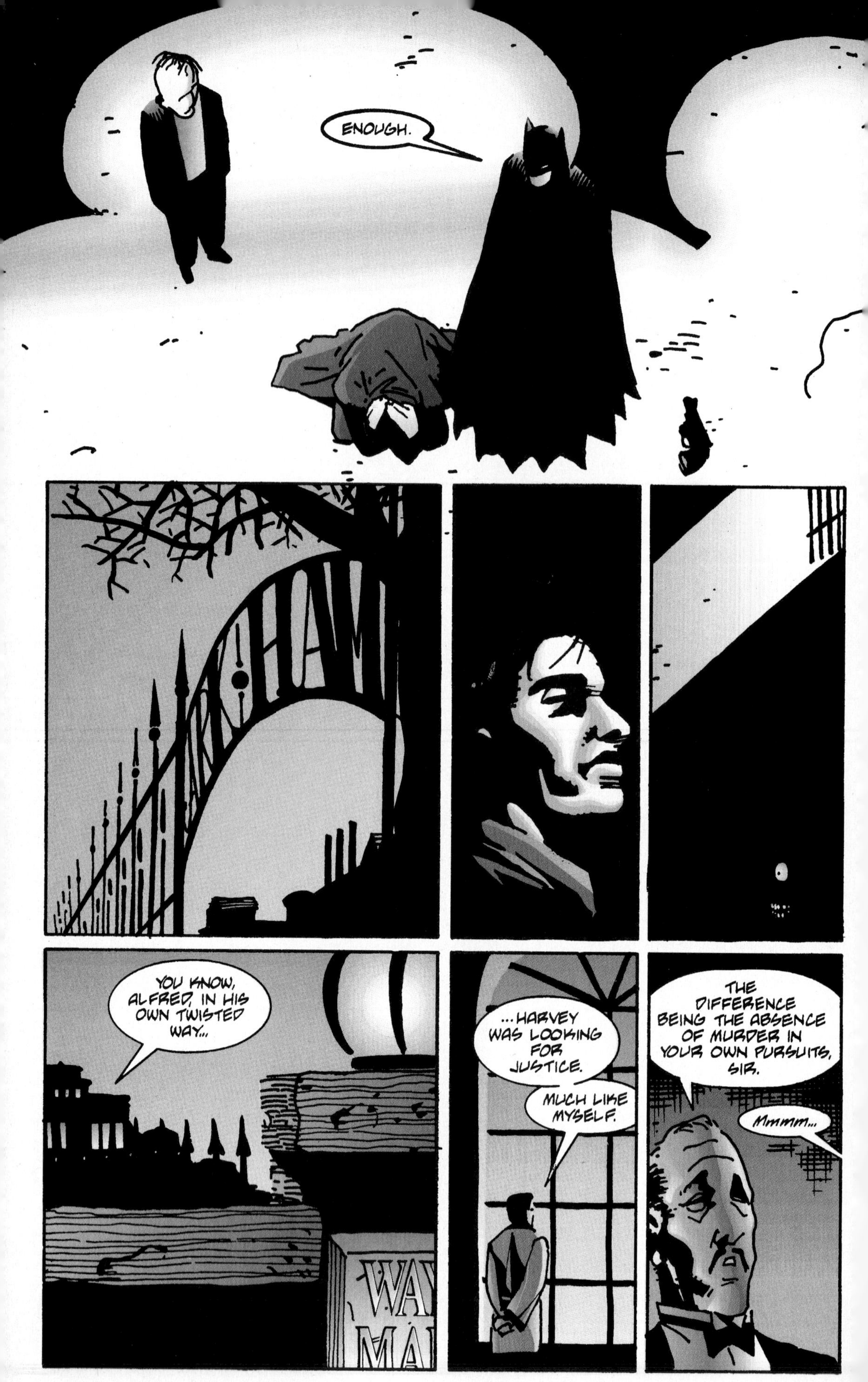
ENOUGH.
YOU KNOW, ALFRED, IN HIS OWN TWISTED WAY...
...HARVEY WAS LOOKING FOR JUSTICE.
MUCH LIKE MYSELF.
THE DIFFERENCE BEING THE ABSENCE OF MURDER IN YOUR OWN PURSUITS, SIR.
Mmmm...

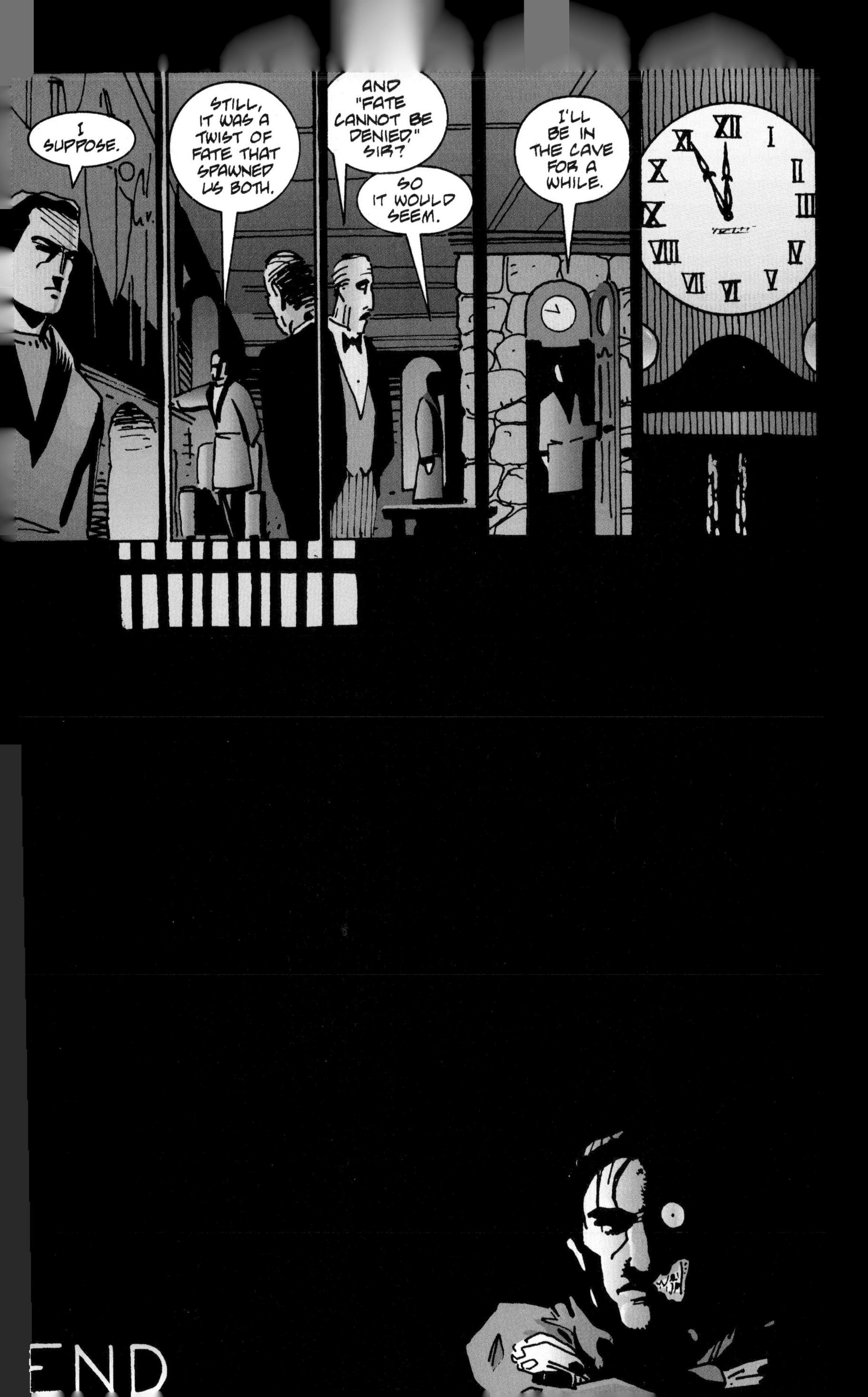
I SUPPOSE.
STILL, IT WAS A TWIST OF FATE THAT SPAWNED US BOTH.
AND "FATE CANNOT BE DENIED," SIR?
SO IT WOULD SEEM.
I'LL BE IN THE CAVE FOR A WHILE.
END

# SKETCHES

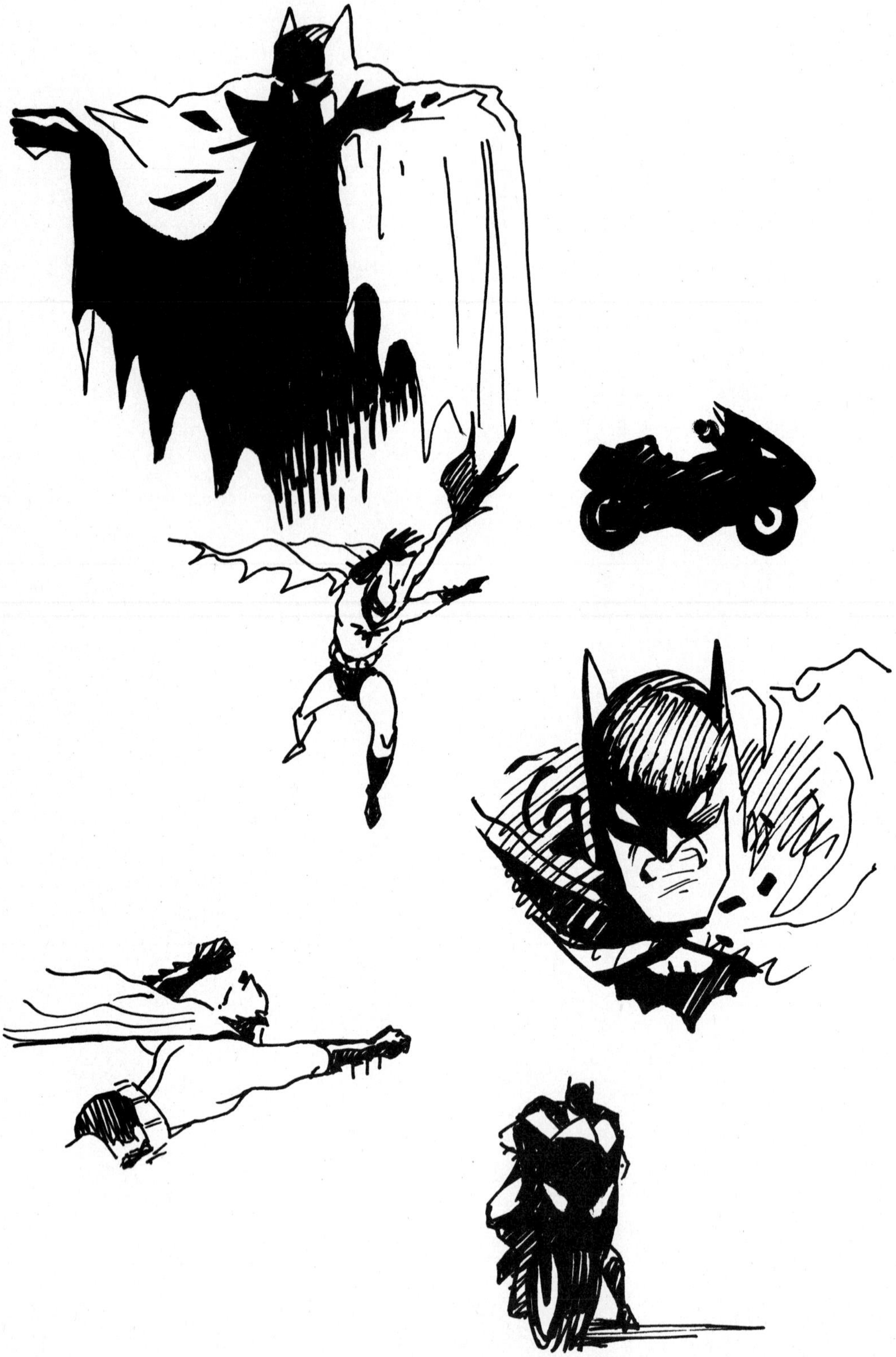

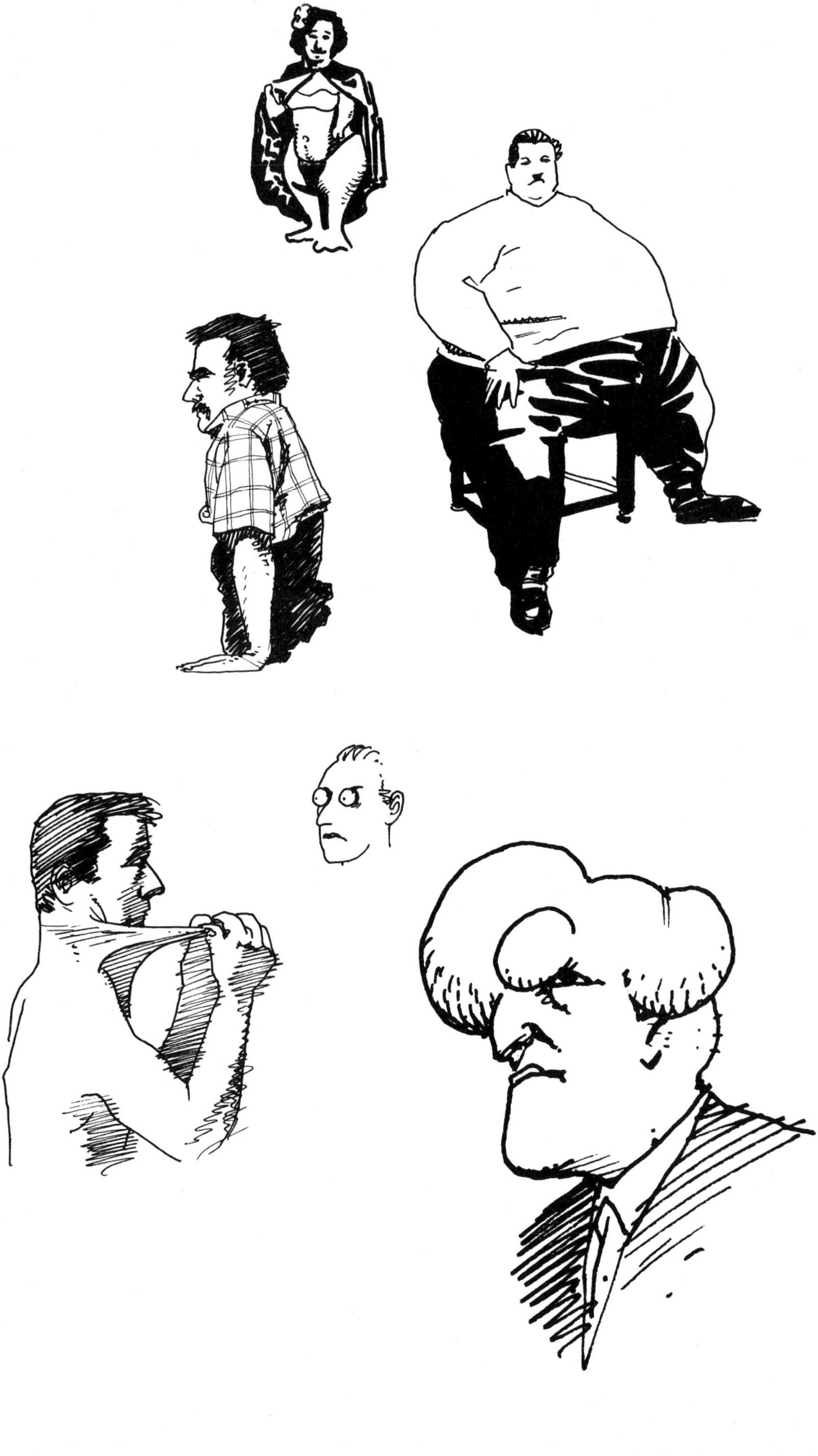

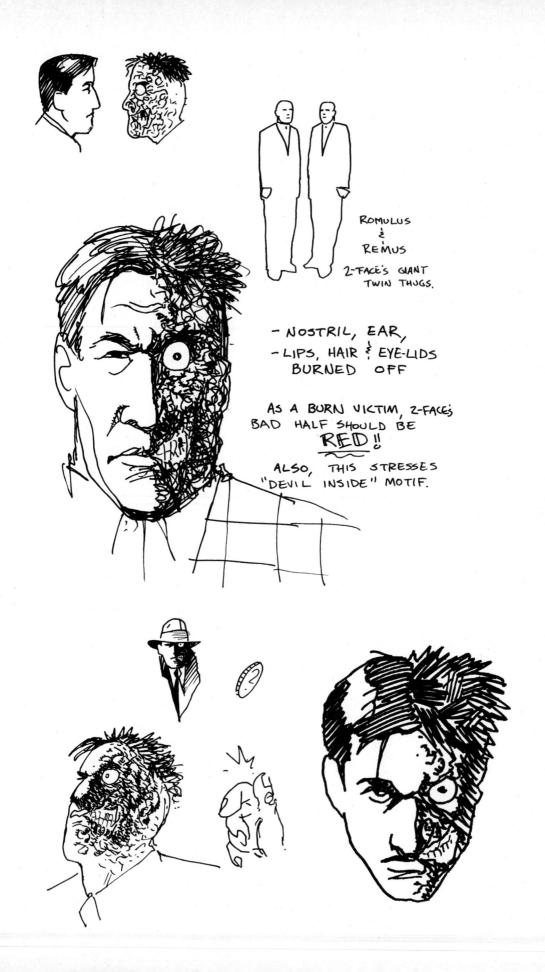

ROMULUS
&
REMUS

2-FACE'S GIANT
TWIN THUGS.

- NOSTRIL, EAR,
- LIPS, HAIR & EYE-LIDS
  BURNED OFF

AS A BURN VICTIM, 2-FACE'S
BAD HALF SHOULD BE
RED!!

ALSO, THIS STRESSES
"DEVIL INSIDE" MOTIF.